New Age Encyclopedia

New Age Encyclopedia brings a much-needed overview to a broad-ranging subject. This book explains a wide variety of topics in the exciting mind, body and spirit movement. It is an essential reference for all those looking forward to a spiritual re-awakening within a golden era for humankind.

New Age Encyclopedia

A
Mind Body Spirit
Reference Guide

BELINDA WHITWORTH

New Age Books

ISBN: 81-7822-239-6

First Indian Edition: Delhi, 2006

First published in Great Britain by Robert Hale Limited

Published by

NEW AGE BOOKS
A-44, Naraina Industrial Area, Phase-I
New Delhi 110 028 (INDIA)
Email: nab@vsnl.in
Website: www.newagebooksindia.com

For sale in South Asia only

Printed in India
at Nice Printing Press
3, Rashid Market Extension, New Delhi-110051

Dedication

For my parents, with love

Acknowledgments

Thanks to the following for permission to reproduce or adapt material: Animal Aid, Association for Neuro-Linguistic Programming, British Anti-Vivisection Association, Chrysalis Books, HarperCollins, Healing Tao Centre, *Here's Health* magazine, David Higham Associates, Hodder and Stoughton, Kessinger Publishing, *Kindred Spirit* magazine, Natural Death Centre, Oxford University Press, Pagan Federation, Penguin Group, Piatkus, Quest Books, (UK) Reiki Association, Sansom & Co., John Seymour Associates, Simon & Schuster, and David Smith. Every effort has been made to contact copyright holders but I apologize for any omissions.

Particular thanks to: King Arthur Pendragon for information on druidry; Bunk for lending her books; Cheryl Critchley for the affirmation exercise and tarot card meanings; Clews Everard, Director, Stonehenge, for information about access; Lisa Hawken, Carol Mathews, and Sowelu for telling their stories; Surinder Whitworth for lending her magazines.

Heartfelt thanks to Frog, Jon Barnes, and Alan Haley for keeping my computer going and without whom this book would never have been finished.

Finally, very special thanks to Cheryl for being a source of such inspiration and to Frog for keeping my feet on the ground.

Introduction

Every two thousand years, the Earth moves into a different sign of the zodiac, and we presently have moved or soon will move (experts disagree on this) from the age of Pisces to the age of Aquarius. This new age, it is said, could bring about our spiritual reawakening and a golden era for humankind.

The New Age movement is concerned with just about every area of existence, but I came to it first through love for Nature and concern about the environment, then complementary health and counseling, and, more recently, meditation and tarot reading. I wanted this book to be a simple introduction to the main themes, but, when I started to write it, I discovered that I knew a lot less than I thought and that the movement was much wider and older than I'd imagined.

If you, too, feel overwhelmed or confused, just remember that one of the basics of New Age thought is that we don't have to take anyone else's word for it but our own anymore—"isms" and "ologies" are things of the past. So absorb what you like from the book and ignore the rest.

Another New Age basic is the belief that we *can* change and that we don't have to suffer to learn. So read on, enjoy, and be happy.

A

Abduction by Aliens

The first reported alien abduction was in Brazil in 1957 and since then they have occurred all over the Western world—in Europe including the UK, Australia, South Africa, Russia, and North America. Although people's experiences vary quite widely, the following features recur:

- Light, especially a beam which draws the person up, and sometimes vibration.
- A spacecraft of some kind.
- Humanoid beings, especially small gray ones with large black eyes, who communicate by telepathy.
- Medical tests being performed and eggs or sperm removed so that human/alien offspring can be produced.
- Lost periods of time and inexplicable small wounds.

Not everyone remembers everything that happens to them and sometimes the full story is only recovered through hypnosis. Many people find the experiences terrifying but according to John E. Mack, a professor of psychiatry who has investigated over eighty cases, some abductees have a sense of entering a different reality and experience great joy. They feel that the aliens are trying to get closer to us and to help us. Some have reported being healed of such serious conditions as leukemia, pneumonia, and polio.

There are striking similarities between alien abduction reports and stories people have been telling for centuries about being kidnapped by **fairies**. (For examples of the latter, see *Fairies: Real Encounters with Little People* by Janet Bord.) It could therefore be that the phenomenon is not new but that each age reinterprets it according to its beliefs.

If you think you might have experienced "spacenap," there are organizations that can help (see Resources) but make sure they are putting your welfare first—not their own research.

See also **UFOs**.

Aborigines

Australian Aboriginal culture is the oldest in the world. The people have inhabited the continent for at least 50 thousand years according to conventional archaeology, but their myths reach back millions of years and they believe that they have been there since time began. According to the Australian novelist and poet James G. Cowan, their tradition represents one of our last links with a truly spiritual way of life, a view also put forward in Marlo Morgan's controversial book *Mutant Message Down Under*. (The word *Aborigine* is used for convenience as there were many different groups living on the continent and the Aborigines themselves have no word for all of them.)

Central to Aboriginal culture is their relationship with the land. The features of the land were formed by ancestral beings in the creation time or "Dreamtime" as they crisscrossed the continent, and every one is recorded in myth and song. The routes the beings took are known as Dreaming tracks or songlines and each person is responsible for a section of a songline, depending on where their mother was when they were conceived or when she first felt them moving in her womb.

They must ensure that the land stays exactly as it was when the ancestors made it and keep it alive by singing its song. Even if they have traveled far away they must return to that part of the land to die. Bruce Chatwin in *The Songlines* suggests that the rhythm and cadences of the songs may actually represent the shape of the land since people from opposite ends of the continent and with different languages can interpret them. He compares them to the territorial songs of birds and wonders if all humans once related to the land in this way.

Your songline determines from which ancestral being you are descended, in other words your "totem" animal, plant, or natural force (clouds, wind, and so on) and no one must kill, eat, or harm their totem being. In this way, not only was the land itself protected but also every living thing on it. Kinship, along a songline, is more important than blood ties, and this helped the different family groups and tribes to live in peace with each other. "Walkabout" is the sacred journey people make along their Dreaming track.

In traditional Aborigine society, people had few possessions, as they considered that goods worked against you if you held on to them. Art was inspired by spirit and was not a personal achievement. Some is found in sacred places in caves and on rocks, on coffin lids, or on "churingas" (secret shields depicting an individual's land responsibilities), but most was drawn temporarily in the earth for ceremonies. It illustrates the land and its myths and is both "map and meditation," in the words of the Australian art critic and historian Robert Hughes.

In common with other native peoples, **Shamans**, known as "clever" women and men by the Europeans, were the spiritual experts and healers. Their power came from one of the most important ancestral beings, the Rainbow Snake. (The American Shaman Lynn V. Andrews describes her work with an Australian clever woman in *Crystal Woman*.)

The first whites reached Australia in 1788, and from then on, Aboriginal culture was under threat. Not only were Aborigines evicted from the land and forbidden to practice sacred ways, but from the 1930s until 1967 children were taken from their parents to be brought up as Europeans. (This horrific practice is described in Marlo Morgan's novel *Message From Forever*.) In recent years, however, the situation has begun to turn around. Some land rights have been restored and in Northern and Central Australia, where the Europeans had less impact, some groups are able to continue their traditional semi-nomadic, gatherer-hunter way of life. Not all Aborigines believe they should remain isolated however. As the clever woman in *Crystal Woman* says:

> *To survive, we must step forward and reach out to all the magicians around our Mother Earth. We must share our dream paintings and our hearts.*

On the other hand, the British writer Howard Jacobson, who has lived and traveled in the country, feels that the Aborigines have "white Australians well and truly on the run." The last word comes from Mudrooroo who has written a book about his people's mythology:

> *Still, in our collective lives, the last 200 years is but a brief spell, a wink of an eye, and whereas the British and other invaders live from day to day, from year to year, we live from epoch to epoch...Perhaps our essential belief is that we belong to this land of Australia, that it is our mother or father and that we must care for her or him. That it was given to us of old and that no one can take it away.*

See also **Didgeridoo**, and **Uluru.**

Acumassage

Massage of acupoints (see **Acupuncture**).

Acupressure

Like **acupuncture**, this works on the body's energy system. It uses light pressure or stroking on the acupoints and gentle manipulation of the limbs. It is less effective than acupuncture but useful for people with a fear of needles. With care, it can also be used at home.

Acupuncture

Part of **traditional Chinese medicine**, this works on the body's energy or **chi**. Chi flows around the body along fourteen main channels called *meridians* and a network of smaller channels. These channels are connected not just to different organs and parts of the body, but also to different emotions or states of mind. At certain points called *acupoints* along the meridians the chi can be manipulated so as to remove blockages or balance the flow. This manipulation is done with extremely fine needles which are inserted from 1/4 inch to 4 inches. These may then be gently rotated and either removed immediately or left in for up to 1/2 hour. As many as 15 needles may be used at one time but four to six is more common.

The insertion of the needles hurts no more than a pinprick but you may feel an ache at the site or along the meridian, and you can feel quite disorientated as the chi rearranges itself although many people feel pleasantly sleepy. After treatment you can feel quite tired.

Moxibustion is a process where heat is applied to acupoints by burning a small bundle of a herb called moxa (Chinese mugwort).

Acupuncture can be used to treat both acute and chronic conditions, and mental/emotional troubles as well as physical ones. It can also be used preventatively. Although full training takes several years, some Western doctors undergo short courses and use acupuncture simply for pain relief.

See also **Acumassage**, **Acupressure**, and **Auricular Acupuncture/Therapy.**

Affirmations

Many of us, as children, pick up negative ideas about ourselves or the world—ideas such as "I am not good enough," or "The world is a tough place." These negative ideas become self-fulfilling prophecies when we are adults. As adults, however, we can reprogram ourselves with helpful ideas and so create for ourselves exactly the sort of life we want and need. These helpful ideas are known as affirmations.

The best affirmations are short, simple, and full of feeling. You will find many suggestions in two classic books on the subject: *Creative Visualization* by Shakti Gawain and *You Can Heal Your Life* by Louise L. Hay. However, the most effective ones are those you invent for yourself. Affirmations should always be in the present tense and contain no *ifs*, *buts*, *whens*, or other conditional words. Finding the right affirmation may take time but you will know when you do because you will feel a sense of relief. One way to find it is to identify what is bothering you and then turn that on its head. For example, if worry or fear is your problem, your affirmation might be "I am safe."

Once you have found an affirmation, write it down, say it to yourself, make it into a poem, or sing it. Keep doing this whenever you remember. You may find that you try to sabotage yourself by bringing up negative ideas to counter the affirmation. Whatever you do, don't try to suppress them as this is all part of the clearing-out process. A superb way of allowing these negative thoughts to surface and then sending them on their way is the exercise that follows.

Write down all your affirmations and date them. Look back at them occasionally and see just how many of them are now part of your life. If they aren't, work on them some more—they soon will be.

Working With Affirmations

Write your affirmation down several times leaving a line of space between each. Read the first example of your affirmation out loud and then, if a contradictory thought comes into your mind, write it down in the first line space. (For example if your affirmation is "I am free," your contradictory thought might be "I have to earn a living.") Then read the next example of your affirmation out loud. If another doubt comes into your mind, write it down and then say the affirmation again.

Continue until you run out of excuses, being sure to end by saying the affirmation. This may take pages, but just keep going. You will come to the end eventually. Be sure to speak the affirmation and write the negative thoughts.

This exercise will leave you feeling enormously relieved and liberated. You will eventually see that all negativity is just a construct of the mind.

Aikido

A modern Japanese martial art where the opponents are taught to flow and cooperate with each other rather than clash. Aikido is practiced as a series of attacks and throws using either bare hands or wooden swords, is completely non-competitive, and is suitable for both women and men. The name means "the way of developing harmony with life energy."

Akasha/Akashic Records

Akasha is **Sanskrit** for space or ether, the psychic dimension of the universe, and the akashic records are a sort of divine filing system containing information on everything—past, present, and future. We unconsciously tap into the akashic records all the time through dreams, premonitions, and intuitions but can bring the process under conscious control by learning skills like **divination**. Through the akashic records we can not only find out about our own past, present, and future or about that of friends or people who are with us, but potentially we can find out about anyone or anything anywhere in the universe.

Alchemy

The science of physical, psychological, and spiritual transformation and the forerunner of modern chemistry. Alchemy is thought to have come from ancient Egypt (see **Hermeticism**). It was brought to Europe by the Arabs in the Middle Ages and then driven underground because the Christian church disapproved. Interest revived in the 19th century, with the psychologist **Jung** spending many years studying alchemical texts and using them to shape his own ideas about the human psyche, and occult groups such as the **Hermetic Order of the Golden Dawn** building their magical rituals around them.

The alchemists believed that there was a "prima materia" or original material from which all life was created. This manifested itself in each of the four **Elements** in turn, from Fire to Water to Air and finally to Earth. The key to this material was the "philosopher's stone," a substance capable of transforming ordinary metals into gold and bestowing immortality. Central to the alchemists' work was their belief in the influence of the planets and the system of **correspondences** between them and earthly components (colors, metals, minerals, and so on). And a vital part of the transformation process was the *sacred marriage*, the union of feminine and masculine, symbolized by the *caduceus*, a wand with two snakes entwined around it.

While many alchemists were undoubtedly charlatans, others are said to have succeeded in their quest. The Flamels, a 14th-century husband and wife team, founded and endowed 14 hospitals, three chapels, and seven churches with the gold from their work and were said to have been seen in Paris in the 18th century. The 20th-century French alchemist Fulcanelli is said to have reappeared in 1937 after his death and warned a physicist about the dangers of atomic energy.

Although alchemy has been hugely influential in the past, today it is practiced largely as a spiritual discipline by just a few people.

Alexander Technique

A way of reeducating you about your posture and the way you move so as to remove pain and tension. Treatment is one to one and a minimum of 20 *lessons* is recommended. (Sessions are called *lessons*, therapists, *teachers,* and clients, *pupils*.) It was developed at the beginning of the 20th century by an Australian actor, Frederick Alexander, who lost his voice through holding his neck wrongly.

Popular with actors, musicians, and athletes, it can also benefit people who get head, neck, or back pain and those with respiratory or digestive disorders. It can free up energy so is useful if you feel perpetually tired, and can sometimes be helpful for mental and emotional problems like anxiety or depression.

See also **Feldenkrais Method**.

Alternative Medicine/Therapies

See **Complementary Health.**

Angels

Conscious beings who exist in a different dimension from us. Their particular role is to be an intermediary between us and the Divine (the name coming from the Greek for *messenger*), to protect us and to help us fulfil our destiny. Like other spirit helpers, they only intervene in our lives if asked.

See also **Spirit Guides.**

Angels and Other Spirit Beings—Lisa's Story

I was a marine artist for many years until 1995, when I came to realize that my heart's desire was to serve through my paintings. I surrendered this to the Divine and was given the idea of painting angels.

After painting these beloved ones for a few months, I received the understanding that I could paint people's guardian angels, and later on came to paint guides, the Ascended Masters, star beings, and Divine Light beings.

I paint from my heart and not my mind. This is the only way the beloved ones work with me. I feel their loving energies around me and in my heart. All these beings come in great love to help and guide us all with our journey through life.

The pictures carry the energies of the beings I paint and often I see sparkles of silver energy flashing in my work. Their message comes symbolically—I am given symbols in their many forms, from

(cont'd)

flowers to sacred geometry, also the colors and their vibration for each person I paint for.

It is such a joy for me to be able to paint these pictures for people, and it has helped me in my own growth. I do not plan my work or my life. I greet each day in surrender to God, and go along with whatever the day brings.

*As I understand it, angels assist us in every way with great love to realize who we are. Along with our guides, the Ascended Masters, star beings, and beings of Light, they are part of our multidimensional selves, the I AM THAT I AM, THE I AM PRESENCE OF GOD**

** This is a way of referring to the divine energy within us all.*

Anima/Animus

These are terms used by the psychologist **Jung**. The *anima* is the latent feminine side of a man and the *animus* the latent masculine side of a woman. Like the **shadow**, these latent qualities need to be brought into consciousness and expressed in our lives in order for us to become fully rounded and psychologically healthy ("individuated" as Jung puts it). Unrealized ("repressed"), they can be harmful—for example leading us either to mistreat the opposite sex or to idealize them. They can also erupt at times of stress, perhaps causing a woman to become opinionated and strident because her *thinking*, a quality from the animus, is not under conscious control, and a man to break down because his *feeling*, a quality from the anima, is not under conscious control. (These of course are generalizations as women may have realized "masculine" qualities and vice versa.)

See also **Archetypes.**

Animals

Animals are our closest relatives and since we first started telling stories and painting pictures we have used them to represent human characteristics, good and bad. Tribal peoples feel guided and protected by their special totem animals, and **Shamans** draw on spirit animals for power (**Power Animals**). Whatever we do to animals, we do to ourselves since it's a short step from saying "it's only an animal," to saying, "it's only a black/white person," or "it's only a woman." And to distinguish between animals and say this animal is good, that one is a pest, is like rejecting parts of our own character.

In industrialized countries the majority of households contain at least one pet and Susan Chernak McElroy, in *Animals as Teachers and Healers,* tells moving stories of the good they bring. Larry, an alcoholic, adopted a stray dog he called Homer and found it hard to keep drinking all hours knowing Homer was waiting for him. "Through my love for him and his unconditional love for me," he said, "change became possible." He now hangs his AA three-year sobriety medal round Homer's neck, not his own. Animals make ideal counselors—apart from offering unconditional love, they're good listeners, they don't judge, they're honest, they're empathetic, and they're physical. Rupert Sheldrake, in *Dogs That Know When Their Owners Are Coming Home*, gives many examples of their extraordinary sensitivity. One couple driving in the Austrian mountains was forced to slow down by their suddenly pawing, howling poodle only to turn the corner and find the road had disappeared in a landslide. Native peoples have always viewed the behavior of animals as portents.

If the Earth is a living entity held together by a complex web of interactions (see **Gaia**), it is very short-sighted of us to think that we can reduce the numbers of a species or eradicate it and escape any consequences. Animals of all kinds have a great deal to teach us, deserve to be treated well, and have as much right to be here as we have.

See also **Veganism**, and **Vivisection**.

Some Ways to Help Animals

The following is adapted from a list produced by Animal Aid, a UK animal-rights charity. It is based on the idea that, however well we treat our pets, farm animals, and so on, we have no right to exploit animals and keep them in captivity.

Diet: *Avoid eating meat, fish, and poultry and, if possible, eggs and dairy products. There are numerous tasty—and more wholesome—*

(cont'd)

alternatives to animal products. Give your pets non-animal food as well, if possible.

Household and personal products: *Choose cosmetics, toiletries, and household cleaners that have not been tested on animals and do not contain animal ingredients (most have and do—see Resources section for specialist suppliers).*

Clothing: *Don't wear fur or leather. The leather trade helps keep animal farming going. Wool, silk, and feathers/down also come from animals. Beware of items that come from endangered species or habitats (e.g. coral, tortoiseshell).*

Health: *Keep fit so that you don't need medical treatment.* All *(whether prescription or over-the-counter) are tested on animals (during both development and manufacturing) and some, such as hormones, come from animals. Instead, use herbal remedies and complementary therapies for both you and your pets. (Animal drugs are also tested on animals.)*

Pets: *Choose your companion animal from a sanctuary or rescue center, not a pet shop or breeder because breeding perpetuates pet-keeping. Don't buy exotic animals—many are completely unsuited to a life of captivity and the trade causes immense suffering and death as well as endangering the species in the wild.*

Environment: *Pick up litter, particularly plastic and glass, as this can harm wildlife. Use the car as little as possible—roads destroy habitat and millions of animals are run over each year. Use humane "pest" control (the Vegan Society—see Resources—can help with this). Leave wild areas in your garden and don't use chemicals.*

Sports: *Choose sports that don't involve animals. This means avoiding dog and horse racing as well as hunting, shooting, and fishing.*

Entertainment: *Don't visit zoos, safari parks, bullfights, rodeos, sea-life centers or aquariums, or any spectacle involving animals. Zoos do not help conservation—captive breeding programs are largely ineffective and the money is better spent preserving natural habitat.*

(cont'd)

Money: *Most banks, building societies, pension companies, and so on, invest their money in companies involved in animal exploitation (for example, vivisection). Put your money in those that don't (see* ***Ethical Consumerism/Investment****).*

Charity donation: *Many medical research charities experiment on animals, so be careful who you donate to. (Animal Aid can supply a list of non-animal research charities.)*

Campaigning: *Do your bit to spread the word. Help an animal charity. Report any cruelty or poaching (of rare birds or birds' eggs, for example) to the police or the American Society for the Prevention of Cruelty to Animals (ASPCA).*

Animal Testing

See **Vivisection.**

Anthroposophy

A spiritual science developed by **Rudolf Steiner** at the beginning of the 20th century.

Aquarian Age/Aquarius, Age of

As the earth spins, it wobbles, and over the course of approximately 26,000 years, its north-south axis describes a complete circle. In **astrological** terms, this means that every 2,160 years (or so) the sun appears to rise in a different part of the sky or "sign of the zodiac." This is known as "precession of the equinoxes" because the sun moves backwards through the signs and because its position is measured at the spring equinox (the old new year). Presently (although there is much dispute as to exactly when) we are set to move or have already moved from the sign of Pisces into the sign of Aquarius and according to astrologers this will bring about major changes in the nature of civilization on earth.

Astrology, or the study of heavenly bodies and their relation to events on earth, is the oldest known science, found as far apart as India, South America, and Egypt, and "the kind of correspondences claimed by astrologers are feasible in principle within the context of the scientifically validated physical world" (John Anthony West in *The Case for Astrology*). Ancient peoples had a detailed knowledge of the heavens, including bodies not visible to the naked eye, and their records went back thousands of years. They also had a vast concept of time: Hindu writings, for example, describe 8,000 *million*-year cycles of explosion and implosion in the universe.

It is possible to see the influence of precession on past cultures. The Sphinx at Giza in Egypt, which is shaped like a lion (with a human head), is now thought by some to have been built between 12,000 and 6000 BCE—the time of the age of Leo (11,000—9000 BCE). Bull worship was prevalent among cultures (such as that of Minoan Crete) during the age of Taurus, and the Old Testament, which is full of references to the sacrificial lamb, corresponds to the age of Aries (the ram) from around 2000 BCE.

With our debased understanding of the influence of the stars, it is difficult to make predictions about humankind's future during the age of Aquarius from astrology alone. (The table at the end of this entry shows some of the basic qualities of Pisces and Aquarius for comparison.) Since the turn of the last century, however, the transition to the age of Aquarius has been looked upon by many as a chance for spiritual rejuvenation. Alice Bailey, who was part of an early 20th-century group who called themselves the Aquarian New Age, foresaw:

- the rediscovery of ancient spirituality.
- a world religion uniting East and West.
- the discovery of the soul by science.
- paranormal abilities, such as telepathy, becoming normal.

The clairvoyant **Edgar Cayce** believed that 1958–98 would be a time of global transformation leading to the dawning of a new age of hope and community for all humankind. Peter Lemesurier, in *The Great Pyramid Decoded,* finds prophecies about a spiritual leader who will usher in an era of spiritual expansion starting in 2076, and whose birth will be preceded by a sign in the sky on October 31, 2015 or 2034. According to Hindu astrology, however, the current age of Aquarius is the last and worst age of the 26,000-year cycle and human transformation for the better won't begin until around the year 4000.

Although astrology does not compare the signs of the zodiac saying that one is better than the other, the new age of Aquarius is a focus of optimism. At the very least it gives us a sense of perspective and helps us picture the sort of future we want.

See also **Maitreya.**

Correspondences of Pisces vs. Aquarius		
	Pisces	***Aquarius***
Element	Water (emotions)	Air (thoughts)
Quality	changeable	fixed
Polarity	negative (feminine)	positive (masculine)
Planets	Neptune, Jupiter	Saturn, Uranus
Function	dissolution	distribution
Keywords	dreams, imagination, intuition, idealism, romance, unworldy, escape, self-deception	originality, freedom, reform, humanitarian, communication, telepathy, honesty, privacy

Archetypes

Idealized images common to all human beings. According to the psychologist **Jung** we have both a *personal* and a *collective* unconscious. The collective unconscious has evolved from the thousands of years of human experience and is something we are born with, unlike the "personal" unconscious which is made up of personal memories and those parts of our character we have not yet been able to express. Archetypes are images from the collective unconscious. They appear in our dreams and visions, religions, myths and fairytales, folklore, and in art, and although different cultures may shape the images slightly differently, the underlying meanings are the same the world over.

The most common archetypes according to Jung are the **shadow**, the **anima/animus**, the *persona*, the *self*, the *wise old man* or *hero*, and the *Earth Mother*. The persona is the part we play in everyday life—the *good wife*, or the *rebel*—and the self is our totality, a combination of our conscious and our unconscious parts. Reconciling the two is a difficult and dangerous process, the chief danger of which "is that of succumbing to the fascinating influence of the archetypes" and becoming "inflated"—for instance, becoming a workaholic because we believe we are a hero. This process is often symbolized as a quest or journey, such as the quest for the grail.

The writer and therapist Caroline Myss believes that the archetypal dimension will become increasingly important to us during the new **Aquarian age**. It will help us to see our personal experiences in terms of human evolution as a whole.

Aromatherapy

This uses the *essential oils* of plants, most commonly in massage. Essential oils are what give plants their scent, so called because they are concentrated *essences* extracted by distillation. The oils have both physical and emotional effects, our sense of smell being directly connected to the emotional center of our brain. As well as in massage, the oils can be used in compresses and baths, vaporized or inhaled, or (**under trained guidance only**) taken internally.

Fragrant plant oils have been used for thousands of years, but their medicinal use fell out of favor in Europe in the middle ages, restricting them to the perfume industry. In the 19th century they began to be replaced by synthetic scents, and it wasn't until the early 20th century, when a French chemist burnt his hand and accidentally discovered the healing power of lavender, that the use of essential oils revived.

Aromatherapy can treat a range of health problems. Hormonal disorders respond particularly well. Aromatherapy massage is enjoyable in itself and is also useful for stress-related conditions, back and neck pain, high blood pressure, headaches, and insomnia. It can also help skin problems such as acne, eczema, psoriasis, stretch marks, scars, and sunburn.

Art Therapy

See **Creative Therapies.**

Arthur, King

The story of King Arthur is a blend of historical fact, **Celtic** legend, and medieval embellishment. It has enthralled audiences for hundreds of years, with each age reinventing it to reflect its own hopes and fears.

The historical Arthur was a 5th or 6th century British chieftain, described briefly in 9th century Welsh texts and revered for his exploits against invading Saxons. In the 12th century, Geoffrey of Monmouth wrote, in Latin, a history of British kings, including Arthur and introduced some of the main elements of the story as we know it, including Arthur's sword Excalibur, the Isle of Avalon, and the characters Guinevere, Mordred, and Gawain. The work is not considered entirely factual.

(See "King Arthur—People and Places" table on page 26.)

King Arthur—People and Places

Avalon: *A mythic and mystic island where Arthur was conveyed after his death. Its connection with Glastonbury is almost certainly due to a 12th-century fraud (see* Glastonbury*).*

Tintagel: *According to Malory, Arthur's mother is Igraine, Duchess of Tintagel in Cornwall, and the Victorian poet Tennyson describes his birth as taking place here. Tintagel castle is 12th/13th-century, but in 1998 huge fortifications of the 5th or 6th century were discovered together with a stone inscribed "Artognov."*

Camelot: *This is the name given to Arthur's headquarters by the 12th-century French poet Chretien de Troyes. Geoffrey of Monmouth places the court at Caerleon in South Wales (although the Roman amphitheater here once thought to be the round table is too early). Malory places it at Winchester (although the round table here is 13th-century, probably created by Edward I to legitimize his claim to the throne). Cadbury Castle in Somerset is the right date and size but that is the only indication.*

Guinevere: *According to Geoffrey of Monmouth she is a noble Roman lady, but she appears in Welsh folklore as the daughter of a giant or a minor goddess.*

Lancelot: *Introduced by Chretien de Troyes, but may be related to the god Lugh (worshipped at the Celtic festival of Lughnasadh).*

Merlin: *Introduced by Geoffrey of Monmouth. Possible connection with a 6th-century British poet.*

Mordred: *Brief mention in historical source.*

Morgan/Morgaine: *In early Arthurian stories, she appears as a goddess of healing and ruler of Avalon. Also an Irish battle goddess. Vilified by medieval writers, in the modern novel* The Mists of Avalon *by Marion Bradley, she is presented as a Pagan priestess fighting to preserve the Old Ways against Christianity, represented by Arthur.*

Sir Thomas Malory's 15th-century romance *Le Morte D'Arthur* was the first work on Arthur in English and a Tudor bestseller, being written at the same time as the invention of the printing press and one of the first printed books. Malory introduces most of the rest of the elements of the Arthurian legends, in particular the pulling of the sword from the stone, the exploits of the Knights of the Round Table, the search for the Holy Grail, and the love affair of Guinevere and Lancelot. He was inspired by both history and legend—some of this very ancient, predating Arthur himself. The grail, for instance, harks back to a cauldron of inspiration and rebirth which formed a deeply significant part of Celtic mythology, and (as suggested by Bronze Age expert Dr. Francis Pryor) the story of the sword in the stone could relate to the way swords were made in the Bronze Age.

Arthur is an ideal of manhood that has persisted from medieval times right up to the present day, combining, as he does, courage and idealism with wisdom and vulnerability. He is also Britain's greatest hero who, it is said, will rise again in his country's hour of need.

Asatru

A **Pagan** religion in the **Northern Tradition.**

Ascended Masters

Highly evolved human beings who have ascended to the spiritual plane, whether through death or not, and who no longer have any need to reincarnate. They remain, however, close to humanity in order to help and guide us, particularly at this time of transition to the new age of **Aquarius**.

Madame Blavatsky and the **theosophists** communicated with (and **channeled**) a whole hierarchy of ascended masters whom they called the great white brotherhood. Different groups recognize different ascended masters, but the list includes Jesus, the Virgin Mary, Moses, and Buddha as well as people who were not famous while on Earth.

Astral Projection/Travel

Deliberate **out-of-body experience**. Although this seems a frightening concept at first, there is a strong link between our astral (**subtle**) and physical bodies, sometimes seen as a silver cord, and this helps us return. According to J. H. Brennan, who trained himself to astral travel, people most likely to learn the skill are those who are self-confident, able to take risks, and good at concentration and visualization. Too much rational questioning, a rigid personality, and lack of confidence will get in the way.

See also **Teleportation.**

Learning Astral Travel

The following is adapted from *What Witches Do* by Stewart Farrar. It is just one method—there are many others. Don't worry if you find the exercises difficult—each of the stages may take days or weeks to achieve.

Method 1:

Concentrate on a finger and visualize its astral double.

Raise your astral finger with the power of your mind and will your physical finger to follow it.

Gradually increase the number of fingers until you can raise both hands by willpower alone. Place your hands under a table and raise your astral hands through *the table.*

Learn to control your whole astral body until you can make it stand up while your physical body is still sitting.

Visualize your astral body sitting opposite you (keep your eyes closed if necessary) and then will your consciousness into your astral body. (This is likely to happen suddenly and unmistakably.)

Method 2:

Take several items (such as tarot cards) and place them around the room. Study the items and their immediate surroundings carefully until you know every detail by heart.

Close your eyes and go on a mental walk around the room and up to each item, noting carefully how you get there and what you see when you do.

Instead of visual items, use smells (an opened scent bottle, incense stick, a spice), sounds (a clock, the hum of a television), textures, or tastes.

Once you are used to your consciousness being separate from your physical body, it becomes easier for you to detach your astral body as well.

Astrology

The science of how heavenly bodies influence events on Earth. The system used in the West comes from Babylonia (where Iraq is now) in the 1st or 2nd millennium BCE. This uses the positions and movements of the planets against the background of the stars and constellations (the zodiac). It was the Babylonians who gave us our seven-day week, based on the seven planets that they knew about. Vedic astrology, used in India, works with the stars and constellations only and **Chinese astrology** with the 12-year cycle of the planet Jupiter. Aztec and **Maya** astrology concentrates on the movements of Venus.

It's not easy to understand how astrology evolved, given that many of the events covered happen so seldom (the 26,000-year change in the Earth's tilt, for example—see **Aquarian Age**), so the science could be a lot older than we think. John Anthony West, in *The Case for Astrology,* makes the further suggestion that the ancients were much more sensitive to the heavenly bodies than we are, and actually felt their different influences so that the system was built up from first-hand experience as well as observation.

It was ancient Greeks and Romans who first started plotting individual birth charts or *horoscopes*. Before that, astrology was used to determine the fate of rulers and countries, and perhaps the timing of religious ceremonies. Like **alchemy**, the science was preserved by the Arabs and taken up by the Europeans in the Middle Ages before declining under the influence of Christianity and then being revived in the 19th century.

While most of astrology is perfectly acceptable to science, there are two main stumbling blocks:

- ❑ Why do the stars and planets cast their influence so strongly at the *birth* of a person?
- ❑ The specific influences of the planets (for more on these, see **correspondences**) and of the signs (divisions) of the zodiac.

As Lyall Watson points out in *Supernature*, babies are much more likely to be influenced at conception and just afterwards when tiny pressures can have huge effects later in life. Astrologer and physicist Peter Roberts suggests that the heavens imprint characteristics on a person at the moment of their birth rather like an image being imprinted by light on a photographic plate.

The 20th century French researchers Françoise and Michel Gauquelin found a strong correlation between prominent planets in people's birth charts and their professions, in accordance with astrological principles. However, this only held true for people who were outstandingly successful in their field and *not* for people whose births were induced. He also made the interesting find that parents and their children tended to have the same planetary influences. Peter Roberts suggests this could mean either that children *choose* when to be born, or there is some other influence at work affecting both us and the planets. He has done research into "time-twins"—unrelated people born at the same time—and has found surprising similarities in their lives.

Astrologers at work are more difficult to assess, but in a series of tests in 1959 by an American psychologist named Vernon Clark, the majority of the participating astrologers were able to match up people, events, and birth charts with complete accuracy.

The West sees ancient astrology as a combination of state religion, science, philosophy, and art—an integral part of the culture. Today it is used simply as a method of **divination**.

Atlantis

A mythical Atlantic island, which vanished in a cataclysm, **may** have had an advanced technological and spiritual civilization, and may have seeded cultures all over the world.

The island was first described by the Greek writer Plato (c. 427–347 BCE) who said the story came from Solon, an Athenian wise man of the 6th century BCE, who'd heard it from some **Egyptian** priests. According to Plato, the priests recounted the following:

- ❑ Human civilization has been subject to periodic destruction and risen and fallen many times.
- ❑ There used to be a string of islands stretching from the Mediterranean to the Americas.
- ❑ Atlantis itself was filled with a great variety of flora and fauna, including many delicious fruit and vegetables, and had natural hot and cold springs. The human settlement was on a plain surrounded by mountains, watered by irrigation ditches, and connected to the sea by a vast canal, some 5 miles long, 295 feet wide and a 100 feet deep.
- ❑ The people had invented writing and created beautiful statues. They conducted extensive sea trade and, at one stage, waged war on the cities of Europe and Asia, but the Greeks defeated them.
- ❑ The Atlantean dynasty was founded by the god Poseidon, but as the people's divinity became diluted, their moral fiber declined and they had to be punished by Zeus. The entire island was destroyed in just a single day and night (around 10,000 BCE).

The story was considered imaginary until the 19th century when the American politician Ignatius Donnelly published his influential *Atlantis: The Antediluvian World*. He proposed and presented evidence for the following:

- Atlantis existed and its peoples colonized parts of South America, the Mediterranean, and the west coast of Europe.
- The universal memory of a place of happiness and plenty (for instance, Garden of Eden) is a memory of Atlantis.
- The goddesses and gods of the ancient Greeks, the Hindus, and the Scandinavians were the queens, kings, and heroes of Atlantis.
- The mythology of Egypt and Peru represented the original religion of Atlantis (sun-worship). The civilization of ancient Egypt was a reproduction of that of Atlantis.
- The island perished in a terrible convulsion of nature and sank into the sea, with just a few people escaping in ships. Their accounts have survived and give rise to legends found all over the world.

The tale was taken up by the prophet Edgar **Cayce** and Madame **Blavatsky**. According to Cayce, the Atlanteans, during their golden age, were able to travel in the air and under the sea as well as on land. They had closer communication with animals than we do, had made a connection between material and spiritual forces, could neutralize gravity, and harnessed the sun's energy with **crystals**. It was misuse of crystal power that caused the cataclysms that sank them. According to Madame Blavatsky, the Atlanteans were spiritually superior to modern humanity, all except for those of the Aryan race who are descended from the Atlanteans. (These ideas were later used by the Nazis.) Cayce also made two predictions about Atlantis: an Atlantean hall of records would be found near the Sphinx in Egypt in 1999, and part of Atlantis would be found near the Bimini islands off Florida in 1967–68.

Although orthodox scientists scoff at the idea of Atlantis, there are many anomalies in the conventional view of human development. For example, why are there similarities between the ancient Egyptian culture and some Central American ones, both mummifying their dead, building pyramids, and using hieroglyphs? How did ancient people have detailed knowledge of planets and stars before they had telescopes, and how did they build such structures as **Stonehenge** or the Great **Pyramids**? Numerous archaeological finds don't make sense (for more on this fascinating subject see *Forbidden Archeology* by Michael Cremo and Richard Thompson) and there is really no satisfactory explanation for the Ice Ages. As Herbie Brennan points out in *The Atlantis Enigma*, a fragment of an exploding star passed close to the earth between 12,000 and 9000 BCE. This could have caused the last Ice Age, the colossal floods described in myths worldwide, and destroyed a continent.

Since 1968, all kinds of stone structures have been spotted near Bimini, elsewhere in the Bahamas and in the Caribbean—roads, walls, arches, stone circles, pyramid bases, steps, and buildings. However, opinion is divided as to whether these are natural or artificial. All of these findings are in the "Bermuda Triangle," the area between Florida, Bermuda, and Puerto Rico, where instruments malfunction and ships and planes disappear. The writer Charles Berlitz suggests there is an Atlantean crystal still there, under-water, still functioning.

Recent theories place Atlantis in the Antarctic after a shift in the Earth's crust (see *When the Sky Fell to Earth* by Rand Flem-Ath) or in South America (see *Atlantis, The Andes Solution* by Jim Allen).

See also **Lemuria.**

Atman

The divine spark within each of us, according to **Hinduism.**

Aura

The **subtle energy** field as visible to some people. In humans, it is egg-shaped and extends from a few inches to several feet or more away from the body. The size, color, and texture of our aura varies with our mood, health, and development, and dark spots or *blocks* in the aura can be early warning signs of illness.

Various scientists have tried to capture the aura on camera, most notably the Russians Valentina and Semyon Kirlian in the 1930s. In the 1980s, a technique called Aura Imaging was developed in America, which uses a computer to translate emissions from the hand into color portraits of energy around the head and top of the body. How much of the aura these techniques show is, however, open to question.

Aura Reading

People able to see the human energy field or **aura** can use this to learn about others' physical and mental health and advise them accordingly.

Learning to Sense Auras and Subtle Energy

Never look directly at the sun. If you wear glasses or contact lenses, remove them for the first three methods.

- ❑ Look up into the sky on a sunny day and notice the myriad specks of dancing light. Notice at night in the dark (indoors or outdoors) that these same specks of light can be seen.
- ❑ The first layer of the aura is a thin band of light. Look at trees from a distance and see if you can see it. Relax your eyes, as if you were looking at a Magic Eye picture.
- ❑ The following is taken from *The Celestine Prophecy* by James Redfield: Hold your index fingers a few inches away from each other against the light. See if you can see the energy like strands of smoke stretching between the tips. (Don't strain or you will produce an after-image, which can be mistaken for the aura.)
- ❑ Say to yourself "If so-and-so had an aura, what color would it be? Are there any dark spots?" Go with whatever comes into your mind.

Aura Soma

See **Color Therapy.**

Auricular Acupuncture/Therapy

This works on the body's energy system like **acupuncture** but through points on the ear only. It can treat a variety of conditions but is most often used for addictions and eating disorders. In these cases, small needles, studs, or magnets are left in the ear for the sufferer to press when they feel a craving coming on.

Autogenic Training

A form of self-**hypnosis** used for a range of chronic and stress-related conditions. Usually taught by health professionals, it consists of learning to relax physically and mentally by focusing on your breathing or imagining heaviness and warmth in different parts of the body.

Avatar

A word from **Hinduism** meaning the incarnation of the Divine, or God in human form. Buddha, Jesus, and Muhammad are all seen as avatars, and Hindus pray to avatars, living or dead, in the same way that Christians pray to Jesus and the saints. Simply being in the presence of avatars is said to have a profound effect on people.

Two living avatars are Sai Baba and Mother Meera. Sai Baba is believed to be the avatar of love prophesied in the Upanishads (c. 600 BCE). He has set up free schools, universities, and hospitals and performs many miracles including producing water out of the taps at the ashram in Puttaparthy, South India, where he lives.

Mother Meera is believed, as is the Virgin Mary, to be an incarnation of the Divine Mother. She says her mission is "to give the joy and strength necessary for change" and to activate the divine light, which is all around us but has never before been used. This light can be received by all who are open, whether or not they have met her in the flesh. She is Indian but lives in a German village.

Avebury

One of the most important prehistoric sites in Europe with the biggest stone circle in the world. A huge bank and ditch (now half their original depth) enclose a stone circle once made up of a hundred huge stones. Within this stone circle there are now two, but were probably once three smaller circles, each with further stones inside them. A stone avenue nearly two miles long (now incomplete) leads to the Sanctuary where there were once concentric circles made of wooden posts and stones. A mile away is Silbury Hill, an enormous artificial mound.

The complex is probably about 4500 years old, which makes it late Stone Age and a little earlier than **Stonehenge**. However, it may have been an important site from as much as 8000 years ago, when people first began to clear the land for farming, and had originally been made up of tree trunks instead of stones. The stones are local and unworked.

The site was rediscovered in the 18th century, by which time half of it had been destroyed by farmers clearing the land, church people wanting to remove evidence of Paganism, or just locals wanting to use the stones (one was found laid out as a fish slab). Luckily many of the stones had simply been buried in their original location, and the monument was reconstructed in the early 20th century.

The stones fall into two types: tall, thin "male" ones and shorter, rounder "female" ones. This has led people to connect the site with fertility rituals. The circles could be related to Sun or **Goddess** worship, and some have seen a **dragon** in the combination of avenues and circles. (The Sanctuary is on Hackpen Hill and *hackpen* means "head of the serpent.") The shapes are also reminiscent of **crop circles,** and as this is prime crop circle country, one researcher has put forward the idea that the monument commemorates an earlier appearance.

Silbury Hill is an even greater mystery. One theory suggests that it was built to influence **Earth Energies**.

Avebury is a lovely site in a small village and you can visit all parts of the monument at any time, except for Silbury Hill (which can't be climbed). It is much less well known than its cousin, Stonehenge, 16 miles away and in the winter you may even be lucky enough to have it to yourself.

Ayers Rock

The same as **Uluru.**

Ayurveda

This healing system is several thousand years old. It is still used in India to treat around 80 to 90 percent of the population and has recently started to become popular in the West. It is renowned for its ability to prolong life (see Deepak Chopra's best-selling *Ageless Body, Timeless Mind*) and deals especially thoroughly with sexual disorders.

Treatment is wide-ranging and comprehensive, including medicines, surgery, **psychotherapy** and **counseling, massage** (*marma*), enemas and emetics, sweating, and bloodletting. The patient may be asked to change diet or alter other aspects of lifestyle, sunbathe, do **yoga** exercises, recite **mantras,** and/or conduct rituals. Diagnosis is through taking a case history, physical examination, taking pulse, and observing urine, sweat, spit, and voice. **Astrological** considerations are also taken into account.

Ayurveda recognizes five Elements—Ether or Space, Air, Fire, Water, and Earth—and three forces or *doshas*. The doshas should be in balance but usually we are dominated by one of them and we need to learn to work with our individual make-up, particularly through what we eat, so as to counteract this imbalance.

Ayurveda—The Three Doshas			
Dosha	**Elements**	**Characteristics**	**Beneficial Food Qualities**
Vata	**Air, Ether**	**nervous, thin**	**cooked, sweet, moist**
Pitta	**Fire, Water**	**competitive, muscular**	**raw, astringent, bitter, sweet**
Kapha	**Earth, Water**	**patient, fleshy**	**hot, spicy, pungent, astringent**

Bailey, Alice

See **Aquarian Age.**

Bates Method

A type of **Vision Therapy.**

Behavioural and Cognitive Therapies

Short-term types of **psychotherapy**, which focus only on symptoms and train you to change your physical and mental bad habits.

Besant, Annie

See **Theosophy.**

Bible Code

Secret messages discovered by Jewish mystics (see **Cabbala**) in the first five books of the Bible and since verified by computer analysis.

Biochemic Tissue Salts

Mineral remedies prepared like **homeopathic** remedies and used by homeopaths, **naturopaths**, and **herbalists**. They are also available over-the-counter for self-treatment.

Biodynamic Agriculture

A specialized form of **organic** gardening and farming developed from the work of the spiritual scientist Rudolf **Steiner** at the beginning of the 20th century.

Unlike organic farming, biodynamic agriculture also recognizes the importance of cosmic forces (the influence of the planets and moon, for example) and of the **subtle energy** of plants and soil. Special preparations are used to enhance compost and for spraying on crops, and each farm or garden is seen as an individual, largely self-contained unit shaped by the relationship between the farmer and the land. As in organic farming, diversity and natural features such as woods and ponds are encouraged in biodynamic agriculture. Food that has been grown biodynamically is sold under the international Demeter label.

The movement has its center in Switzerland but there are biodynamic farms and gardens in more than 30 countries and associations in 26. The *biodynamic bible* consists of the yearly moon charts produced by Maria Thun in Germany.

Bioenergetics

Exercises to unlock defensive bodily postures and their corresponding emotional states, taught individually, at first, and then in groups. Developed by **psychotherapists**.

Biotechnology

The same as **Genetic Engineering.**

Blavatsky, Madame Helena

Russian mystic, writer, and founder of the **Theosophical Society**. She was born in 1831 and died in 1891.

Bodhisattva

A word from **Buddhism** meaning someone who has reached spiritual maturity (*enlightenment*) but who remains on Earth in order to help others. Neale Donald Walsch describes this sort of person in *Conversations with God*:

You can tell them apart at once. Their work is finished. They have returned to Earth simply and merely to help others. This is their joy. This is their exaltation. They seek naught but to be of service.

You cannot miss these people. They are everywhere. There are more of them than you think. Chances are you know one, or know of one.

(Reproduced by permission of Hodder and Stoughton Limited.)

Bodywork

Holistic massage—physical therapies which affect body, mind, and spirit and involve massage, manipulation, and movement reeducation.

Bowen Technique

A type of **bodywork** developed recently in Australia, which uses gentle rolling movements on specific points on the body to realign muscles, soft tissue, and energy. It can be done through clothes, takes only about half an hour, and two or three treatments are usually enough. It is said to work very well for all kinds of pain and injury, including sciatica, migraine, Repetitive Strain Injury (RSI) and frozen shoulder as well as asthma, menstrual irregularities, and colic.

Buddha/Buddhism

Buddhism is the world's fastest-growing religion, although under threat in many of its Asian homelands. It stems from the teachings of Siddhartha Gautama who was born into a rich Hindu family in Northern India around 560 BCE. At the age of 29 he abandoned his wife and baby son to live a life of poverty. After much soul-searching, he came to the following conclusions, which he called the four noble truths: all life involves suffering; suffering is caused by desire and by attachment to things that are impermanent; suffering ends when desire and attachment end; we can stop desire and attachment by following the eightfold path. This path should follow a middle way between the extremes of self-indulgence and asceticism and consists of: right understanding (that is, accepting the four noble truths); right aims; right speech; right actions; right livelihood; right effort (controlling the mind); right thinking (calming the mind); and right concentration (**meditation**).

Although Buddhists may use wise and enlightened people (**bodhisattvas** and buddhas) as examples, there is no god in Buddhism. It is through the control of our own minds, in particular through meditation, that we achieve freedom—if not in this lifetime then in a future one. We have no permanent self since, like the rest of life, we are constantly evolving into new forms.

The earliest form of Buddhism (Theravada), which is still followed in South-East Asia, stressed withdrawal from the world and considered that only monks were likely to reach enlightenment. The later form (Mahayana), found today in China, Japan, and Tibet, holds that salvation is available to all.

Buddha's teachings were originally passed on by word of mouth and weren't written down until a few hundred years after his death. The oldest and shortest text, the *Dhammapada*, contains the essential Buddhist philosophy. The three *Pitaka* (baskets) deal with monastic discipline, the story of Buddha, and advanced philosophy.

See also ***Tibetan Book of the Dead***, and ***Zen***.

A Buddhist glossary

Bodhisattva: *Someone who has nearly reached enlightenment (buddhahood) but who delays passage so as to help others.*

Buddha: *An enlightened person. There are many who have reached this state in the past and there are many who will do so in the future. The Buddha is Siddhartha Guatama, the founder of Buddhism. The Buddha nature is the root mind or soul of all sentient beings.*

Dharma: *The Buddha's teachings.*

Enlightenment: *Total wisdom, total compassion, and total mastery of desire.*

Maitreya: *The Buddha to come.*

Nirvana: *The state of bliss when desire ceases. Freedom from the cycle of death and rebirth. Between being and not being.*

C

Cabbala, Cabala

This mystical form of Judaism flourished from the early centuries after Christ until the Middle Ages. Originally an oral tradition only, some of its teachings were written down in medieval times, most notably by Moses de Leon, who produced a work called *Zohar* or *The Book of Splendour* in about 1290. The 16th-century prophet **Nostradamus** is thought to have been influenced by the Cabbala. The cabbalistic idea of the Tree of Life was revived and expanded by the **Hermetic Order of the Golden Dawn** in the late 19th century, and **gematria** or the practice of reading secret meanings into words, particularly those of the Old Testament, received new impetus with the advent of computers.

The Tree of Life represents both the universe and humans. It is portrayed roots up and describes the emanations of God or the progression of spirit towards matter and matter back to spirit. The tree contains 10 (or sometimes 11) *sephiroth* or spheres, which are levels of divine manifestation, and these are connected by 22 paths. The Golden Dawn related the sephiroth and paths to Greek, Roman, and Egyptian gods; Christian and Jewish spirits; astrology; the tarot; and colors, scents, stones, and animals and used these correspondences in their meditations and magical practices. The psychologist

Jung also became interested in the Cabbala and the following table shows the traditional interpretations of the Hebrew names for the sephiroth, as well as modern psychological ones.

The 11 Sephiroth or Levels of the Cabbala Tree of Life		
Hebrew Name	*Translation*	*Psychological Interpretation*
Kether	crown	divine connection
Hokmah	wisdom	revelation
Binah	understanding	reason
Daath	knowledge	spirit
Hesed	mercy	compassion
Geburah	judgement, severity	discipline
Tiphareth	beauty, harmony	self
Netzack	glory, victory	practice
Hod	power, splendor	theory
Yesod	foundation	ego
Malkuth	kingdom	body

Cabbalists supposed that the first five books of the Old Testament had been received directly from God by Moses, and to contain within them hidden meanings accessible by assigning numbers to each of the Hebrew letters and then making connections between words with the same numerical value. Computer analysis of this Bible code, as it is known, has revealed predictions hidden in the writings. The Hebrew alphabet can be related to the 22 paths of the Tree of Life and this gives Hebrew words extra layers of meaning, much like **Egyptian** hieroglyphs.

Castaneda, Carlos

A Californian academic who went to Mexico in 1960 to study medicinal herbs and became drawn by the sorcerer Don Juan into the strange and disturbing world of native **Shamanism**, about which he has written many books. These are considered, by some, to be fiction.

Cayce, Edgar

This devout and unassuming son of a Kentucky farmer discovered, at the age of 21, that he had the ability to go into trance and describe people's health problems and the appropriate treatment. He went on to do *readings*, as they are called, for 43 years for over 8000 people until his death in 1945.

Although at first limited to health, his readings later covered such topics as reincarnation and past lives, **Atlantis** and ancient **Egypt**, crystals, dream interpretation, and **meditation**. His information, he said, came directly from the **Akashic Records** and many of his readings were "travelling" ones, that is, for people not present. He also made prophecies about Earth changes—for example, a shifting of the Earth's axis (tilt) at the end of the 20th century which would cause Japan and the "upper portions" of Europe to be submerged and Los Angeles, San Francisco, and New York to be destroyed. Prophecies that have come true include the Wall Street Crash, the assassination of Kennedy, and the formation of Israel.

In 1931 Cayce (pronounced *kay-see*), with his family and supporters, set up the Association for Research and Enlightenment in Virginia. This still exists, has kept transcripts of most of his readings, and in the 1960s, began publishing selections of his work by theme (under the editorship of his son Hugh Lynn Cayce and grandson Charles Thomas Taylor Cayce).

Celts

The Bronze Age people of Europe whose vibrant culture has left a lasting impression in spite of Roman occupation and Christianity. The **Druids**, who may have descended from the Shamanic Stone Age people who preceded the Celts, acted as their priests, scholars, poets, musicians, counselors, magicians, and healers. For their rituals they used the stone circles and other megalithic monuments of these earlier people, as well as clearings (groves) in forests.

The Celts' spiritual experience was closely bound up with nature. Trees were particularly important, featuring in their alphabet (**ogham**) and their system of lunar astrology. Caves and water—for example springs and pools—were also revered. Their year began with the start of winter (October 31), and each new season was celebrated as well as the year's solstices and equinoxes.

Celtic Festivals

These were adapted for use by Christianity and form the basis of modern-day Paganism. Four are related to the sun (solstices and equinoxes), and the other four mark the changing seasons and would probably have been celebrated at the full moon, so the dates are approximate. The Celtic day started and finished at sunset.

Samhain (pronounced* sow-in*)

October 31

New year and start of Winter. A major festival and time when the door to the Otherworld opens. Celebrated with

(cont'd)

fire as all lunar festivals, and a time for acknowledging death. Continued today as Halloween and (in the United Kingdom) as Bonfire Night (November 5).

Yule

December 21

Winter solstice (shortest day). Rituals connected with rebirth. Absorbed into Christmas.

Imbolc, Imbolg, or Oimelc

February 1, 2

The start of Spring. A time to honor the Goddess, particularly Brigid, goddess of Fire and Water. The Christian Candlemas.

Eostre/Ostara

March 21

Spring Equinox (day and night equal length). Became Easter.

Beltane/Beltain

April 30, May 1

The other major festival (besides Samhain) and the start of summer. Continued today as May Day.

Midsummer

June 21

Summer solstice (longest day of the year). Worship at stone circles and prehistoric monuments aligned with the sun such as Stonehenge.

Lammas/Lughnasadh (pronounced **loo-nassa*)***

July 31, August 1

The start of autumn.

Autumn Equinox

September 21

Day and night are equal length. The Christian Harvest Festival.

The Celtic Otherworld was the magical realm where you met heroes, goddesses, gods, and fairy folk. At certain times of year, and in certain places, the veil between this world and the other was thinner, and you could move between the two.

Celtic culture was a largely oral one, so what is known comes from archaeology, the Romans (who wrote about the colorful warrior race they had come up against), and medieval storytellers who used Celtic legends. The Celts were hard to shift and Christianity had to graft itself on to indigenous beliefs. So, for example, churches were built on Celtic sacred sites, Celtic festivals became Christian ones and Celtic deities became saints or, as in the case of the horned god Cernunnos, devils. Folklore also reflects Celtic—and earlier—practices and beliefs, particularly in the Far West and North (Ireland, Scotland, Wales, Cornwall, and Brittany) where the culture continued undisturbed for longer.

See also **Arthur**.

Centering

Deep inside we are all happy, peaceful, and wise, and centering is a way of getting in touch with that part of ourselves. As Shakti Gawain says in *Creative Visualization*, life is about being, doing, and having, in that order, but so often we do it back to front or forget the "being" part, and the result is misery and exhaustion. The simple techniques in the following box may help to put things right. They don't need to take very long because all you are doing is reminding yourself of something that is always there.

See also **Meditation**.

Centering—Some Suggestions

- ❑ Create a beautiful place in your imagination, whether indoors or outdoors, and go there whenever you feel the need.
- ❑ Create a small shrine or sacred space in your house.

(cont'd)

- ❑ Sit quietly, preferably outside, and feel the four Elements—Fire (sun), Air (wind), Water (moisture, the sound of running water) and Earth (ground).
- ❑ Sit quietly, preferably outside facing South and be aware of the four compass points.
- ❑ See how long you can stand on one leg with your eyes closed. Change legs.
- ❑ Close your eyes and breathe deeply. Inhale for a count of four, hold for a count of four, exhale for a count of four, hold for a count of four. Repeat.

Chakras

Points on the body where life energy (**subtle energy**) is taken in, processed, and given out, much as our lungs do with air. The word is **Sanskrit** for wheel, the chakras having first been described by Indian **yogis** thousands of years ago and looking like cone-shaped vortexes.

There are seven main chakras, each processing a different part of the spectrum of energy and, therefore, relating to a different area of our experience. They respond to different colors and musical notes and are connected to different organs, glands, and physical systems (such as blood circulation).

You can also see the chakras as reflecting our development from childhood to old age and the development of humankind as a whole. For example, Caroline Myss, in *Why People Don't Heal and How They Can*, sees the first three chakras as producing a tribal mentality. With the birth of Christ, humankind became able to access the energy of the next four chakras and learned about the importance of individual experience. As we enter the age of **Aquarius** she sees us moving into a new eighth chakra (in the **energy** body above the head) which will lead us to see our individual experiences in universal or **archetypal** terms.

Working with the chakras ensures that energy flows freely throughout our body so that we stay physically, mentally, emotionally, and spiritually healthy. It helps us to understand that we are creatures of many parts, and to keep a balance between them. It also helps us to understand why other people and other countries are different from us, and to respect them whatever their level of development.

See also **Kundalini**.

The Seven Main Chakras

Understanding the role of each chakra helps us to pinpoint areas of weakness. Because physical problems are usually the last to show up, they have not been listed here. You will find slight variations in people's interpretation of the functions of the different chakras.

Name and Location	Color	Function	Symptoms of Imbalance	Helpful Activities
Base Extending down from the groin	red	physical survival	feeling insecure or ungrounded, violence	work, competitive sports, conventional medicine
Sacral Below navel	orange	social and sexual conection, giving and receiving	too empathetic or clinging, giving or recieving too much	massage, gentle flowing exercises, such as dance, yoga, or t'ai chi
Solar Plexus Above navel	yellow	Ideas, willpower, self-image	Chasing, novelty, feeling of not enough time, addiction, arrogance, poor self-esteem	Affirmations, finishing things, psycho-therapy (especially congnitive and behavioral)

(cont'd)

Name and Location	Color	Function	Symptoms of Imbalance	Helpful Activities
Heart In the middle of the chest	green	emotions	Feeling numb, being dominated by negative emotions, such as fear and anger	Looking after children and animals, music, psycho-therapy, especially humanistic
Throat Below navel	sky blue, turquoise	Organiza-tion, sense of duty, self-expression	Living in the past, bigotry, repression	Meditation, laughter
Third Eye In the center of brow	indigo	Intuition, psychic abilities. wisdom	Living in the future, lots of plans but no action	*Doing* anything, especially if practical or physical, divination
Crown Extending up from top of the head	violet	Connection with the Divine, channeling, compas-sion, creativity	Depression, confusion	Spiritual and creative activity of all kinds, selfless service, fasting, healing, silence

Chakra visualization

This can help correct areas of imbalance.

- ❑ Close your eyes and calm your mind in your usual way or see *meditation.*
- ❑ Work through each of the chakras, in turn, from the base to the crown. Imagine them spinning freely (in clockwise direction as you look at the body) and extending outwards from both the front and back of the body.
- ❑ See the colors of each of them, and as they spin, imagine them throwing out accumulated dust and debris so that energy can pass freely into and around you.
- ❑ If you find one of the chakras refuses to spin properly spend a little extra time imagining sending warmth and light to that area of your body.
- ❑ When you have finished, feel the connections between the chakras, and the energy spreading throughout your body. Give thanks.

Channeling

Receiving and passing on information from spirit beings. According to Sanaya Roman and Duane Packer, authors of the classic *Opening to Channel*, many of us can do this. All it takes is a strong desire to do so, and the ability to relax and hold the concentration. **Meditation** can be valuable training here. We can channel information both for ourselves and for other people. Therapists and artists can use channeling in their work. It can also help **divination**.

We lay ourselves open to channeling through "raising our vibrations." This means that we are very unlikely to attract lower and unhelpful spirits. If we do, we will know them immediately because they tell us what to do and make us feel worse, and we can simply ask them to go away. Some people channel in trance and remember nothing afterwards, but it is better to try and stay conscious because, in this way, channeling will expand our normal consciousness and enhance our life as a whole. It can be a good idea to record, at the time, the information that comes through, either with a tape recorder or by repeating it to someone who can write it down.

Channels have gone by various names in the past—oracles, seers, prophets, **Shamans**—but in the last 150 years, many more of us are finding we have the power. This, some say, is because the vibrations of the Earth are changing and because many higher souls are choosing to incarnate. With their ability to explore other realms they create a doorway for the rest of us. As Orin and DaBen, the guides of Roman and Packer, say, "This is a time in which people who put their energies into growing spiritually will be abundantly rewarded...The golden age of man is coming."

See also **Spirit Guides**.

Cheirology/Cheiromancy (also Chirology Chiromancy)

The same as **Handreading**.

Chi

The Chinese word for life energy or **subtle energy**. Chi (pronounced *chee*) flows around our body through channels called *meridians*, nourishing every organ and influencing our emotions and states of mind. The flow can be upset by both internal and external factors—including illness, injury, lifestyle, weather, and climate. It is adjusted through **traditional Chinese medicine**, in particular **acupuncture**.

Chi Kung/Qi Gong

A type of exercise related to **t'ai chi** that has been practiced for thousands of years in China. It consists of simple postures and movements, breathing, meditation, and visualization. Its purpose is to develop **chi** or life energy in order to enhance vitality and extend life span.

Childbirth, Alternative Options

Although the technology of hospitals can reassure us that we will be taken care of should anything go wrong, hospitals are not the ideal places in which to give birth. The stress of the surroundings can affect both labor and the baby, and it is all too easy to be coerced into medical intervention we don't really want. According to the noted childbirth educator Sheila Kitzinger, the lack of control that some women feel in hospital can affect them for decades, and several studies have shown a link between medical intervention and postnatal depression. Alternatives are home birth, special birthing centers, and small hospitals.

For several hundred years, women were forced into giving birth lying on their backs, but now, thanks to women's insistence and the work of Dr. Michel Odent, mothers are allowed to move about and find more natural positions such as sitting, squatting, and standing. Dr. Odent also introduced the birthing pool. This can help with pain and is a less traumatic way for the baby to enter the world. Birthing pools can be hired for use at home as well as in hospitals.

More and more women are choosing to use **complementary therapies** during labor, even bringing their therapists into hospitals. Therapies used include acupuncture and acupressure, homoeopathy, herbalism, aromatherapy and massage, reflexology, hypnotherapy, and flower remedies. These can help to induce an overdue baby, stimulate contractions, relieve fear and pain, expel the placenta, and promote healing. Some of them can be practiced by companions during labor as well as by therapists.

Dr. Frederick Leboyer's beautiful book *Birth without Violence* describes birth from a baby's point of view and shows what a terrifying transition it can be. He makes many suggestions as to what we can do to make a baby's entry into the world as gentle as possible, in particular delaying cutting the umbilical cord until it stops pulsating so that the baby can gradually start breathing on its own. He maintains it is our unconscious memory of our own traumatic first breath that makes us insist the cord be cut as quickly as possible and the baby slapped to make it breathe (a trauma that is addressed in **rebirthing**, which uses special breathing techniques to heal us).

Chinese Astrology

Like Western **astrology**, this has 12 character types or signs but, unlike Western astrology, these relate to the 12-year cycle of the planet Jupiter (not the sun, month by month). Each new year begins on a slightly different date so you need to consult a detailed chart if your birthday falls in January or February (otherwise you can use the information from the chart provided).

The *year* of your birth gives your dominant sign—your main characteristics and the face you present to the world. The *time* of your birth gives your ascendant sign—your inner self and characteristics that modify your dominant ones. The *month* of your birth is your love sign—the characteristics you bring to intimate relationships.

The signs are represented by 12 animals, and each of the animals is influenced by a different Element, of which there are five in Chinese tradition (for more on these see **feng shui**). Each *year* is also connected to an Element, so you are likely to have more than one Element in your astrological profile. As in Western astrology, signs are either feminine or masculine (**yin or yang**).

Chinese Astrology—the 12 Signs

Sign and Element	*Main Characteristic*	*Years and Elements*	*Month*	*Time*	*Energy*
Rat Water	Intelligent	1948 1960 1972 1984 1996 Earth Metal Water Wood Fire	Dec	11 pm–1 am	Yang
Ox Earth	Patient	1949 1961 1973 1985 1997 Earth Metal Water Wood Fire	Jan	1 am–3 am	Yin
Tiger Wood	Brave	1950 1962 1974 1986 1998 Metal Water Wood Fire Earth	Feb	3 am–5 am	Yang
Hare Wood	Diplomatic	1951 1963 1975 1987 1999 Metal Water Wood Fire Earth	March	5 am–7 am	Yin
Dragon Earth	Dynamic	1940 1952 1964 1976 1988 Metal Water Wood Fire Earth	April	7 am–9 am	Yang
Snake Fire	Wise	1941 1953 1965 1977 1989 Metal Water Wood Fire Earth	May	9 am–11 am	Yin
Horse Fire	Independent	1942 1954 1966 1978 1990 Water Wood Fire Earth Metal	June	11 am–1 pm	Yang
Sheep Earth	Adaptable	1943 1955 1967 1979 1991 Water Wood Fire Earth Metal	July	1 pm–3 pm	Yin
Monkey Metal	Fun-Loving	1944 1956 1968 1980 1992 Water Wood Fire Earth Metal	Aug	3 pm–5 pm	Yang
Rooster Metal	Resillient	1945 1957 1969 1981 1993 Wood Fire Earth Metal Water	Sept	5 pm–7 pm	Yin
Dog Earth	Loyal	1946 1958 1970 1982 1994 Fire Earth Metal Water Wood	Oct	7 pm–9 pm	Yang
Pig Water	Optimistic	1947 1959 1971 1983 1995 Fire Earth Metal Water Wood	Nov	9 pm–11 pm	Yin

**Consult a more detailed chart if born in January or February or outside range of years shown here.*

Chinese Medical Massage

See **Tui Na.**

Chiropractic

Regulated by law like **osteopathy**, this therapy involves correcting the position of joints with quick "thrusts." Diagnosis is likely to be by X-ray.

McTimoney, McTimoney-Corley, and applied chiropractic are gentler and more **holistic** forms, which do not use X-rays.

Clairaudience/Clairsentience/Clairvoyance

Different forms of **extrasensory perception** (ESP). In *clairaudience* you hear voices or sounds, either in your head or externally like normal sounds; in *clairsentience* you feel emotions and bodily sensations that belong to another person, place, or time, or know things intuitively; in *clairvoyance* you perceive literal or symbolic images, or in some cases, writing.

Codependence/Codependency

A term used by **psychotherapists** for unhealthy dependence on other people—living our life through, or for, other people. It is used especially for the families of addicts—people who get so used to caring for someone else that they become dependent on having someone dependent on them. Another word used in the same context is *boundaries*—we have to be clear where we end and other people begin. Becoming healthily dependent rather than codependent is part of the process of growing up.

An organization set up specifically to help the families of alcoholics is Alcoholics Anonymous (AA).

Avoiding Codependence

Some people may need professional help, but here is what you can do for yourself.

- ❑ If you help other people, don't be attached to the outcome. Do what you can and then set them free. Don't give advice unless asked.
- ❑ Don't blame others for *your* feelings. If you are talking to someone about something they have done that has upset or angered you, use "I" rather than "you." For example, "I get lonely without you," not "You are unkind to leave me alone so much."
- ❑ Learn to enjoy being on your own.
- ❑ Develop your spiritual side.

Cognitive Therapy

Short-term **psychotherapy**, which focuses on symptoms only and offers simple techniques, such as **affirmations**, for changing things in the here and now, particularly the way you think.

Cohousing

See **Communities**.

Colonic Hydrotherapy/Irrigation/Lavage

The colon or large intestine is the last part of our digestive system. Some **complementary therapists** believe that malfunction here can lead not just to digestive and bowel problems but to illness throughout the body. Causes of malfunction include bad diet, not drinking enough water, lack of exercise, stress, drugs, and pollution. The therapy involves cleaning out the waste matter that has become stuck by using water at low pressure. It is quite painless, and safe if done by someone who is properly trained. Afterwards, herbs and probiotics (helpful bacteria) are implanted so that the process of digestion can get going again properly. Although some nurses and doctors are trained in the therapy, others are skeptical about its value.

Color and Light Therapy

Like plants, we are sensitive to light. For example, natural light causes the level of cholesterol in our blood to drop, and not enough can lead to depression. The hormone *melatonin*, which makes us sleepy, is secreted by our bodies in the absence of light. And we are also sensitive to color, whether or not we can actually see it. Most of us can be trained to distinguish colors through touch alone. Ultraviolet rays enable the body to manufacture vitamin D, and red light has been found to speed up the circulation and raise blood pressure.

Color and light therapy are used within both conventional and **complementary medicine** for both physical and mental problems. It is a vast subject, which has only ever been researched piecemeal. In Indian **ayurvedic** medicine, color and light have been used for millennia and are related to the **chakras** (the body's energy centers), each of which responds to a different color and is connected to different organs of the body and different types of mental and emotional activity.

Complementary therapists shine beams of colored light on parts of or the entire body, and advise on the colors of clothes, furnishings, and food. In Aura-Soma therapy you choose from an array of colored oils. Your choice is then used by the therapist to advise you on your physical and emotional health, and you take the oil away to use on your body. Colorpuncture directs beams of light on to **acupuncture** points. A Monochrome Dome developed in Sweden bathes you in the entire spectrum of colors and is used to treat depression, phobias, stress, and anxiety.

Light therapy is sometimes used by doctors for skin conditions such as psoriasis, acne, and skin cancer. In the 1920s, a variety of ailments including wounds and scars, asthma, hay fever, pneumonia, and cataracts were treated with light therapy and its wider use is coming back into favor. Sufferers of the winter depression known as seasonal affective disorder (SAD) are treated with bright light therapy, and equipment for home use is available. This can also help eating disorders, addictions, and infertility.

Color and Light—Self-help

- ❑ Pay attention to the color of your clothes, furnishings, and food. Go with your instincts when making choices.
- ❑ Irradiate your drinking water with different colors by placing it in sunlight in a colored container.
- ❑ Use different colored crystals (see **crystals/crystal therapy**).
- ❑ Use color in your meditations. For example, choose a color and direct it in your imagination to a part of your body that needs healing. Or, imagine your chosen color penetrating deep inside you and bathing you from head to foot.
- ❑ Try to have at least an hour's exposure to natural light per day on as much of your body as possible. If you are not used to the sun, build up gradually (and bear in mind current medical advice about the need to protect skin with sunscreen).
- ❑ Indoors use "natural light" bulbs.

Chromotherapy

The same as **Color Therapy.**

Communities

Intentional communities are formed for a variety of reasons. One of the most common is the environmental benefit. American research shows that communards use 36 percent less gas and 82 percent less electricity per person compared to their non-communal neighbors. Shared land, money, and person power mean that communities can try out alternative energy sources such as windmills and solar panels, recycle their own sewage (e.g. in reed beds or compost toilets), and produce their own organic food.

Another common reason is the spiritual. One of Britain's oldest and best-known communities at **Findhorn** in Scotland sees their ideological focus as "celebrating the divinity in all of life," and has a busy program of courses attended by people from all over the world. The Pilsdon Community in Dorset is a group of 45 Christians who offer a temporary home to people facing a crisis in their lives, such as homelessness or addiction. The Camphill movement, inspired by the work of Rudolf **Steiner**, has almost one hundred centers worldwide where people of all ages with developmental disabilities can live, learn, and work with others.

There are Hindu, Buddhist, monastic, feminist, and socialist communities as well as communities developed to provide low-cost housing, home-based children's education, and craft facilities.

Community living—Carol's story

I first visited an intentional community when I was 18. I was on vacation in Denmark and visited a Danish friend who lived with four other families. Each family had their own house plus use of a communal house and communal grounds, including a beautiful courtyard where we had supper under the stars. My sense of the residents' mutual love has remained with me to this day. This was the beginning of my dream of making a more communal lifestyle for myself, and on my 30th birthday I celebrated the fulfillment of this dream with a big shared supper under the same stars in the cobbled courtyard of my new home at Beech Hill in Devon.

Beech Hill is one of many intentional communities in England. It has a large old house, several other smaller houses around the courtyard, plus beautiful gardens. It offered more than the shared houses that I had been living in until then—everyone is actively choosing to share their living arrangements and so there is much better motivation to reach agreement about the usual niggles like cooking, washing dishes, and cleaning. Also, being a cooperative, which owns and manages the property, there is much more scope for working together to improve the place and to develop environmentally-sustainable projects. And for children (and adults who enjoy being around children), communal living is a great way to learn from a wide variety of adults and other children.

The good things about Beech Hill are:

- ❑ *I love the people who live here.*
- ❑ *I am strengthened by the things we achieve as a group that I could not attempt alone.*
- ❑ *I am proud of the ways we work collectively—no one is in charge.*
- ❑ *I devour our tasty, organic, home-grown vegetables.*
- ❑ *I am richer because we share domestic and garden equipment.*
- ❑ *I revel in our shared swimming pool.*
- ❑ *I am sustained by our beautiful grounds and buildings.*
- ❑ *I get exhausted when we work hard together.*
- ❑ *I hear laughter and music every day.*
- ❑ *I have fulfilled some of my dreams at Beech Hill.*

Things I don't like include the many meetings—frequently in an evening after I have been at work all day; the continually infinite list of work to do around the place and some of the guilt I feel when I feel I haven't done enough; and the exhaustion that can come from sharing the emotional highs and lows of 20 people.

On the other hand, living in a community has taught me so much about how humans interact; about my needs and the needs of others; about communication and respect. Beech Hill has made me who I am and I am very grateful for it.

Many people join communities simply for the company or to save money. Often a community has a combination of aims. They are found in towns and countrysides all over the world.

Two more recent trends are ecovillages and cohousing. Ecovillages are communities with a strong environmental focus whose inhabitants are likely to work within the village—which is not always the case in other communities. The main focus of cohousing is social. People live in individual houses but share facilities such as gardens, workshops, guestrooms, and cars.

If you want to join a community, you need first to find out if they have space for new members. Both the United Kingdom and the United States publish directories (see Resources section) of communities and international contact addresses. Many communities run visitor weekends during which you have a chance to join in the life of the community and see whether it is for you. Others let prospective members come and stay for progressively longer periods.

Complementary Currencies

See **LETS**.

Complementary Health/Medicine/Therapies

The use of complementary medicine has grown enormously in the last few decades, and in the United Kingdom there are now more complementary therapists than general practitioners (family doctors). In fact, 40 percent of GPs refer patients to complementary therapists and 20 percent have therapies available at their surgeries.

The main differences between conventional and complementary medicine are:

- ❑ In complementary medicine, people are treated as individuals, so two people with the same disease might be treated differently.

- Complementary therapies take into account mind, emotions, and spirit as well as the body, and aim to have an effect on all levels.
- Complementary treatment does not inflict further harm and aims to support the body's own natural healing ability.
- It treats the causes of ill health, not the symptoms. Symptoms are seen as evidence of your system trying to reestablish a healthy equilibrium and not usually something to be suppressed.

In other words, complementary medicine is *holistic*—it takes the whole picture into account. It is also sometimes described as *natural* medicine because it's low tech, and before it started to become absorbed into the mainstream it was known as *alternative* medicine.

The best way to find a therapist is by word of mouth. Alternatively, you can check out local advertisements or contact umbrella and therapy organizations (see Resources) who can send you lists of registered practitioners. However, few therapies are regulated by law so the only real way to judge a practitioner is through your own instinct or the testimony of someone who has been treated by them. Some therapists offer a short initial consultation free of charge.

Complementary treatment may take longer than conventional, especially if you've been ill for a long time, but you should be consulted at all stages as to how you want the treatment to proceed. The first session normally takes at least an hour while the therapist finds out all about you. You will then be expected to take part in your own cure, if necessary, by modifying your lifestyle—diet, exercise, amount of relaxation, and so on. Sometimes during treatment you may find that your symptoms get worse for a short while. This is known as a *healing crisis* and is usually seen as a good thing because it is a sign that your defenses are being mobilized.

Complementary treatment is best at treating chronic illness and symptoms that are uncomfortable but not something you would go to a doctor about, such as poor sleep, frequent colds, or headaches, since these are seen as early warning signs of "imbalance" or disease. It is also increasingly used for animals. A big advantage of complementary medicine for many people is the fact that none of the remedies is tested on animals, although a very small number (see **homeopathy** and **herbal medicine**) do come from animals. This book covers the better-established therapies and those with a reasonable record of success. New therapies are being developed all the time but often these are just variations on older ones.

See also **Dentistry.**

Complementary Therapies

The therapies listed below are those covered in the book. Those in parenthesis are the related or less well-known therapies provided, either in a separate entry or under the main entry.

The animal ratings relate to the situation at present. However, it is changing very quickly as people increasingly turn to complementary medicine for their animals.

Therapy	How it Works	Use on Animals
Acupuncture (Acumassage, Acupressure,Auricular Acupuncture/Therapy)	S	*
Alexander technique (Feldenkrais Method)	B	
Anthropological Medicine	B,M,E,S	
Aromatherapy	B	*
Ayurveda	B,M,E,S	
Chiropractic (McTimoney, McTimoney-Corley and Applied Chiropractic)	B	*
Colonic Hydrotherapy/ Irrigation/Lavage	B	

(cont'd)

Therapy	How it works	Use on animals
Color and Light Therapy	S	*
Counseling	M,E	*
Creative Therapy (art, dance, drama, music)	B,M,E,S	
Crystal Therapy (electro-crystal therapy)	S	*
Flower Essences/Remedies	S	**
Healing (Radionics, Theraputic Touch)	S	***
Herbal Medicine (Western and Chinese)	B	**
Homeopathy (Biochemic Tissue Salts)	S	***
Hypnotherapy (Hypnoanalysis, past-life regression)	M,E	
Kinesiology (Touch for Health)	S	*
Magnet Therapy	B	***
Massage and Bodywork (Bioenergetics, Bowen Technique, Craniosacral Therapy, Do-In, Hellerwork, Indian Head Massage, Looyenwork, Marma, Rolfiung, Swedish Massage, Thai Massage, Trager, Tui Na, Zero Balancing)		
Naturopahty (Hydrotherapy/ Flotation, Iridiology)	B,M,E,S	*
Nutritional Therapy	B	*
Osteopathy (Craniam Osteopathy)	B,S	**
Polarity Therapy	B,M,E,S	

(cont'd)

Therapy	How it works	Use on animals
Psychotherapy (Analysis, Behavioral and Cognitive, Bioenergetics, Clinical Psychology, Existential, Gestalt, Humanistic/ Human Potential, Inner Child Work, Neurolinguistic Programming, Person-centered, Primal, Psychiatry,Psychoanalysis, Psychodrama, Psychodynamic, Psychospiritual, Psychosynthesis, Rebirthing, Transactional Analysis, Transpersonal)	(B) M,E (S)	
Reflexology (Metamorphic Technique, Vacuflex)	B,S	*
Reiki (Karuna, Tera-Mai, Seichem, Seichim/Sekhem)	S	***
Shiatsu	B,S	
Sound Therapy	S	
Traditional Chinese Medicine (Acupuncture, Herbs, Tui Na)	B,S	
Vision Education/Therapy (Bates Method)	B,ME	

Key

B	through body	*	occasional use, some animals
M	through mind	**	moderate use, some animals
E	through emotions	***	well established for use on a variety of animals
S	through spirit/subtle energy		

Correspondences

Connections between large and small or general and specific used in the West for **divination** and **magic** and in the East for healing. Traditional Western correspondences derive from classical writers (who were perhaps influenced in their turn by the ancient **Egyptians**) and focus on the planets and the Elements. The sun and moon are counted as planets and there are four Elements—Earth, Air, Water, and Fire. Eastern systems such as **ayurveda** and **traditional Chinese medicine** use five Elements.

Like **dream** symbols and **archetypes**, correspondences are both universal and specific, so when working with them, use a traditional system but enrich it with your own experience.

The Planets and Some of Their Correspondences

You will see that Uranus, Neptune, and Pluto don't have as many correspondences as the other planets. This is because they weren't discovered until relatively recently (18th, 19th and 20th centuries, respectively).

Planet	Qualities	Color	Metal	Day	Astrological Sign
Sun	joy, creativity, vitality	yellow	gold	Sunday	Leo
Moon	intuition, dreams, psychic sensitivity, emotions, fertility	white	silver	Monday	Cancer
Mars	assertiveness, competitveness, anger, struggle	red	iron	Tuesday	Aries
Mercury	communication, flexibilty, thought, science	grey	mercury	Wednesday	Gemini

(cont'd)

Planet	Qualities	Color	Metal	Day	Astrological Sign
Jupiter	leadership, success, responsibility, expansion, optimism	blue	tin	Thursday	Sagittarius
Venus	sharing, pleasure, love, beauty	green	copper	Friday	Taurus
Saturn	discipline, trials, introversion, idealism	black	lead	Saturday	Capricorn
Uranus	nonconformity, higher consciousness, anarchy				Aquarius
Neptune	mysticism, self-sacrifice, illusion, prophecy,				Pisces
Pluto	drastic upheaval, transformation, ends and beginnings				Aries

The Elements and Some of Their Correspondences

Element	Area of Experience	Direction	Season	Tarot Suit	Astrological Sign	Concentrated In
Earth	physical, material	North	Winter	Pentacles	Taurus, Virgo, Capricorn	caves, standing stones, soil
Air	mental, intellectual	East	Autumn	Swords	Gemini, Libra, Aquarius	windy and high places, smoke, incense
Water	emotional	West	Spring	Cups	Cancer, Scorpio, Pisces	springs, pools, rivers, lakes, seas
Fire	spiritual, creative	South	Summer	Wands	Aries, Leo, Sagittarius	candles, fires, sun

Counseling

A form of **psychotherapy**, often for people undergoing some sort of crisis in their lives but also for long-standing mental and emotional problems. Counselors help by giving you their complete uncritical attention, which is therapeutic in itself. Through carefully directed questioning, they lead you to find your own solutions and give you back a sense of control. With couples and groups, they can act as a sort of referee, turning painful conflicts into constructive discussions.

Many counselors have specific training in dealing with particular issues, or special knowledge that can help you make difficult decisions. Areas covered include bereavement, rape, finances, addictions, medical issues, partnership and family problems, sexual difficulties, and problems with study or work. Counseling is available over the phone as well as face to face.

Craniosacral Therapy

The spine and brain are cushioned by fluid, which flows in slow rhythmic waves, which if disturbed, can put pressure on nerves and cause pain. The therapist aims to correct this by lightly touching your lower back and head. This can help a variety of conditions including neuralgia, migraine, and pain from head injuries. Like cranial **osteopathy**, it is very gentle and so particularly recommended for those in severe pain, the elderly, babies, and children.

Creative Therapies

Non-verbal forms of **psychotherapy**, involving art (such as painting, sculpture), dance (sometimes called dance movement therapy), drama (sometimes called psychodrama) and music. They are used within conventional medical circles for people with severe emotional problems, children, the terminally ill, or people with mental or physical handicaps, but are also a good way for anyone to relax, release emotions, and find out more about themselves. Done either individually or in a group, no special talent, previous experience, or any particular level of fitness is needed.

In dramatherapy you can find out what it feels like to behave differently from your usual self or explore ways of dealing with difficult situations. A popular form of dance therapy is Gabrielle Roth's "five rhythms." In this you are encouraged to move completely freely to five different types of music—flowing, staccato, chaotic, lyrical, and still. The aim is to put you in touch with your body and with the present so that you liberate your natural creativity, spontaneity, and joyfulness.

Crop Circles

In 1980, a Wiltshire farmer found two circles of neatly flattened oats in one of his fields and called in UFO researchers. They contacted a local physicist, and between them, they came to the conclusion that the circles were created by small stationary whirlwinds. Over the next couple of years, other circles and simple shapes appeared in the same area, and from about 1983, the shapes started to get more and more complicated and the numbers of circles increased to as many as 50 per year. They also started to appear all over the world—in the United States, Canada, Australia, Russia (in grass), Japan (in a paddy field), Ireland, and Holland.

In 1991 two Hampshire artists, Doug Bower and Dave Chorley, announced that they had started the whole thing and that the shapes could be made quite easily with boards and string, although they personally were responsible for only about 100 (10 percent) of the circles that had appeared in Wiltshire. Other people have also confessed to making circles. However, as UFO writer Nick Pope points out, it is difficult to see how so many crop circles could have been made without any hoaxers ever having been caught at it—some must be "genuine." Indeed, experts say that there are differences between faked and authentic circles: A faked circle's edges are rougher; faked circles have broken corn, real ones don't; and faked circles don't respond to **dowsing** rods, but real ones do.

It may be that the phenomenon is not new at all. Doug and Dave, as they are known, say they got their idea from a circle of flattened reeds found in Queensland, Australia, in 1966 after a UFO sighting. Apparently (according to paranormal researcher Jenny Randles) there is a tradition of circles in that area and the Aborigines tell of strange lights appearing in the same places as the circles. A document in the British Museum describes a "mowing devil" who created circles in Hertfordshire in 1678. It has even been suggested that prehistoric stone circles commemorate crop circles. Interestingly, Britain's two largest stone circles, **Avebury** and **Stonehenge**, are found in the same area as the majority of crop circles.

Unusual lights have also been reported in connection with Britain's crop circles, which has led some people to connect the phenomenon with fairies and fairy rings (which are also accompanied by unearthly lights in many stories). The theory that the circles were caused by **UFOs** landing and taking off had to be scrapped once the complicated shapes started appearing (as did the whirlwind theory). In any case, UFOs traditionally leave scorch marks and craters. However, some of the very complicated shapes are like mathematical symbols called Mandelbrot sets and could be a form of communication, mathematics being a universal language. But who are these messages from? **Nature spirits**, gods, and aliens are just some of the suggestions. Or it could be the Earth herself. Wiltshire has the highest number of **ley** crossings in the country, which could mean that it is rich in **earth energies**.

Whatever the explanation, circles are still appearing. A current group of self-confessed circle-makers believes that their crop circles "catalyze paranormal events"—they have seen strange lights and other phenomena while making circles. And, as Doug and Dave say, the mystery still remains as to why they did it. Who or what inspired them all in the first place?

Crowley, Aleister

A notorious magician and writer who lived from 1875 to 1947 and was, at one time, a member of the ritual magic society, the **Hermetic Order of the Golden Dawn**. His indulgence in sex and drugs scandalized Victorian society and continues to give **magic** a bad name.

He was a prolific writer and among his works are the influential *Magick in Theory and Practice* and *The Book of Thoth*, which is about the tarot and contains his own striking card designs (executed by Frieda Harris). He wrote two (just about readable) novels: *Moonchild* which contains caricatures of members of the Golden Dawn; and *Diary of a Drug Fiend*, which consists of an idealized portrait of himself and his experiences with drugs.

Crystals/Crystal Therapy

Crystals are precious and semi-precious stones of all shapes, sizes, and colors. They store, transmit, and amplify **subtle energy,** or life force, and have been used by shamans and in Eastern healing systems like ayurveda for thousands of years. Although these subtle powers cannot yet be demonstrated scientifically, crystals do have many intriguing scientific properties. When compressed they give off electric signals and light, and they vibrate when an electric current is passed through them. (Clear quartz is used in electronics because of this.) Like living systems, they grow by reproducing themselves and when subjected to some outside force, such as heat, light, pressure or electricity, they are able to restore their internal stability. Some crystals, such as lodestone, are magnetic.

According to the clairvoyant Edgar **Cayce**, the Atlanteans harnessed the sun's energy with crystals and it was misuse of crystal power that caused the cataclysms that eventually sank their continent. The reason we are rediscovering crystals now is because many people from **Atlantis** are being reincarnated.

Although several different sorts of therapists may work with crystals (including **color therapists**, **healers**, and **kinesiologists**), they are ideal for home use. Holding crystals in your hand can help you when you **meditate**—you may find they become very hot or start emitting a pulse like a weak electric fence. You can also place them on or around you in what are sometimes known as *nets*. On the body, crystals can sometimes feel unnaturally heavy. You can of course wear crystals as jewelry, keep them in your pocket, or hang them in a pouch round your neck, and you can place them around the house and garden.

Choose crystals that appeal to you or go by the colors of the **chakras**. If you want to know more about the properties of individual types, consult the crystal bible, *Love is in the Earth* by Melody. The shape and size of crystals affects *how* they work but does not make them any *less* effective. They can be tumbled (polished), shaped, rough cut (natural), or in clusters. Crystals that taper towards a faceted point are known as *wands*. Point them where you want the energy to go. For instance, point them away from you if you want to calm down or clear out stale energy, or towards you if you need revitalizing or healing. Clusters work well around a room, and small polished and shaped stones are nice to hold.

Clear quartz is a universal cure-all and enhances the effects of all the others. It is traditional to use it for *scrying*, or divination from a reflective surface, and it is the ingredient of true crystal balls. However, because of the expense, glass is more often used now.

You will need to cleanse crystals when you first acquire them and then at regular intervals after that—as a rough guide, crystals around a room should be cleansed every week and those you wear or use for meditation and healing every few days. If using them on different people cleanse after each person. Here are some methods:

- Hold under running water and then dry in the sun.
- Bury in sea salt for 24 hours. (Don't use salt water as this can dissolve some crystals.)
- **Smudge** them—waft fragrant smoke towards them (this is a good way of cleansing very heavy crystals) or pass them through the smoke.

- ❑ Use pure sound such as that made by a tuning fork, bell, gong, or "singing bowl."

See also **Electro-crystal Therapy.**

Using crystals

- ❑ Balance your energies by placing a crystal of the appropriate color on each of the chakras.
- ❑ Enhance your drinking water by keeping a clear quartz crystal in it.
- ❑ Neutralize radiation from electrical appliances (such as computers and televisions) by placing a crystal next to them. (*Don't* use clear quartz here as it will make things *worse*.)
- ❑ Help your plants by putting a crystal or crystals around their base.
- ❑ Attach crystals to the collars of your animals.

Crystal Skulls

In the Museum of Mankind (part of the British Museum) in London, the Musée de l'Homme in Paris, and the Smithsonian Institute in Washington are near-life-size replicas of the human skull made out of transparent quartz **crystal**. As carbon-dating techniques cannot be used on stone, their age is a mystery, and little is known about where they come from. According to the British Museum, their skull may have been brought from Mexico at the end of the 19th century. The French skull was acquired around the same time, and the American one came from an anonymous donor in 1993.

A superb life-size crystal skull with a moveable jaw (just like the real thing) was found by the daughter of the explorer Frederick Mitchell-Hedges in 1924 when they were excavating **Mayan** ruins on the coast of Central America. Mitchell-Hedges believed the skull to be **Atlantean** and at least 3,600 years old.

According to Chris Morton and Ceri Louise Thomas, who have written a book on the subject, crystal skulls have long been spoken about by indigenous peoples as far apart as Australia, Russia, and America. Their legends tell of 13 ancient skulls, one for each of 12 planets originally inhabited by human beings and one to connect all the others. They are repositories of ancient wisdom and will reappear when humanity is ready to receive their messages.

D

Dance (Movement) Therapy

See **Creative Therapies.**

Death

Few of us today have much first-hand experience of dealing with people who are dying, and when someone close to us falls seriously ill, we don't know how to behave. Hospitals, for all their sophisticated equipment, can make the process of dying lonely, frightening, and protracted. Yet, as the American psychiatrist Elisabeth Kübler-Ross has shown, what the terminally ill want most of all is companionship and a sense of control over what happens to them.

The natural death movement started in the 19th century with hospices. These provide a home-like atmosphere with expert pain control, emotional and spiritual counseling, and help for relatives. However, only four percent of the dying use hospices and those who do are mostly cancer patients. The Natural Death Centre, which started in London in 1991, believes that we should all be able to die at home if we want to. They have made many radical suggestions including:

- ❑ Midwives for the dying.
- ❑ Neighbourhood Care schemes with neighbors taking turns to help families with someone terminally ill at home.

- Beds available in hospitals so that friends and family can stay.
- Access to nature for those dying away from home—whether this means taking them outside or bringing animals, trees, and so on, inside.
- The use of psychoactive drugs such as LSD to help the dying with their fears.
- Legal leave of absence from work for the bereaved.
- Death days, like birthdays, when we remember a person who died.

In living wills or advance directives, people can set out the kind of medical treatment they wish to receive or not receive and save themselves, as far as possible, from a slow, painful death. In addition, these can also cover the sort of burial and funeral we want. Increasingly popular are environmentally-friendly coffins and woodland burial sites where people are commemorated with trees, not gravestones. Do-it-yourself funerals are also becoming less unusual because these are more personal, and you can tailor them to particular spiritual beliefs (as well as being a great deal cheaper).

According to Elisabeth Kübler-Ross, the dying go through five stages: denial, anger, bargaining, depression, and acceptance. The same could probably be said about any uncomfortable occurrence in our lives. However, death is the biggest challenge any of us have to face. For our own sakes, as well as the sakes of people who are dying, we need to bring it back home instead of leaving it in the hands of professionals.

See also **Near-death Experience.**

Dentistry, Teeth

Mercury is one of the most toxic substances on earth and yet it has been used in our teeth for two hundred years. Silver *amalgam* fillings are about 50 percent mercury, and there is now scientific evidence that this is released from our fillings into the rest of the body and can be linked with kidney problems,

Alzheimer's disease, and neurological disorders. Some dentists also believe it may play a part in autoimmune diseases, chronic fatigue, multiple chemical sensitivity, and allergies. Seven countries including Sweden, Germany, and Canada (but not the United Kingdom or the United States) have recently taken steps to phase out its use.

Taking out amalgam fillings can release huge amounts of mercury vapor so it is not advisable to do so unless you have a health problem that you can link with mercury sensitivity. For this you may need special tests. (See Resoursces section for details of organizations that can help.) Mercury fillings should be replaced with white "composite" ones made of either formaldehyde-free resin or porcelain. Don't use other metals (such as gold, platinum, or palladium) as these can also cause health problems. If replacing fillings because of poor health, it is essential to find a dentist experienced at dealing with mercury sensitivity who can prepare you with dietary supplements beforehand, take the necessary precautions while removing your fillings, and support your health afterwards. Otherwise, you risk making matters worse.

We are normally advised to see a dentist once or twice a year. However, a survey by the Consumers' Association found that you stand a better chance of keeping your teeth if you only go to the dentist when you have a problem. However, you must go at the first sign of trouble and if your teeth form scale you must get this removed regularly. (You'll know you form scale if your teeth tend to feel "furry" or if the dentist scrapes between your teeth with a small pick whenever you visit.)

There are alternatives to conventional treatment in dentistry as well as medicine. For instance **homeopathy** can be used to deal with both mercury sensitivity and a variety of other problems such as gum disease (gingivitis), tooth decay, pain, and fear of treatment.

Fluoride in drinking water is another controversy since it can affect bone density, the thyroid, the kidneys, and the immune system. Evidence that it makes teeth less liable to decay is questionable, and some people maintain that pressure to put it in our water comes from industry since it is a waste product it would have trouble disposing of otherwise. In the United Kingdom only about 12 percent of the population has fluoridated tap water but in the United States it is closer to 50 percent.

Devas

Spirit beings who control the essences or blueprints of everything in existence and channel the energy necessary for things to come into being and evolve. There are devas, for example, of the Elements, plants and animals, countries, places, organizations, homes, projects, and machines. The word comes from **Hinduism**, where devas are seen as lesser gods who direct divine energies down to the level of material existence. It was first used in the West by Dorothy Maclean at **Findhorn** for the spirit intelligence she came into contact with, and which helped the founders of the community create a garden on previously barren land.

As humans we have a role to play in creation and we can work *with* devas rather than trying to control things simply for our own ends. For example, in the garden we can contact the deva of a plant or insect that is becoming a pest and ask it to go elsewhere. We have to be quite specific about this though, suggesting exactly where it can go, and we have to do it for the greater good—for the creation of something of beauty, for instance. It is no good being angry or doing it as an experiment.

Dorothy Maclean sees cooperation with devas as the only way we can save the environment. She says (in *Far Out: The Dawning of New Age Britain*):

> *We have polluted the planet and we are only now realising to what extent. At Findhorn we started dealing with nature in a different way. We've got to change our viewpoint completely and if we can recognise that there's an intelligence we can cooperate with, what a difference it will make to the planet.*

See also **Morphic Resonance**, and **Nature Spirits**.

Didgeridoo/Didgeridou

Also called a *yidake* (or *yidaki*), this is an Australian **Aborigine** musical instrument traditionally made from a dead tree branch naturally hollowed out by termites. Not easy to play, it makes an extraordinary booming drone and in some tribes is considered sacred to men (therefore women shouldn't play it). Modern didgeridoos can be made from a variety of natural and man-made materials.

Another Aboriginal instrument is the bull-roarer, a piece of wood on a string that creates a strange humming when whirled and is used to call the spirits or is seen as the voice of the spirits. Sometimes it is carved with secret information about an individual's Dreamtime heritage.

Divination

Obtaining knowledge about the past, present and future by non-rational means. There are several ways that this happens or can be explained:

- ❑ Everything in the universe is connected, and the small reflects the large. So the way cards fall, for example, actually shows us what's going on in the world at large or, conversely, heavenly activity mirrors and influences what's happening on Earth.
- ❑ Through our intuition we have access to all the knowledge in the world—the more skilled we are in using it and listening to it the more knowledge we can tap into. A divination tool is simply a way to focus our intuition.
- ❑ The divination tool is a way for our spiritual self or a higher power to communicate with our everyday self, and our spiritual self or the higher power influences the runes, cards, dowsing rod, etc..
- ❑ **Spirit Guides** talk directly to us.

Learning and using a divination technique can benefit our lives in all sorts of ways. It puts us in touch with our deeper, wiser self. It is a way to help other people. It strengthens our faith in and knowledge of the unseen, spiritual world.

Divination methods covered in this book	
astrology	numerology
aura reading	ogham
channeling	psychometry
dowsing	remote viewing
handreading	runes
I Ching	tarot

Divining

Another name for **Dowsing**.

Do-In

A modern Japanese form of self-**massage** focusing on the body's energy points and **meridians**. Pronounced *dough-in*.

Dowsing

Also called *divining* or *radiesthesia*, this is used for finding things and answering questions. There are two sorts of tool—the *rod* and the *pendulum*.

The rod tends to be used outside for locating underground water, archaeological remains, minerals, oil, and so on. The most common types of rod are a forked stick (you hold a fork end in each of your hands) or two L-shaped pieces of metal (you hold the shorter sides). Hazel is the traditional wood used, but apple, willow, and peach are also good. To keep them from snapping, they should be freshly cut and green rather than dry. Metal rods can be made out of wire coat hangers.

Pendulums are for answering questions. Anything reasonably symmetrical will do so long as it is not too heavy (which hampers the swing) or too light (so that it gets blown in a breeze). You could try a pendant, a threaded needle stuck into a cork, a button, a ring on a piece of cotton, or even a bath plug.

Dowsing seems to work by sending unconscious knowledge into the muscles (making a forked stick rod move up and down, parallel metal rods move together or away from each other, and pendulums swing). Rod dowsers may be sensing the different frequencies or patterns of **subtle energy** given off by different substances, or the **Earth energies** of different places. They have a better prospecting record than geologists and are employed by many large companies.

When starting to dowse with a pendulum you need to *program* your tool—that is, find out what type of swing means yes and what means no. Holding the pendulum lightly between your thumb and forefinger, ask questions to which you know the answer, for example, "Am I wearing blue shoes today?" or, "Do I have a cat?" The two types of swing are usually backwards/forwards and circular (clockwise or counterclockwise). You may also find a swing that means, *I'm not answering that question*—try asking your pendulum whether it tells the truth.

We are probably all capable of dowsing. The art is to be relaxed and not think too much about what you are doing. When pendulum dowsing for yourself, don't allow wishful thinking to intrude and frame the questions carefully—simple, straightforward ones are best. For example, "Should I take up this job offer?" not, "Will I be a success in such and such a field of work?"

Working at a distance is also possible, for example asking your pendulum questions about someone who is not present, or dowsing over a map. Some people like to use a *witness* which is a small piece of whatever they are looking for, or a photograph of a person or something that belongs to them.

Dowsing—Some Suggestions

In all cases, be very clear what it is you want to know and then put it to the back of your mind. The more serious your intention, the better the results.

- ❑ Find lost objects by dowsing through your house or over a map.
- ❑ Diagnose the source of illness by dowsing over a person's body or a diagram of the body.
- ❑ Discover the sex of an unborn child by using a pendulum over the mother's abdomen.
- ❑ Find out whether different sorts of food or drink are good for you by pendulum dowsing over them or over their name written on a piece of paper.
- ❑ Use a rod in the garden to find the best places for new plants.
- ❑ See if you get any unusual responses near prehistoric monuments (such as stone circles) or crop circles.

Dragons

Dragons and serpents appear in legend and art all over the world. In British folklore they guard and fly between hilltops and prehistoric sites and have been linked with **leys** and **earth energies**. In **kundalini** yoga, human energy is seen as a serpent coiled at the base of the spine ready to be awakened as we mature. Serpents and spirals are a dominant motif in the sculpture and mythology of the ancient **Goddess**-worshipping cultures of Europe and the Near East.

What are they and where do they come from? One theory is that dragons are an attempt to describe what we call **UFOs**. Another is that they are dinosaurs, and that dinosaurs died out much later than we think (the Loch Ness monster being a survivor). Or, alternatively, that *we* actually go back a lot further than we think and once coexisted with dinosaurs. The scientist

Lyall Watson presents a psychological explanation—dragons represent the older, instinctual part of us (because we have evolved from reptiles) which the newer and more rational part of us both fears and loves.

Drama Therapy

See **Creative Therapies.**

Dream Body

A name sometimes given to our energy field or **subtle body.**

Dreamcatcher

A Native American device to trap bad dreams (which then dissolve in the morning sun) and let through good ones. Inspired by spiders' webs, it consists of a round frame woven with a net and decorated with feathers, shells, stones, and beads. The feathers are particularly important because they are antennae to the spirit world.

Dreams, Dreaming

According to the sorcerer Don Juan (who taught Carlos **Castaneda**), dreaming is the "gateway to infinity." Part of Castaneda's training was to learn to dream at will and while awake. Before we can do this, however, we have to learn to recall and use our sleeping dreams, and perhaps to dream *lucidly*—to gain some conscious control over the content of our dreams by being aware while dreaming that we are dreaming.

Marlo Morgan's Aborigine friends in *Mutant Message Down Under* say that we, in the West, dream while asleep because we don't dream enough while awake. The spirit teacher Seth, **channeled** by Jane Roberts, says that by sleeping in one single session we separate our conscious self from our unconscious self—we would do better to have two or three sessions of sleep each 24 hours and have part of the night awake. Working with dreams is a way to unite our waking and sleeping, or conscious and unconscious selves.

Working With Dreams

Remembering Dreams

The only way to do this is to record them or tell them to someone as soon as you wake up, even if it's the middle of the night. If you are going to record them you will need to keep a notebook and pen or tape recorder and perhaps a light next to the bed. Whatever method you use you need to send a clear message to your unconscious before you go to sleep that you want to remember important dreams. Affirmations (see ***affirmations****) such as "I am ready to listen to my dreams" can help. You can also put something under your pillow that represents, to you, the power of your unconscious such as a crystal. Both of these methods are also good for overcoming any reluctance we might have about exploring the deeper levels of our mind.*

Understanding Dreams

The first step is to look at the emotions they contain. Dream language is largely symbolic, so some people also recommend keeping a dream dictionary. In this you write down all the features in your dream that you don't understand—people, places, colors, seasons, objects—and their associations for you as well as their universal meaning. For instance, a cross is related to Christianity but it might remind you of school, a particular churchyard, or a piece of jewelry. In this way you can start to understand what your dreams are telling you and recognize recurring symbols. Often dreams don't make sense right away, so look back over your dream diary from time to time (and remember to date all the dreams you record).

Dealing With Bad Dreams

As psychologist Ruth Berry says, these are good signs because they show that you are ready to work on the issues they raise, and as you start to do so, you will find that the dreams disappear. Try using visualizations (see **visualization***) to deal with them. While awake, return to your dream in your imagination and visualize yourself dealing with the problem—in whatever way seems most appropriate. It is often helpful here to think in mythical terms. For instance, turn the problem into a monster and yourself into a hero, or imagine yourself finding your way out of a labyrinth to whatever prize you desire.*

Lucid Dreaming

This is an extension of visualization. Most of us have had the experience of being aware that we are dreaming, especially during particularly pleasant or unpleasant dreams. Next time this happens, don't be in such a hurry to wake up. The lucid-dreamer Stephen LaBerge recommends getting into the habit of carrying out "reality checks" while awake—examining your environment for unusual phenomena—as this makes it more likely that you will do the same while dreaming and so realize that you're dreaming. The next stage involves waking up earlier than usual, recalling your last dream and then going back to sleep with the intention of reentering that dream. Alternatively there are eye masks available that signal to you when you are dreaming without waking you up.

Dreamtime

The Australian Aboriginal word for the spirit world.

Druids/Druidry

Druidry is usually associated with the **Celts** but it may be the United Kingdom's original spirituality, dating back to the Stone Age. It has even been linked with **Atlantis**. Druids were educated, priestly elite women and men, who fell into three types. The bards passed on myth and tradition through poems, stories, and songs. Ovates practiced magic, divination, and healing, and the Druids, with both bardic and ovate skills, were teachers, counselors, and judges. All Druids were highly respected and traveled freely between the warring Celtic tribes since the penalty for harming them was death. Training began at the age of nine or 10 and could take up to 20 years. Everything was passed on by word of mouth as the Druids considered it sacrilege to commit their teachings to writing. Their alphabet—**ogham**—was used for inspiration and magic.

The Druids, along with the rest of Celtic culture, were supplanted first by the Romans who occupied Britain from the 1st to the 5th century, and then the invading Anglo-Saxons and Christianity. However, bardic colleges continued in Wales, Ireland, and Scotland until as late as the 17th century. Towards the end of the 18th century, Druidry began to be revived, particularly through the work of a Welshman called Iolo Morganwg, who discovered some ancient documents (not considered genuine) and wrote extensively about the Welsh bardic tradition. He started the Welsh bardic festival, the Eisteddfod, and the Druid rituals, or Gorsedd, at Primrose Hill in London, both of which continue to this day.

Modern Druidry, like other **Neo-Pagan** movements, centers on respect and love for nature, with some Druid groups (*orders* or *groves*) actively involved in environmental protest. Other groups are more concerned with researching the tradition and passing it on, and others with the ritual, spiritual, Shamanistic, or magical elements. The majority of Druids worship the old goddesses and gods of Britain, Ireland, and Scandinavia, but others combine Druidry with another faith such as Christianity or Buddhism. A key concept is *awen*, an old Welsh/British word meaning flowing spirit or Divine inspiration, which is brewed by the Welsh mother goddess Ceridwen in her cauldron of wisdom and rebirth. As Emma Restall Orr, Joint Chief of the British Druid Order says:

Spirit to spirit, consciously we reacknowledge how we are connected, tree to bird to cat to woman to man, through the land, through time, to our ancestors and gods. Consciously, with respect, we allow the perfect fluidity to flow once more, unchecked, revitalizing our souls and all the world.

Earth Acupuncture

Prehistoric monuments, in particular standing stones, may have had a specific function, with regard to the Earth's **subtle energy body**, working in the same way that the needles of **acupuncture** do on the human energy body. An idea developed by the **dowser** Tom Graves.

See also **Earth Energies**.

Earth Energies

If the Earth is a living being (see **Gaia**) she may have an **energy** body like other living beings. In **acupuncture** there are fixed spots (*acupoints*) on the human body where the energy flows closer to the surface and can be manipulated, and in yoga there are energy vortices, called **chakras**, where energy is taken in and given out. It may be that ancient sacred sites relate to similar points on the Earth's surface, either marking and amplifying energy-rich areas or correcting energy black spots. Standing stones may work in the same way as acupuncture needles and the **Celts**' beacon fires, lit on special dates at special places, may have worked in the same way as moxibustion (burning herbs on acupoints to create energy.)

The rock that was used in prehistoric monuments is often magnetic, rich in quartz **crystal**, or brought from far afield, and therefore may have been chosen for its particular effect on Earth energies. Landscaping and building that seems to have no purpose, such as Europe's largest artificial mound, Silbury Hill near **Avebury**, or the Egyptian **pyramids**, could have been created with the specific purpose of altering Earth energies.

A system of Earth energy manipulation, or geomancy, still in existence is **feng shui**. This works on the principle that the flow of subtle energy, or **chi,** varies in accordance with the landscape, and buildings are sited and arranged in order to take advantage of this.

Guy Underwood, who **dowsed** a huge variety of natural and ancient man-made features in Britain, found that similar features gave similar results and that the main energy patterns are straight or wavy lines, circles, and spirals. Geomancy expert Nigel Pennick and Earth energies enthusiast Paul Devereux have found examples of these motifs all over the world. In Europe there are the mysterious stone-age "cup and ring" rock carvings which show concentric circles intersected by lines, as well as prehistoric stone circles, avenues, and mazes. Throughout the Great Plains of America there are thousands of prehistoric stone rings, and in South America at **Nazca** there are huge ground etchings showing straight lines and spirals as well as other geometric shapes and animal figures. In addition to tracing out energy patterns, all these features could have been used as ritual pathways, with people increasing or changing their energy (such as state of consciousness) by aligning it with the Earth's energy.

See also **Earth Lights**, and **Leys**.

Experiencing Earth Energies

When out walking in the countryside:

- ❑ Do some places feel better than others?
- ❑ Do you have sudden emotions at certain spots?
- ❑ Do you have favorite places for sitting down?
- ❑ Build up a relationship with a particular place by clearing it of litter and meditating there.

When visiting prehistoric sites:

- ❑ Do you see, hear, smell, or otherwise sense anything unusual?
- ❑ Do you feel different?
- ❑ What images come into your mind?
- ❑ If you have animals or children with you, how are they reacting?
- ❑ Touch any stones that are part of the monument. What do you feel? Do the stones vary? Touch individual stones in different places.
- ❑ How does the site relate to the landscape? Why is it the shape it is?
- ❑ Does the vegetation at the site differ from that of the surrounding area?
- ❑ If you are able to sleep at the site, do you have any unusual or powerful dreams?
- ❑ Conduct your own tests, such as with a magnet, dowsing rod, pendulum, camera, or tape recorder.

Earth Lights

There are many unexplained light phenomena. At Marfa, in Texas, colored globes are seen so often in the sky that there is a warning to motorists. Earth mysteries researcher Paul Devereux calls these phenomena Earth lights, and has discovered that they occur most often over rifts in the Earth's crust where the rock is under stress. This may be because when rocks are subjected to pressure they give off electrical signals that can ignite atmospheric gases. This physical explanation, Devereux believes, may account for many paranormal events such as ghosts and **UFOs**.

However, researchers at Hessdalen in Norway have found that Earth lights can lead to poltergeist activity, sensitize people so that they are more likely to see things psychically, and move and change shape according to the mind of the observer. Another interesting find, by geologist Paul McCartney, is that every single prehistoric stone circle in England and Wales is within a mile of some sort of rock fault.

Earth Mysteries

See **Crop Circles**, **Earth Energies**, **Earth Lights**, **Leys**.

Ecopagan

A **Pagan** who works to preserve the environment.

Ecovillage

A **community** with strong environmental focus—in the buildings, the power sources, and the occupations of the inhabitants.

Egypt

Ancient Egypt is one of the oldest civilizations with written records still in existence, and its culture had an enormous influence on the ancient Greeks, Romans, and Hebrews who, in turn, influenced us. It is also thought to be the fountainhead of Western mysticism and **magic**, and perhaps a link with the lost continent of **Atlantis**.

Egyptian culture was deeply symbolic. They had a special sacred script (hieroglyphs) consisting of pictures, which also represented sounds, and this meant that each word could have many layers of meaning. For example, the word for the underworld was *duat*. The letter D meant "body" and was drawn as a mummy, and the letter T meant "eternity" and was drawn as a serpent.

The full word *duat* was drawn as a mummy with a serpent curled round it. Their temples were constructed of materials representing the four **Elements** and were perhaps designed to mirror the human body or the human body and soul, with inner rooms where the public could sleep when they wanted dream guidance and an innermost room where the god dwelt, accessible only to the priest. The human being was seen as consisting of nine parts or layers—three physical ones, three mental and emotional ones, and three spiritual ones. The rich had their tombs built to imitate this, with increasingly elaborate containers within containers. The **pyramids** are thought to be tombs, but since no body has ever been found in them they may also be symbolic structures.

The Egyptians had a plethora of deities whose functions and character tended to change over time. The myths about them may encapsulate astronomical events since the Egyptians had a sophisticated knowledge of the stars. Osiris, for instance, is associated with Orion, and Isis with Sirius. Thoth was the fount of all knowledge, in particular written and magical knowledge. The Greek **Hermetic texts**, which underpin alchemy and Western magic, were attributed to him.

Some Egyptian Deities and Symbols

Isis

Supreme goddess. Depicted wearing a solar disc on her head and holding an ankh (see upcoming definition). Her hieroglyph and that of the throne of Egypt are the same. Pharaohs were depicted sitting on her lap, suckling from her. Taught humankind agriculture, medicine, marriage, spinning, and weaving. Sister and lover of Osiris; conceived their son Horus with the artificial phallus she made for him when the real one was lost (see following). Associated with the star Sirius.

Osiris

God who presided over the underworld. Killed by his brother Set but found (minus phallus) by Isis, who made an artificial one for him and restored him to life. His death and resurrection were reenacted each year. Associated with star Orion.

Thoth

God who brought language, writing, astronomy, mathematics, and magic. His temples kept records on myths and rituals as well as on medicine, geometry, architecture, astronomy, and law. Sometimes shown as a baboon or ibis.

Maat

Goddess of truth and order, involved with the judging of the dead in the underworld—their heart would by weighed against a feather from her hair to see if it was heavy with sin.

Hathor

Goddess sometimes represented as a cow, with a pharaoh suckling from her, or wearing a headdress of horns and solar disc. Sometimes seen as married to Horus. Gives birth to sun every morning.

Horus

Sun god. Child of Isis and Osiris. Depicted as a falcon or falcon-headed. Eye of Horus an important symbol (far-seeing, channeling sun?)

Anubis

Jackal or jackal-headed god who guided souls in the underworld.

ankh

Looped cross (T with a loop on top) representing life.

scarab

Type of beetle representing rebirth, growth, and transformation (because its young emerge miraculously from a ball of dung, and because it looks like a skull).

It is from the ancient Greek writer Plato that the connection between Egypt and Atlantis springs. His knowledge of the lost civilization, he said, came from Egypt where priests had records of it. The priests also maintained that Egyptian civilization went back to 9000 BCE (the current conventional dating is 3000 BCE) and this has led to the suggestion that Egypt was founded by Atlantean refugees and that these might later have been mythologized as deities.

The Egyptian *Book of the Dead* is a collection of prayers, incantations and rituals for the dead to use as they made their way through the underworld to the afterlife. Like The ***Tibetan Book of the Dead*** it was read aloud to the dying and the dead, and copies were placed in tombs. Its Egyptian title translates as "Chapters on coming forth by day," referring to the fact that the transition to the afterlife began the morning after a person's death. (It is hard to see how this fits in with mummification, thought to have been done to preserve bodies for the afterlife, since the transition would have begun—and perhaps been completed—before the mummification had even been started.) *The Book of the Dead* has also been a source of inspiration to modern magic.

Women played a significant role in the priesthood. Temples dedicated to goddesses were always served by women priests, although the head priest was a man. In all temples they were involved in music-making, particularly as singers and dancers. Within the population at large, although there were few jobs for women, and wives were virtually slaves to their husbands, property was inherited by daughters, not sons. The pharaohs were held to be descended directly from Isis through the female line and, in order to preserve the royal blood, marriage within the family was common, with women marrying their brothers or fathers. There was only one woman pharaoh, Hatshepsut, and her monuments were defaced after her death by her successor (who was also her husband and her half-brother).

Electro-Crystal Therapy

Healing with **crystals** that were previously stimulated with an electric current in order to increase their power.

Elements

See **Correspondences**.

Energy

See **Subtle Energy**.

Energy Medicine

See **Complementary Medicine**, and **Subtle Energy**.

Enneagram

A graphic device used for understanding human nature, developed from **Sufi** ideas by George Gurdjieff in the early 20th century and the Chilean Oscar Ichazo in the 1960s.

The device itself is a nine-pointed star, each point equating to different personality types or traits. We acquire our personality in stages. We are each born with one particular *holy idea*. As we grow, we develop a *fixation* and a *passion* in order to cope with life's challenges. Our *acquired personality* is the final stage. The enneagram is unusual in that it links personality and spirit.

The Main Ingredients of the Enneagram

Holy Ideas	Passions	Fixations	Personality Types
1. Perfection.	1. Anger.	1. Resentment.	1. Perfectionist/ Reformer.
2. Freedom.	2. Pride.	2. Flattery	2. Caregiver/Helper.
3. Hope.	3. Deceit.	3. Image/Vanity.	3. Achiever/Performer.
4. Idealism/ Originality.	4. Envy.	4. Melancholy.	4. Romantic/Artist.
5. Omniscience.	5. Greed.	5. Stinginess.	5. Observer/Intellectual.
6. Faith.	6. Fear.	6. Cowardice.	6. Questioner/Cynic.
7. Work.	7. Gluttony.	7. Planning.	7. Optimist/Bon Viveur.
8. Truth.	8. Lust.	8. Vengeance.	8. Confrontationist/Leader.
9. Love.	9. Sloth.	9. Indolence.	9. Mediator/Peacemaker.

ESP

See **Extrasensory Perception**.

Essential Oils

Plant essences used in **aromatherapy**.

Ether

The same as **subtle energy**, or the dimension in which subtle energy exists. The etheric body is the same as the **subtle body** or, sometimes, one particular layer of the subtle body.

Etheric Projection

The same as **Astral Projection**.

Ethical Consumerism/Investment

Most players in the financial world, especially the big ones, put profit before any other considerations such as human and animal welfare or the environment. Through our day-to-day spending, bank accounts, mortgages, insurance policies, pensions, savings, and tax payments we are part of this unless we deliberately seek out alternatives.

Ethical investment is the fastest-growing section of the U.K. stock market and is increasing by about 34 percent a year. It is not just a fringe activity any more—trade unions, churches, and universities are all ethical investors. Ethical investments perform as well or better than non-ethical and may be a lot safer in the long run as environmental and employee laws become more stringent.

Ethical products can be more expensive, but by substituting just one of our normal purchases each week we can make a difference. Chloroflurocarbons (CFCs) were withdrawn from use in the 1980s largely because people stopped buying products that contained them. The current debate about the genetic modification (GM) of food (see **genetic engineering**) has been stimulated by consumers.

How to Be an Ethical Consumer

Ethical products are increasingly available in mainstream shops, but see Addresses for specialist suppliers.

- ❑ Buy organic, fair trade and cruelty-free products.
- ❑ Buy local products (saving on transport and supporting smaller industries).
- ❑ Avoid over-packaged items.
- ❑ Choose products that can be recycled or are made from recycled materials.
- ❑ Avoid products that contain harmful chemicals (such as weedkillers, some household cleaners, dyes, and drugs).
- ❑ Be an "eco" and ethical tourist—go independently so that the money you spend benefits the locals, or choose a travel company that supports the local environment and community.

How to Be an Ethical Investor

See Resources section for further information.

- ❑ Use ethical banks and building societies.
- ❑ Use ethical insurance companies if possible (although these are hard to find).
- ❑ Choose an ethical pension; if you are in a company pension, find out about investment criteria.
- ❑ Use ethical financial advisers and ethical investment companies.
- ❑ Research companies yourself or get a specialist organization to do this for you.
- ❑ Be an active shareholder, commenting on what your company does.

Areas of concern include human rights (including the treatment of women and ethnic minorities), animal welfare, trading policy (for instance, whether suppliers in developing countries get a proper deal and whether local communities and indigenous people are supported or exploited), pollution and environmental damage, tobacco, alcohol, weapons, pornography, and gambling.

Existential Therapy

A **psychotherapy** that aims to help us fully understand the present so that we can deal with it constructively. Related to existential philosophy which holds that there are no universal values, and we have to create any sense of meaning for ourselves.

Extrasensory Perception (ESP)

The ability to obtain information—about people, places, objects, the past, present, and future—by non-normal means. ESP is probably dormant in all of us and able to be developed with training and encouragement. Sometimes we acquire it at times of crisis or extreme emotion.

See **Clairaudience/Clairsentience/Clairvoyance**, **Divination**, and **Telepathy**.

Eyes

See **Iridology**, and **Vision Therapy**.

F

Faeries/Fairies

A type of **nature spirit.**

False Memory Syndrome

Sometimes **psychotherapists** are accused of (inadvertently) implanting false memories—often about sexual abuse—in their patients and it can be very difficult for someone at a vulnerable stage in therapy to know what to believe. It is as well to remember that some memories, especially those uncovered by techniques like **hypnosis** that reach into the unconscious, may be symbolic (like dreams) rather than literally true. However, the emotions can be just as real.

Feldenkrais Method

Movement and posture reeducation taught both in groups and one-on-one. It is similar to the **Alexander Technique** but concentrates on the entire body (rather than the head/neck/spine). The founder, Moshe Feldenkrais, was an engineer, physicist, and judo expert who developed the method through teaching himself to walk again after serious knee injuries.

Feng Shui

The ancient Chinese art of placement. Originally used for situating tombs, it went on to be applied to building, landscaping, and the interior arrangement of houses. Although the practice is now dwindling on the Chinese mainland under the influence of Communism, it is still practiced in Chinese communities elsewhere and has recently become popular in the West.

There are many different schools of feng shui but all use the eight trigrams from the **I Ching** to assess what activities are best carried out in which part of a building. Each of the trigrams represents a different type of energy and in a home these are usually listed (with variations) as: journey (the progress of one's life in general), relationships, elders (relatives), fortunate blessings (luck), helpful friends, creativity, wisdom, and illumination. The trigrams are arranged around an octagon called the *pa kua* with a section in the middle for health and this octagon is placed over a plan of the house.

Chi is the energy that shapes the Earth. Some shapes are harmonious and others are not. This is why the location and orientation of a house is of the utmost importance. Within a house, chi is interrupted by sharp corners, clutter, and dust. Corridors and doors opposite each other cause the chi to flow too quickly. Simple devices like mirrors, plants, lights, clocks, wind chimes, and water features can be used to mitigate problems both inside and out.

The concepts of **yin and yang** and the five Elements (Wood/Tree, Fire, Earth/Soil, Metal, and Water) are used to bring balance to interiors and exteriors. In feng shui astrology, also known as "nine star ki," a person's birth date is used to determine their personal Element and their personal number, each of which has a different quality. A house can then be planned or adapted to suit these astrological profiles. (Feng shui astrology can also be used on its own to give help with relationships, decision-making, the timing of important occasions, and travel.)

The Chinese Elements and Their Use in Feng Shui					
Element	Characteristic	Season	Direction	Shape	Color
Wood/ Tree	growth	Spring	East	tall, narrow	green
Fire	passion	Summer	South	triangular, zigzag	red
Earth/Soil	comfort	early Autumn	center	low, wide	yellow
Metal	organization	late Autumn	West	round, oval	white, gold, silver
Water	flexibility	Winter	North	wavy, irregular	blue, black

Findhorn

A **community** in Northeast Scotland, famous in the 1960s for its pioneering work with **nature spirits** and now for its educational activities and developing **ecovillage**.

Floatation

A **complementary therapy** which involves floating in a dark soundless chamber in warm water filled with mineral salts to give buoyancy. This makes most people profoundly relaxed but can sometimes induce panic so it's best to be supervised.

Flower Essences/Remedies

Infusions of wildflowers, garden flowers, trees, and fungi from all over the world for the self-treatment of emotions. Prepared like **homeopathic** remedies, they work on our **subtle**

energy and are normally considered completely safe. Unlike homeopathic remedies, they don't work by exaggerating symptoms but by providing the qualities we are lacking.

The first remedies were created by the English doctor and homeopath Edward Bach (pronounced *batch*) who found himself suffering different negative states of mind one by one, and then being led intuitively to the plant which could help him.

Some Bach Flower Remedies	
Rescue Remedy	A combination of five remedies for using before or after stress and trauma.
Agrimony	For those who hide worries behind a brave face.
Crab Apple	For self-disgust.
Larch	For lack of self-confidence.
Vervain	For fanaticism.
Wild Oat	Helps you determine your path in life.
Willow	For bitterness and resentment.

Flower remedies are widely available in health food shops and natural health centers and are popular for animal treatment as well as for people.

Fortune, Dion

A writer of fictional and nonfictional works on magic and mysticism. At one time involved with the **Hermetic Order of the Golden Dawn**, she later set up her own Fraternity of Inner Light, which still exists as the Society of the Inner Light. She was born in 1891, made her home in **Glastonbury**, England and died in 1946.

G

Gaia

In 1969 the scientist James Lovelock presented the theory that the Earth is a living being because it regulates itself. He called this theory Gaia after the Greek goddess of the Earth. Just as we keep our body temperature constant by sweating and shivering and regulate the oxygen in our blood by varying the activity of our lungs and heart, the temperature of the Earth and the chemical make-up of the atmosphere and oceans have remained roughly the same for millions of years. This is achieved by enormously complex interactions between every single mineral, vegetable, and animal inhabitant.

If Lovelock is right, it means that humans are no more or less important than any other species. This flies in the face of evolutionary theory, which puts humankind at the pinnacle of creation. It also adds another dimension to the environmental debate because it means that we have a moral duty to treat the Earth well, not simply a practical one.

As far as the future is concerned, opinion is divided as to whether humans have the power to damage the Earth's systems beyond repair or whether we could simply make the Earth uninhabitable for ourselves, leaving Gaia to live on in another form. The biologist Rupert Sheldrake suggests that humans are the nervous system and consciousness of the Earth, part of the preexisting plan according to which the Earth is developing, in much the same way as lettuce seeds develop into mature lettuces and human babies into people.

Lovelock's theory unites many scientific disciplines—geology, geophysics, oceanography, climatology, ecology, biology—and offers a global perspective on the functioning of the Earth. He believes that it could do the same for us:

> *It may be that the destiny of mankind is to become tamed, so that the fierce, destructive and greedy forces of tribalism and nationalism are fused into a compulsive urge to belong to the commonwealth of all creatures which constitutes Gaia. (Reproduced with permission of Oxford University Press.)*

By treating the Earth as a whole, we can regain our own sense of belonging. However imperfect, we are still part of the web of life.

Gematria

The practice of reading secret meanings in words by replacing letters with numbers and switching words with the same numerical value. In this way the **cabbalists** discovered prophecies hidden in the Old Testament, and words that had been kept secret because their sound was so powerful.

Genetic Engineering/Genetic Modification (GE/GM)

Genetically engineered organisms (GEOs) only came on the market in 1996. However, many people believe that the technology is too powerful to unleash on the natural world without a great deal more testing, that we should not be eating GM food until we know more about any health risks, and that in any case it is the wrong way forward.

Biotechnology, at present, is imprecise and unpredictable. Scientists don't really know how genes interact or understand the consequences of the changes they are making. Once transgenic (GM) organisms have been released into the wild they are part of the planet forever, unlike harmful chemicals which are eventually diluted or broken down by natural processes and can be withdrawn from use. Nobody yet knows what the effect on wildlife might be. Testing for consumption is minimal or nonexistent because if producers can prove that GEOs are "substantially equivalent" to an unmodified organism they don't have to do any. GM food is being sold before tests have been completed.

Scientists and biotech companies say that GE is essential for solving the problems of malnutrition and starvation. However, others point out that companies are patenting not just GM crops but also crops that have been staple foods for centuries, thus potentially making the lives of poor farmers worse, not better. Farmers are forbidden to save seed from GM crops, and GM crops need pesticides sold by the companies who supply the seed. In *Genetic Engineering, Food and Our Environment*, Luke Anderson explains that the world already produces 50 percent more food than is needed and food shortages are a political not a practical problem. Ethiopia, for example, was actually exporting food to Europe during the famine of 1984, and 78 percent of malnourished children live in countries with food surpluses.

Plants are being genetically engineered to be resistant to pesticides. This is so that *more* pesticides—which harm both wildlife and us—can be used. Animals are being engineered for research (**vivisection**), a practice to which many people object, and so that their organs can be transplanted into humans, something many people would find distasteful.

As the gardeners at **Findhorn** discovered, we don't have to change nature by force. Cooperation is infinitely more beneficial in the long term. The GM debate has highlighted, like nothing else, the split between those who want technological and economic progress at any cost and those who don't.

Avoiding GM food

Nothing can be guaranteed free of GM contamination, but the following guidelines will help you minimize your exposure—and send a message to the powers that be.

- ❑ *Read the label.* In the United Kingdom (at time of writing) GM food has to be labeled as such unless the GM content is less than one percent.
- ❑ *Know your supplier.* Some manufacturers, supermarkets, and restaurants are guaranteeing that their produce is non-GM.
- ❑ *Buy organic* because all organic food is non-GM. This applies to meat and dairy products just as much as fruit and vegetables, because non-organic animals may have been raised on GM food.
- ❑ *Avoid processed food* as this is very likely to contain GM additives. Not all the ingredients in *organic* processed food are necessarily organic so read the label. Alcoholic and nonalcoholic drinks, bread, and dairy products, even organic versions, may have been produced with GM enzymes.
- ❑ *Supplements and medicines.* Increasingly likely to be GM.

Geomancy

The art and science of building and landscaping in order to bring about changes in people or the world at large.

See also **Earth Energies**, **Feng Shui**, and **Magic**.

Gestalt

A type of **psychotherapy** using different methods (including art, reenactment, movement, and talking) to discover bits of you that you have repressed and get you used to expressing them again. Treatment is either one on one or in a group.

Glastonbury

A small market town in Southwest England that has been a spiritual center for thousands of years.

The town was once surrounded by marshy and flooded land and the "ines" part of the old Welsh name for it, Ineswytrin, means island. In 1191 monks discovered two skeletons in the Abbey grounds and identified them as belonging to King **Arthur** and Queen Guinevere, thus connecting the town with Avalon, the mystical island where Arthur was conveyed after his death. The discovery was almost certainly faked, a ploy either to attract tourists or to encourage loyalty to the king. Only the ruins of the 10th or 11th century Abbey remain today, but it was once the largest church in Britain.

Legend has it that the first Christian settlement in Britain was established in Glastonbury by Joseph of Arimathea. Before doing this he climbed Wearyall Hill and planted his staff, which sprouted into a thorn tree, a descendant of which can still be seen today. Thorn trees, especially single ones, were sacred to the **Celts**, and legendary thorns are also to be found in the Abbey grounds and near Chalice Well, which suggests that these sites were important before Christianity.

Joseph brought with him the Holy Grail, Jesus' cup from the Last Supper. It is said to be buried in the hill whose spring feeds Chalice Well. According to pre-Christian legend, these waters have healing power, and according to Christian legend they are red because the cup contained Jesus' blood. (A modern twist to the tale of the Holy Grail is to be found in *Bloodline of the Holy Grail* by Laurence Gardner. He sees the blood as symbolizing the descendants of Jesus and Mary Magdalene who are presumably still alive and well and living in Glastonbury.)

It is said that the dramatic Tor (*tor* is a Celtic word for hill) used to be crowned with a prehistoric stone circle, but the stones were removed and placed in the foundations of the Abbey. The hill is encircled with a labyrinth of ridges which some believe were made by prehistoric peoples and used in their ceremonies. (The official view is that they are either the result of land slippage or were created for farming in medieval times.) A nearby hill, Burrow Mump, has similar ridges, and both hills are topped with the remains of a church of St. Michael. St. Michael was a **dragon** slayer and it may be that these spirals represent serpents, motifs found in stone-age art throughout Europe. Stone-age remains have been found on the Tor but not enough to say what the site was used for. It was certainly a religious site from about the 10th century, although the present ruins are 14th century.

One of the longest **leys,** or energy lines, in the country passes through both these hills as well as St. Michael's Mount in Cornwall, several other churches of St. Michael and a church of St. George (another dragon slayer). It is known as the dragon line.

A zodiac (a circle of **astrological** symbols—fish, crab, lion, and so on) was noticed in the early 20th century in the pattern of roads, tracks, rivers, ditches, field boundaries and woods to the south of the Tor. Glastonbury itself is in **Aquarius**. If this was deliberately created it would have been an incredible feat, not least because it can only be appreciated on a map or from the air. Some say it is the origin of the legend of the round table but, as it must have been created after the marshy land surrounding Glastonbury was drained, Glastonbury cannot simultaneously claim to be Arthur's *Isle* of Avalon.

The massive midsummer music festival is held outside the small village of Pilton a few miles away.

Gnosticism

A spiritual tradition that rivaled early Christianity and has been given new impetus by the discovery in 1945 in a cave in Egypt of 53 Gnostic texts. Not only do these shed new light on Gnosticism but they also reveal that the Christian church in its infancy encompassed many views and was very different from what it later became.

The Gnostics drew their ideas from various sources, including Christianity. Their main tenet was that spirituality is a question of knowing (*gnosis* being Greek for knowledge) rather than faith. It is through personal experience that we come to the divine, not through dogma and priests, and the world will only be transformed if we all make an effort to transform ourselves—it is no good waiting for a divine miracle. One of their stranger ideas was that the real god is hidden, and the world has been created by a false god. Everything material is therefore bad and humankind is a divine spark trapped in a body.

Gnosticism, along with other heresies, was crushed by the early Christian Church, with vast numbers of books being destroyed, including a great library at Alexandria in Egypt in the year 387, and until the discovery of the Gnostic texts, our knowledge of it came largely from what its detractors had written. It was the Gnostic attitude to women as well as their attitude to priests that outraged the establishment. The Gnostics held that the feminine aspect of god, which they called *Sophia*, meaning wisdom, is as important as the masculine. The Gnostic texts, some of them gospels which predate the New Testament, present a picture of Mary Magdalene as one of the most important figures in the early Christian movement. One scandalized 2nd-century churchman said of Gnostic women: "They teach, they engage in discussion; they exorcise; they cure." Not only that, but they performed rites of baptism as well.

Gnostics divided people into three kinds—fleshly, partially enlightened, and spiritual—seeing themselves, of course, as spiritual. In contrast to this elitism, however, their meetings were open to all people ("even Pagans" as the previously quoted churchman put it), and they drew lots at each meeting for leaders. Riane Eisler, in *The Chalice and the Blade*, suggests that the suppression of Gnosticism is just one more example of the destructive dominator or "blade" culture taking over from the partnership or "chalice" culture which served humanity so well during its early millennia (see **goddess**).

The Gnostics hid their texts because they were a threat to the emerging Church. They are obviously still a threat since their publication was delayed for over 45 years after they were found. You can read many things into Gnosticism—mysticism, feminism, egalitarianism—but, without doubt, it represents a lost facet of our spiritual heritage. As one bishop put it (quoted in *Kindred Spirit* magazine in reaction to *The Jesus Mysteries*, a book about the lost mystical aspects of Christianity by Tim Freke and Peter Gandy), Christian orthodoxy "is not orthodoxy because it is right, but because it won."

Goddess

We know from the art and artifacts they left behind that early agricultural people in Europe and Asia worshipped a female god, and because they have left no weapons or fortifications behind we presume that they lived in peace with each other. This golden age came to an end when they were invaded by nomadic horse-riding tribes (Aryans) with a culture of violence and male dominance, whose influence affects us to this day.

The **Hindus** and **Celts** merged the two cultures and had male as well as female gods, as did Christianity, to begin with, until it was adopted as a state religion (see **Gnosticism**). As this hierarchical and authoritarian type of Christianity took hold in Europe, women were tortured and murdered en masse in the witchcraft persecutions of the 16th and 17th centuries, and in India the life-denying and male-led philosophy of **Buddhism** was born.

Modern Goddess worship is an attempt to put humanity back on track after its "5,000-year androcratic detour," as Riane Eisler calls it, and for women to reclaim their spirituality and sense of self-worth. There are no rules to Goddess worship and no book of dogma, but Starhawk identifies the following main characteristics in *The Spiral Dance*:

- ❑ Everything is sacred. Humans are not better than the rest of nature, and the mind is not better than the body. Neither women nor men are better than each other.
- ❑ The self is celebrated, not denied. We are all goddesses and gods.

- ❑ Individuality and diversity are encouraged, not conformity.
- ❑ Life is spiral and interconnected, rather than linear and discrete. This means accepting that suffering and death are part of the natural cycle and necessary to make way for new life.

The Goddess herself has numerous names in numerous different cultures—the Virgin Mary, **Gaia**, Ceridwen, Shakti—but often three faces, like the phases of the moon: maidenhood, like the new and waxing moon; sexuality, creativity, and motherhood, like the full moon; old age and wisdom, like the waning moon.

Sometimes she has a male consort, symbolized by the bull or the stag, who is sacrificed but comes back to life, like crops that are harvested but grow again. Some say this is the origin of the story of Jesus' crucifixion and resurrection. The theme also appears in the ancient **Egyptian** myth of Isis and Osiris, in the Greek myth of Theseus and the Minotaur, and in the legend of King **Arthur**. The Old Testament bull-worshippers harangued by Moses may well have been trying to follow the ancient Goddess-centered religion. The serpent is also associated with Goddesses in myth and art, and the story of Eve's temptation by a serpent and expulsion with Adam from the Garden of Eden can be read as propaganda for the new male-dominated culture.

Men, as well as women, are involved in Goddess worship, although a few groups such as those of the Dianic movement (named after the Roman hunter goddess) do restrict men and have a strong political and feminist intent. Others are concerned with the environment and healing the earth. Many draw on **Shamanism** and **Paganism**, and the U.K. Pagan Federation calls women's spirituality "one of the richest and most dynamic forces in modern Paganism."

Golden Dawn

See **Hermetic Order of the Golden Dawn**.

Graphology

Also called *graphoanalysis*, this is handwriting analysis. It is used by therapists and businesses for insight into people's character and health, and by the law in criminal investigations and to authenticate signatures. You can also consult a graphologist as an individual to find out more about yourself.

It developed largely through the work of a 19th-century French monk called Michon who collected thousands of examples of handwriting over 30 years and studied them in minute detail. An Austrian called Alfred Kanfer explored the relationship between handwriting and health during 1950–71, and although much of his work was inadvertently destroyed after his death, researchers in America are trying to continue it.

Significant features of writing are: size, slant, angles, spacing, connections, and the upper and lower *zones* (the parts of a letter that hang down or extend upward). The signature is a particularly rich source of information.

Training is usually through a graphology organization, although in Italy, there is a university degree course. Children's handwriting is a specialized branch.

Grounding

It is important when doing any regular mental or spiritual practices such as **meditation** to keep your feet on the ground. After all, the true test is whether it enhances your everyday life. Symptoms of being "ungrounded" include:

- ❑ An inability to put plans into action.
- ❑ Being too secretive about your spiritual life or feeling a big gap between your spiritual experiences and the rest of your life.
- ❑ Thinking you have all the answers.
- ❑ Feeling "floaty," not fully in your body, or unable to handle practicalities.

Some Ways to Staying Grounded

- ❑ Start your meditations by feeling your connection to the Earth wherever your body is touching it. Imagine roots growing down from you deep into the ground.
- ❑ Start your meditations by drawing deep red Earth energy up through the whole of your body and back down again. Feel its warmth and strength.
- ❑ Use affirmations like "I am," "I belong," and "I have a right to be here."
- ❑ Carry or wear a dark red or black crystal.
- ❑ When you eat, concentrate on the food, not something else.
- ❑ Don't scorn your share of the practical things of life like cleaning, cooking, watering plants, feeding animals.
- ❑ Be outside in nature as often as you can.
- ❑ Go barefoot.
- ❑ Keep fit.

Gurdjieff, George

A Russian psychologist and spiritual teacher who lived from 1877 to 1949 and was responsible for bringing **enneagram** personality analysis to the West.

H

Handreading

Handreading or palmistry is a form of **divination**. Everything about the hand is taken into consideration—texture, color, shape, state of nails—but the most important aspects are: the nine mounds of flesh, or *mounts*, below each finger and thumb and across the palm; the creases, or *lines*, on the palm; and the patterns of ridges and furrows (as used in fingerprints).

Handreading has an ancient heritage and is found all over the world, with references to it in the **Hindu** Vedas (texts which date back 3,000 years), the Old Testament, and classical Greek and Roman writings. It was condemned by the Christian Church but revived in the 19th century largely through the work of a man who called himself Count Louis Hamon or Cheiro after the Greek for hand. (Handreading is also called *cheirology* or *cheiromancy*.) He learned the art in Bombay and went on to read the palms of the rich and famous, often with great accuracy.

Both left and right hands are read, the left hand being seen as a person's basic character and potential, their childhood, and their inner or unconscious self, and the right as the face they present to the world, their adult and conscious self, and what they've made of themselves. (In a left-handed person, this is reversed.) The main lines are:

- ❑ The life line—a map of the main events in a person's life.
- ❑ The head line—a person's mental powers.
- ❑ The heart line—their emotional life.
- ❑ The fate line—the amount of good luck or contentment in a person's life.

Timing of events can be judged from the position of a particular feature on a line.

Hand markings do grow and change throughout our lives, often within a matter of days, and scientists have discovered connections between hand markings and illness. Hands may be special because they have so many nerve endings in proportion to their size compared with the rest of the body. Cheiro says, in *Cheiro's Language of the Hand*:

> *If we study it aright, we hold within our hands the keys of the mysteries of life. In it are hereditary laws, the sins of the fathers, the karma of the past, the effect of the cause, the balance of things that have been, the shadow of things to be.*

Healing

Spiritual, psychic, or faith healing, often simply called healing, is the transference of the natural healing power of the universe by one person to another through the hands or through thought and prayer. This natural healing power goes by many names—love, **subtle energy**, God—and healers themselves come from a variety of religious backgrounds. As the recipient of healing you do not have to believe, but it certainly helps to be open to whatever is happening, to feel positive about it and to want to get better.

Although healing is as old as humankind, it was forbidden outside the Christian Church for many centuries and was only permitted again in Britain in 1951. Since then the practice has exploded, and in the United Kingdom, healing is now available on the National Health Service. In the United States, it is still illegal to heal for money so healing goes by other names such as **therapeutic touch**.

During a healing session, you sit or lie, fully clothed, while the healer places their hands on or just above your body. You may feel heat, cold, tingling, sleepiness, relaxation, or nothing. Both mental and physical problems can be helped, and children and animals respond as well or better than adults. Some healers charge for their services and some ask only for donations.

Healing by thought—known as absent or distant healing—can be equally effective and many healers have lists of people to whom they send absent healing.

See also **Psychic Surgery, Reiki.**

Absent healing

We can all become healers with practice. Sending healing to people is one of the best ways there is to help them because we are not interfering in their lives in any way but simply adding to their strength and well-being. We can also send healing to our past self, if there are episodes in our past still causing us grief, and to our present self by making a note in our diary for, say, six months in the future, asking our future self to send healing backwards in time.

Put yourself in a relaxed frame of mind in your usual way or see ***meditation****, and think of the person to whom you wish to send healing. Imagine light and love pouring into them from the universe or imagine them encased in a bubble of love and light. You can, if you like, imagine the energy going through you on its way.*

You will find this exercise lifts your own spirits as well.

Hellerwork

A type of **bodywork** consisting of gentle manipulation and movement reeducation to make you aware of the relationship between your emotions, attitudes, and body. Takes 11 sessions.

Hemp

This environmentally-friendly and versatile crop, sometimes called "industrial hemp," was banned in the West at the beginning of the 20th century, officially because it is related to the marijuana plant but actually because it stood in the way of the new plastic and wood pulp industries. In the last decade, however, it has made a comeback.

Hemp has been used for thousands of years for textiles, rope, sails, fishing nets, and paper. It can be made into various toiletries, fuel oil, paint, as well as plastic- and concrete-like materials. It can also be eaten (the seeds are tasty and full of nutritious essential fatty acids). Just about the only thing that you cannot do with it is smoke it, because it has virtually no psychoactive content. It can be grown without pesticides and herbicides on a variety of soils throughout the world, provides three times as much fibers per acre as cotton, and takes only a hundred days from sowing to harvest. Cotton, on the other hand, uses 26 percent of the world's pesticides, even though it is grown on only three percent of the world's farmland.

In 1994 the British government allowed industrial hemp to be grown again under license. Most other Western nations, with the exception of the United States, have made similar moves. Hemp products of all kinds are now available, and even car manufacturers are researching its uses. In fact, as Rowan Robinson, editor of *The Great Book of Hemp*, says, "the key to our individual and ecological health may lie in the hands of this once demonized weed."

Herbal Medicine

Also called medical herbalism and phytotherapy, it is as old as humankind and still used today by 80 percent of the world's population. Many modern drugs are derived from plants or synthetic imitations of plant medicines, but herbalists believe their treatment is safer and more effective. Natural substances are easier for the body to deal with than artificial ones. Plants contain many active ingredients and these can enhance or balance each other: For example, dandelion leaves, used as a diuretic, also contain potassium, which replaces that lost in the urine. In addition, like other **complementary therapists**, herbalists aim to treat the root cause of illness, not just the symptoms, and tailor each treatment to the individual.

You can consult a herbalist for any of the problems that you would normally take to your doctor. However, the slower and more profound action of herbal medicines works particularly well for chronic conditions. Medicines prescribed by herbalists are often tinctures that you drop on your tongue or dissolve in water. You might also be prescribed pills, teas, or ointments. You should only treat yourself with herbs for minor conditions and for short periods. It may not be a good idea to mix conventional medicines with herbal ones.

Chinese herbal medicine uses the same principles and methods of diagnosis as other types of **traditional Chinese medicine**. It has grown rapidly in popularity recently in the West, and demand for herbs has outstripped supply, so they have occasionally been contaminated or of poor quality—to avoid this, consult a registered practitioner. Some of the remedies come from animals (including endangered species such as the tiger or bear—although this is very unlikely in the West), and you need to say if you want to avoid these. Remedies are usually *decoctions* which involves you simmering dried herbs in water and then drinking the liquid. These taste fairly disgusting. Chinese herbal medicine can probably be used for an even greater range of illnesses than Western herbalism, but is particularly noted for its success with skin problems and infertility.

Hermetic Order of the Golden Dawn

A ritual magic society whose members were responsible for reviving much ancient knowledge, including **Egyptian** spirituality, **alchemy**, **astrology**, the **cabbala,** and the **tarot**. It started in London in 1888 and spread to other United Kingdom towns and Paris, eventually foundering around 1918.

Under the influence of **Rosicrucianism** and freemasonry, the society was highly secretive and hierarchical, with 10 grades into which members had to be initiated in sequence. Its most famous member is **Aleister Crowley**, who joined in 1898 but was forced to leave two years later because he was so unpopular. Other noted members include the poet W.B. Yeats, the scholar A.E. Waite (nicknamed Dead-Waite by Crowley), who designed the standard modern tarot deck known as the Rider-Waite tarot, and Dion **Fortune**, who soon left, finding the society cliquey and stuffy, and being of the opinion that we should work *with* cosmic forces and not try to dominate them with magic.

Hermeticism/Hermetic Texts

The Hermetic texts are an important collection of works on philosophy, **astrology**, **alchemy**, and **magic** written in Greek and dating from the 2nd and 3rd centuries. Also called the *Corpus Hermeticum*, they are attributed to Hermes Trismegistus (thrice great), the Greek name for the **Egyptian** god Thoth, and so may contain influences from earlier sources including **Egypt**. Hermeticism is the magical theory derived from these texts.

Hinduism

The religion of India, dating back some 5,500 years. Its most sacred book, the *Rig Veda*, is the oldest religious text in the world. It is a collection of hymns thought to have been written down around 1500–1000 BCE. Other sacred texts are the *Upanishads,* which discuss Hindu philosophy, especially

reincarnation. These date from about 600 BCE. The best-known and best-loved work is the *Bhagavad Gita*, a poem of spiritual advice from the god Krishna. This is part of an epic verse tale, the *Mahabharata*.

Although Hinduism encompasses an enormous variety of different beliefs, deities, and practices, at heart it recognizes one unchanging reality—the brahman. The universe is seen as ever-changing and rhythmic with vast cycles of manifestation and dormancy. The divine is in everything but we are prevented from seeing this by our limited understanding. The most important goal of life is enlightenment, expanding our consciousness to see this unity, but other more mundane goals are also important—fulfilling our responsibilities, material well-being, and pleasure. The three main ways to reach enlightenment are actions, love and devotion to a deity, and knowledge.

The earliest Indian civilization that we know about existed between about 3,500 and 1,600 BCE. After this time the continent—and much of Europe—was invaded by Aryan nomads. Their language, Sanskrit, is related to Greek and Latin, and to Germanic, Celtic, and Slav languages, and the gods of Hinduism have their European counterparts. For example, one of the earliest gods of the *Rig Veda* is Dyaus Pitar ("sky father"), who can be related to the Greek Zeus, the Roman Jupiter, and the Norse Tui. In Hinduism, therefore, Europeans return to a spiritual root.

A Hindu Glossary

ashram	A spiritual community. The retreat of a holy person who passes on their wisdom.
avatar	The incarnation of a god. (See **avatar**.)
atman	The divine spark within each of us.
brahman	Absolute unchanging reality.
darshan	The healing presence of a holy person.
deva	A minor god. (See **devas**.)
dharma	An individual's duty or role in life. The natural law of the universe.
enlightenment	The expansion of consciousness beyond individuality. The discovery of our true self.
guru	Spiritual teacher, literally "one who dispels darkness." There is no formal qualification for this—gurus are simply people followed by others because of their holiness.
karma	The natural law of cause and effect. The accumulated results of our past actions which determine what happens to us and our rebirth. (See **karma**.)
maya	The magic which created the universe and our illusion that what we see with our limited perception is reality.
moksha	See previous entry for enlightenment.
om	The sound from which the universe came forth. The basic unity of the universe. Pronounced a-oo-m, and chanted to bring unity.
prana	Life energy, particularly as present in the breath.
sadhu	A holy person, usually a man. A cross between a monk and a shaman.
samadhi	The happiness that comes when we are totally absorbed in something and forget ourselves. We all experience this from time to time, but practices like yoga (see yoga entry) are designed to make it happen more often.
Sanskrit	The spoken language of Northern India until about 2,000 years ago when it became a written language only, used for scholarly and religious texts, such as those about yoga (see next entry).
yoga	A path to enlightenment (see enlightenment entry)—the way of action—with many branches. (See **Yoga**.)
yogi	Someone who practices yoga.

Some Hindu Deities	
Brahma	The creator. Not worshipped as such.
Shakti	Goddess representing all kinds of female power. Often depicted in a sensuous embrace with Shiva (see next). As Parvati she is Shiva's dutiful wife. As Durga she slays demons. As Kali she represents the frightening, terrible, and furious aspects of life.
Shiva	The consciousness of the universe and the destroyer. Often depicted dancing, but with a calm face, symbolizing the movement of the universe or of human life around a still center. Consort of Shakti.
Vishnu	The sustainer or preserver. The god who controls human fate and incarnates to help us. Buddha, Jesus, and Muhammad are all seen as avatars of Vishnu.
Krishna	A heroic, wise and mischievous avatar of Vishnu about whom there are many stories.
Lakshmi	Goddess of prosperity and beauty. Consort of Vishnu.

Holistic Medicine/Therapies

See **Complementary Health.**

Homeopathy

This was developed about 200 years ago by Samuel Hahnemann, a German doctor, who was concerned about the side effects of conventional medicines. Homeopathic remedies are prepared by diluting ingredients many times and shaking or *succussing* them. No biological trace of the original substance is left which makes the remedies very safe, but it is thought that the succussing leaves an energy imprint in the liquid and this is what affects us.

Unlike conventional drugs, all the remedies are tested on humans not animals. The constituents are mostly plants but also include minerals and some animal substances (such as insects, snake venom, cuttlefish bone). The remedies work on the principle of "like cures like." So, for example, if you couldn't sleep you might be given a homeopathic remedy of something like caffeine that normally causes sleeplessness. This stimulates the body's own powers of healing (and may mean that your symptoms get worse before they get better).

Like other **complementary therapies**, homeopathy can treat the mind and the body, and it is effective for acute as well as chronic illness. In fact, its first major successes came during a cholera epidemic in the 1830s. Homeopathy is also a popular treatment for animals.

Humanistic/Human Potential Therapies

Types of **psychotherapy** that are "person centered"—you are treated as an individual, not an example of an illness, and encouraged to find your own answers. Examples are **counseling**, **creative therapies**, and **rebirthing**.

Hydrotherapy

Healing with steam and hot and cold water, often with the addition of herbs and minerals. Compresses, baths, and jets are used to stimulate, relax, remove toxins, and relieve pain and inflammation. It is a staple of **naturopathy** and is also prescribed by **osteopaths** and physiotherapists.

See also **Floatation**.

Hypnoanalysis

See **Hypnotherapy**.

Hypnosis/Hypnotherapy

Hypnosis is a state of deep relaxation when we become more susceptible to suggestions and more in touch with our true feelings. It can therefore be used to deal with all sorts of bad habits and negative thought patterns as well as for uncovering and releasing painful episodes in our past (when it is sometimes called *hypnoanalysis*).

Nearly all of us are capable of being hypnotized and, apart from its immediate therapeutic benefits, hypnosis is a good way of learning to reach deeper levels of consciousness on our own.

See also **False Memory Syndrome**, and **Psychotherapy**.

I

I Ching

This ancient book forms the heart of Chinese culture. The name is pronounced *ee jing* and the term translates as "the classic book of changes." Written down over several centuries, from about 1000 BCE, the book covers material in use for probably a couple of millennia before that. It consists of commentaries on 64 *hexagrams* (six-part diagrams) which represent the movement of life. You use the book for **divination** by finding out the hexagram that is in play at the moment. Originally this was done by throwing yarrow stalks but today people use coins.

The hexagrams are built from eight basic *trigrams* (three-part diagrams), whose associations are summarized in the box. The trigrams are built from combinations of broken and unbroken lines. These represent **yin and yang**, the two opposite forces of the universe, which are in constant dynamic interplay. Dramatic changes are revealed in *unstable* arrangements of lines, which represent yin becoming too yin, in which case it turns into yang, and vice versa.

The Eight Trigrams of the I Ching

Trigram	*Name*	*Meaning*	*Natural Force*	*Direction*	*Attribute*	*Family Member*
☰	Chien	creative, strong	Heaven	Northwest	masculinity	father
☷	Kun	receptive, yielding	Earth	Southwest	femininity	mother
☳	Chen	arousing	Thunder	East	change	first son
☵	Kan	danger	Water	North	flowing	second son
☶	Ken	stillness, steadiness	Mountain	Northeast	resting	third son
☴	Sun	gentleness	Wind, Wood	Southeast	penetrating	first daughter
☲	Li	depen-dence	Fire	South	light-giving	second daughter
☱	Tui	joy	Lake	West	serenity	third daughter

The practicalities of using the I Ching can be tricky to start with, and the commentaries are not always easy to understand. Nevertheless, the book is said to repay careful study, and since its translation in the 19th century, it has been taken up by many people including the magician Aleister **Crowley** and the psychologist **Jung**.

Using the I Ching

Use three coins and throw them six times. Build your hexagram from the bottom upwards. Number the unstable arrangements as these have special commentaries.

3 heads	— —	yin unstable (becomes yang stable)	6
2 heads, 1 tail	— —	yin stable	7
2 tails, 1 head	——	yang stable	8
3 tails	——	yang unstable (becomes yin stable)	9

Indian Head Massage

Head **massage** has been practiced in India for hundreds of years. It involves squeezing, strumming, and stroking and works on shoulders, neck, face, and scalp, as well as the top three **chakras**. In addition to relieving headaches, eyestrain, blocked sinuses, and muscle stiffness, it is good for the hair, may improve the intelligence of children, and can give you a mental "lift." An average session takes about 20 minutes, and the massage can be done with or without oil.

Inner Child

Unresolved emotional pain from our childhood can affect us as adults. Often this childhood pain is too great for us to be conscious of it, but it can manifest in any number of ways, from addiction, chronic illness, and relationship problems to simply feeling that life is mundane and pointless. Inner Child work, whether alone or with a **psychotherapist**, is a way of reconnecting with our child self so that the pain can be released.

Everything we have ever been remains inside us, like the layers of a Russian doll, and we as adults are ideally placed to give our child selves exactly what they need. The best way to learn to be a good parent—and a happy person—is to practice being a good parent to ourselves.

Connecting With Your Inner Child

- ❑ Ask your child self to write a letter to you as an adult telling you what they most need from you. You may find it easier to do this with your left hand (if you are right handed), as this connects to the emotional, unschooled part of you. Reply, writing with your normal hand, promising to give your child self what they have asked for.
- ❑ Put yourself into a relaxed frame of mind in your usual way (or see **meditation**) and imagine yourself as a child. You will probably find that you

(cont'd)

instantly return to a particular point in your childhood. Go up to your childhood self and ask them what they need. Give it to them if you can, whatever it is, whether a hug, attention, understanding, guidance, security, or someone to play with.

- ❑ Check out your inner child whenever you feel stressed or unhappy. Be a nurturing parent to yourself at all times.

Iridology

The study of the markings on the colored part of the eye (iris) and how they change in order to assess someone's basic constitution, their current state of health, and whether they have any problems affecting specific parts of the body. The system was drawn up by a 19th-century Hungarian doctor and developed by the U.S. doctor and **naturopath** Bernard Jensen in the 1950s. More recently, eye markings have been related to personality types.

J

Jung, Carl Gustav

A Swiss psychiatrist who lived from 1875 to 1961. Jung brought a spiritual dimension to the study of the human mind and rediscovered ancient systems of wisdom such as alchemy. He coined the term **synchronicity** for "meaningful coincidence" and devised many concepts, such as **archetypes**, **anima/animus**, introversion/extroversion and the **shadow**, which are still important today. At one stage a colleague of Sigmund Freud, he later split with him because he considered that Freud put too much emphasis on sexuality and was too pessimistic about human nature. Like Freud, however, he was fascinated by the part of our mind which is unconscious and which is manifested in dreams and creative work.

Psychotherapists who use the ideas of Jung are called *analytical psychologists*.

K

Kabala(h), Kabbala(h)

See **Cabbala**.

Karma

The natural law of cause and effect, of reaping what we sow, or the debt we carry as a result of our past. If we harm someone, then eventually—if not in this lifetime then another—we will have to pay the price, and conversely all our good deeds will be returned to us. Because of this we need never worry about taking revenge on people who harm us—the universe takes care of it. And if we do someone a good turn and they don't repay us it doesn't matter—something somewhere will.

Karma is not a question of punishment, but of the balance of the cosmos being restored, so we don't have to blame ourselves for our misfortunes or others for theirs. Misfortunes are part of a larger picture and an opportunity for us to relieve ourselves of karma.

Emotions and thoughts as well as actions create karma, so we should be free of ulterior motives and shouldn't expect to be paid back for good deeds or wait for our enemies to receive their just desserts. Understanding and repentance can be enough to liberate us from the consequences of things we've done wrong, and we don't have to suffer to learn.

Ultimately, karma means taking responsibility for our lives and knowing that everything will come out right in the end.

See also **Hinduism**, and **Reincarnation**.

Kinesiology

A **complementary therapy** developed by a U.S. **chiropractor** in the 1960s. He discovered that muscles are related to **acupuncture** meridians (energy channels). By testing the strength of different muscles you can find out about the health of mind and body. Health can be restored by gentle pressure or massage along the meridians.

Kinesiology is best known for the detection and treatment of allergies, but it can actually be used for anything. It is completely painless and the muscle tests simply involve you trying to resist light pressure from the therapist—they are not tests of muscle development. It also works through a surrogate so, for example, your child or pet could be tested and treated through you.

"Touch for health" is a simplified form of kinesiology developed for use at home.

Kirlian Photography

A method of photographing **Auras**.

Kundalini

A yogic term for the life energy (**subtle energy**) of a human being which in its unawakened form lies like a coiled serpent at the base of the spine. As we develop, it rises through the **chakras** (energy centers) awakening each of them in turn. Kundalini yoga uses breathing exercises, postures, symbolic gestures (*mudras*), and meditation on the chakras to encourage its ascent.

Kundalini visualization

For this exercise, you will need a basic knowledge of the chakras and their associations (see **chakras**).

- ❑ Put yourself in a relaxed frame of mind in your usual way or see *meditation*.
- ❑ Imagine the fiery red energy of your base chakra. Breathe in and picture it rising through each of the chakras in turn right to the crown and then, as you breathe out, falling back to the base chakra.
- ❑ Imagine the warm orange energy of your sacral chakra. As you breathe in and out, take it up through your body to the crown chakra, down to the base chakra, and then back up to the sacral chakra.
- ❑ Do this with each of the chakras in turn. When you get to the crown chakra, reverse the procedure—take the energy down to the base while breathing out and then back up as you breathe in. Be sure to take the energy of each of the chakras back to its proper place.

You should now feel well balanced and full of energy. Give thanks.

L

Left Brain/Right Brain

Roughly speaking, the two sides of our brain have different functions. The right side deals with pictures, emotions, and intuitions, and the left with analytical thinking, speaking, writing, and reading. The right side of our body, however, is controlled by the left side of our brain, and the left side of the body by the right brain.

When the two sides of our brain are working in harmony (that is, with identical wave patterns) our consciousness alters, and we reach a deeply relaxed state. However, because of our culture (which favors "left-brain" activities) and because most of us are right handed (which develops the left brain), this is a rare occurrence.

Why we should be right-handed is a mystery. Animals use both paws and Stone Age people were ambidextrous. It was only when humankind started farming that tools became right-handed. As if to counter this, the connections between the two sides of the brain have been steadily thickening during our evolution (and women have more connections than men.)

Exercises for synchronizing the left and right brains

- ❑ With your left hand, write down a word and then everything that comes into your mind connected with that word. (For right handers only.)
- ❑ Draw an upside-down picture.
- ❑ Close your eyes and listen to all the sounds going on around you. Hear them as rhythm, not as things making a noise.
- ❑ Make a tape that plays beats into each of you ears alternately (a method used by the out-of-body experience researcher Robert Monroe).

Lemuria

There is mythological, geological, and archaeological evidence that an advanced ancient civilization once existed on a continent in the Pacific (see, for example, *Lost Cities of Ancient Lemuria & the Pacific* by David Hatcher Childress).

The seer Edgar **Cayce** called the people the Mu and said that the Lemurian civilization coexisted with that of **Atlantis**, but was destroyed earlier in a cataclysm that occurred about 28,000 BCE. The name Mu was also used in the book *The Lost Continent of Mu* (1926), that its writer, James Churchward, claimed was true but which is presumed to be fiction. Madame **Blavatsky** described Lemuria's inhabitants as humanity's third "root race" as we descended from the spiritual to the material (with Atlanteans as the fourth and us the fifth). She placed the continent in the Indian Ocean, however.

More recently, Lemuria has been connected with the state of California, in particular Mount Shasta, an extinct volcano sacred to Native Americans. Survivors of the continent are thought, by some (including Robert Stelle), to be living in a subterranean world beneath the mountain.

Also called Pacifica and Pan, the continent received its most usual name from the lemur, a primate used as evidence in the 19th century that there was once a continent linking Africa and India.

LETS (Local Exchange and Trading Systems)

We tend to think of money, like time and space, as one of life's absolutes, but it too is relative. As things stand at the moment, money is issued by governments and banks to make profits for themselves and the system can only be maintained by constant economic growth. The system is inherently inefficient because when prices are rising we spend rather than save, and this makes prices rise still further. When prices are falling we save, which makes money scarce and trading even more difficult. In fact, as the economist Richard Douthwaite puts it, the present world monetary system is an "unsustainable, unstable global monoculture." He suggests that we need four different types of money—an international currency, a national or regional currency, a reserve currency, and local currencies. All should be created *for* the users, not by people wanting to profit from them, and the international currency, to which all the others would be related, should represent a scarce natural resource and therefore be directly linked to the state of the environment.

A local currency scheme known as Local Exchange and Trading Systems, or LETS, was started in Canada in the 1980s. There are now over 1,000 LETS schemes throughout the world, including 450 in the United Kingdom. Communities create their own unit of currency, which they exchange for goods (sometimes) or services (more usually). LETS are very useful for people with time, but no money—such as the retired, unemployed, and charities—and are a good way of bringing a community together. Their disadvantage is that they are not legally enforceable, so some people are able to build up an unfair amount of debt. Services can be valued either according to time (for example, one hour of babysitting = one hour of car repair work) or according to their conventional value (10 hours of babysitting = one hour of car repair work).

Leys (Leylines)

In 1921, the respected businessman, photographer, and amateur archaeologist Alfred Watkins was out riding in his native Herefordshire when he had a vision of the countryside covered in a network of straight lines like fairy chains. These connected prehistoric sites and natural features like tree clumps, ponds, and stray lumps of rock, and he later called them *leys* (pronounced *lays*), after the common place-name element (also spelled lay, lee, lea, or leigh). This word is attached to a variety of ancient sites and Watkins felt that its meaning had never been properly explained, so he linked it with his vision. He thought these alignments might have been paths, or at least direction-finding devices, with many of the natural features created and tended by prehistoric people. The painstaking research, which backed up his vision, appeared in his classic work, *The Old Straight Track*.

In his 1969 book *The View over Atlantis*, John Michell suggested that leys were part of an ancient worldwide system of energy manipulation perhaps inherited from **Atlantis**. This sparked off a huge interest in what came to be known as **Earth energies** and led to research of all kinds at prehistoric sites and along leys, including **dowsing** and testing for known energies such as radiation and radio waves. Computer analysis discovered that ancient sites in the United Kingdom were in fact aligned much more often than chance alone would allow.

A more recent idea about leys is that they are spirit paths. Ley expert Paul Devereux has discovered that old straight tracks are found all over the world, and that they are often connected with religious or funeral ritual. In Europe, including England, bodies used to have to be conveyed along "dead" straight paths to their burial sites. Such straight lines could be a portrayal of, or maps for, **Shamanic** or **out-of-body** flight.

You can plot leys on a map for yourself, bearing in mind that over about 50 miles the curvature of the Earth means that straight lines on the map are not straight on the ground. Other problems are: large-scale maps don't cover a big enough area; small-scale maps don't have enough detail; and if your area has changed a lot recently, you may have to look at old maps in your local history library. You can include churches as well as prehistoric features in your alignments as they were often built on previous sacred sites, and you may find that crossroads and older domestic buildings fall on leys When out walking look for sudden vistas, markstones hidden in the undergrowth, or notches cut out of hills on the horizon. Watkins believed that the beautiful Scots pine, native only to Scotland, might have been planted to mark leys so look out for this too (the present ones being descendants). Folklore is another source of information. For instance, as Janet and Colin Bord suggest in *Mysterious Britain*, leys could be connected with the many legends about secret passages.

Life Energy

The same as **Subtle Energy**.

Light Therapy

See **Color and Light Therapy**.

Looyenwork

A type of **bodywork** developed recently in the United States. It uses deep, precise pressure to release physical and emotional tension and allow the body to return to its natural balanced state.

M

Macrobiotics

A way of living concerned with diet, in particular, and based on ancient oriental approaches to health. The idea was developed by the Japanese philosopher George Ohsawa at the beginning of the 20th century. He brought it to the West after World War II, and when he died, his work was continued by his friends Aveline and Michio Kushi. Macrobiotic practices can cure as well as prevent disease (Ohsawa cured himself of tuberculosis) and aim to create mental as well as physical health.

The essence of the macrobiotic lifestyle is moderation and simplicity. Eating is seen in terms of **yin and yang**. These two forces are found in everything, including food and food preparation methods, and the ideal diet is one in which they are balanced. The best foods are fresh, local, and in season as these are adapted to your environment and the current weather, so are most likely to provide the type of nourishment you need.

Macrobiotics—Food Choices

Choose food from the center of the spectrum. (Don't try to balance extreme yin foods with extreme yang ones.)

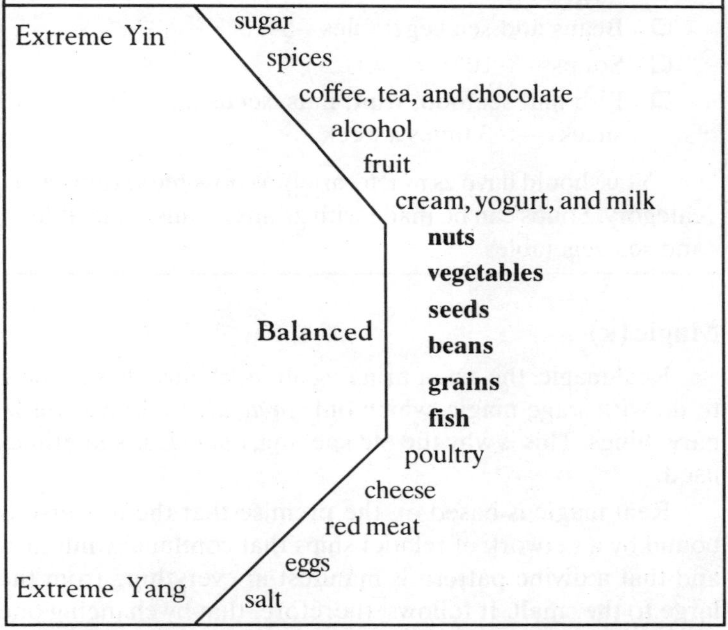

The guidelines in the boxes are for the average healthy person living in a temperate four-season climate. However, the macrobiotic diet can be adapted for anyone, whatever their constitution, condition, or environment, and detailed help can be obtained from the organizations listed in the Addresses section. You may also find that macrobiotic advice is given during **complementary health** treatments such as nutritional therapy, shiatsu, acupuncture, and Chinese herbal medicine.

Macrobiotics—Food Proportions

Food should be eaten in the following proportions:

- Whole grains—50%
- Vegetables—20–30%
- Beans and sea vegetables—5–10%
- Soups—5–10%
- Fish and seafood; fruit; nuts, seeds and natural snacks—1–3 times a week.

You should have as much variety as possible within each category. Soups can be made with grains, beans, vegetables, and sea vegetables.

Magic (k)

Real magic, the art of bringing about change, has nothing to do with stage magic, which only *pretends* to do extraordinary things. This is why the old spelling, *magick*, is sometimes used.

Real magic is based on the premise that the universe is bound by a network of relationships that continually interact, and that a divine pattern is manifest in everything from the large to the small. It follows, therefore, that by changing one thing, we can change something else. For example, by visualizing something—creating something on the imaginative plane—we can make it happen in reality, on the material plane, or by changing a detail in the layout of our homes, we can affect our lives (the basis of **feng shui**).

The difference between magic and wishful thinking is the amount of power involved. We *raise power* by working in a group, by putting our whole selves—body, mind, heart, and soul—into the magic, and through supernatural help, from goddesses and gods, ancestors, **spirit guides**, fairies, and so on. Magic also uses **correspondences**, cosmic connections which help us find our way around and amplify our actions.

Ritual is important in magic for many reasons. It stimulates and fixes the concentration. It takes you away from the everyday world and reminds you of previous magical experiences. It brings people together and it stimulates the emotions. The ritual might involve music, dancing, drumming, and chanting as well as special clothes (or none), special tools, incense, herbs, and **crystals**. "High" magic is likely to use a complex blend of ancient **Egyptian**, **cabbalistic**, and medieval **Hermetic** practices, whereas simpler "nature" magic tends to focus on the seasons, the Elements, the cycles of the moon, and plant and animal spirits. This is the sort of magic found in **Pagan** religions. Many magical rituals take place in a circle, either a natural one such as a stone circle, one created specially for the occasion, or an imaginary one. This is another way of increasing power and gaining protection.

Like most things, magic can be used with good or bad intention. However, you only harm yourself if you use magic for destructive ends as everything rebounds on you sooner or later. In fact, there is a tradition that, whereas ordinary action simply rebounds with equal force, magic rebounds *threefold*. The best use of magic is for healing and to expand our consciousness.

Magnet Therapy

A form of healing using magnets attached to the body or electromagnetic radiation. Popular for animals, as well as people, it is largely known for its soothing effect on pain and stiffness and for its ability to speed healing, such as after a fracture, but it may benefit illnesses as well. It can also be used to aid sleep and ease anxiety, and athletes use it to enhance performance.

Magnet therapy is prescribed by doctors and physiotherapists as well as **complementary therapists**. For home use there is a wide range of products available (for both people and pets), including pillows, cushions, mattresses, shoe insoles, belts, necklaces, bracelets, patches, and magnets to put in drinking water.

Maitreya

A Buddhist word for messiah, used by some for the spiritual leader they believe will appear to help us make the transition into the new age of **Aquarius**. The **theosophists** identified an Indian mystic Krishnamurti (1897–1986) as the maitreya but he refused to take on the mantle. The Aetherius Society, formed in London in 1955, believes that the maitreya arrived from outer space in the 1980s and will reveal himself when the time is right.

Mandala

Sanskrit for "magic circle", this is any concentrically arranged figure, that is, a symmetrical pattern that radiates from a central point. Such figures are found in sacred art all over the world.

In **Hinduism**, beautifully colored mandalas are used for concentration and meditation. Medieval Christian mandalas show Jesus surrounded by the four evangelists. The psychologist **Jung** found mandalas arising in the dreams and visions of his patients and saw them as symbols of the self.

Mantra

A word or phrase chanted or repeated inwardly to uplift and fix the concentration. Mantras are chosen for their sound as well as their meaning since it is believed that certain sounds have the ability to alter consciousness. The classic **Hindu** mantra is "om mani padme hum," which translates as "the jewel in the lotus" and means the soul. The shortened version "om" is seen as the sound from which the universe was created.

See also **Affirmations**, and **Sound Therapy**.

Marma

Vigorous **massage** of **ayurvedic energy** points.

Massage and Bodywork

There is an enormous variety of massage and bodywork (**holistic** physical therapy) systems, old and new. Those based on Western medical ideas tend to be physically-oriented and moderately rigorous. They can improve circulation, tone muscles, ease joints, and provide pain relief. Modern intuitive systems are usually quite gentle. These are the ones to choose for stress and emotional release. Types that work on the body's (subtle) energy circulation system are often, but not always, from the East. They range from gentle to extremely rigorous and can help sort out many deep-seated physical and mental problems.

Massage and Bodywork Systems Covered in This Book

Therapy	How It Works
Acumassage	S
Acupressure	S
Alexander Technique	B, M, E
Applied Chiropractic	B
Aromatherapy Massage	B, E
Bioenergetics	B, E
Bowen Technique	B, S
Chiropractic	B
Cranial Osteopathy	S
Craniosacral Therapy	S
Do-In	B, S
Feldenkrais Method	B, M, E
Healing	S
Hellerwork	B, M, E
Indian Head Massage	B, S
Kinesiology	S
Looyenwork	B, E
Marma	B, S

(cont'd)

Massage and Bodywork Systems Covered in This Book *(cont'd)*

Therapy	How It Works
McTimoney Chiropractic	B
McTimoney-Corley Chiropractic	B
Metamorphic Technique	S
Osteopathy	B, S
Polarity Therapy	S
Reflexology	S
Reiki	S
Rolfing	B
Seichem/Seichim/Sekhem	S
Shiatsu	B, S
Swedish Massage	B
Thai Massage	B, S
Trager	B, E
Tui Na (Chinese medical massage)	B, S
Zero Balancing	B, E

Key

B Through Body ***E*** Through Emotions
M Through Mind ***S*** Through Subtle Energy

Maya

These people lived on the Yucatán peninsula of Central America (Mexico, Belize, and Guatemala) from about 2600 BCE. They built stepped pyramids and elaborate temples, which were staffed by a priestly elite, used a hieroglyphic script, and had a sophisticated system of mathematics. Their knowledge of astronomy was matched only by that of the ancient **Egyptians**, and because of the similarities between the two cultures some have suggested either that the Maya culture derives from the Egyptian or that both come from an earlier one—perhaps even that of **Atlantis**. Other evidence for this theory includes early Central American legends about white people from across the sea who brought them knowledge and wisdom, and the fact that the letter combination "atl" (as in "Atlantis") is rare in all languages except those of Central America.

The Maya calendar goes back to 23,000 BCE. It is divided into 5000-year cycles, each of which ends with a disaster from the heavens that destroys civilization on Earth and forces humankind to start again. Cultures all over the world have a similar cyclic view of human civilization, but the Maya myths are distinguished by their precise dating: the current cycle is due to end on December 23, 2012.

We know that life on Earth has been dramatically changed from time to time by collisions with asteroids (big chunks of space debris) and meteorites (smaller chunks), and that this could happen at regular intervals as the orbit of the Earth coincides with that of a particular cloud of debris. However, we have never been able to predict such collisions thousands of years in advance and with pinpoint accuracy. Whether the Maya could remains to be seen.

Meditation

Meditation is a way of stilling the mind so as to get in touch with the happiness and calm we all have deep inside us. As the Buddhist writer Gyatso says, "When the turbulence of distracting thoughts subsides and our mind becomes still, deep happiness and contentment arise naturally from within."

Although many (if not most) religions recommend meditation of some sort or another, it does not need to have any religious connotations and you don't have to believe in anything to start practicing.

We all know what contentment is like and how impossibly fickle it is—no sooner do you realize it's there than it's gone. The ultimate aim of meditation is to make it such a habit that it happens all the time.

Meditation—Some Tips

- ❑ Briefly and often is best. Try to meditate once or twice each day, even if just for two minutes.
- ❑ Don't get too attached to any experiences you have while meditating, however enjoyable they may be. The aim is to simplify your life, not complicate it, and it's the practice that matters, not what happens.
- ❑ Try and meditate at approximately the same time each day. This makes it habitual, and therefore easier.
- ❑ Don't turn meditating into a chore. A little bit of discipline is necessary, but if you get really fed up, have a break for a few days or even weeks.
- ❑ Sit, rather than lie, as this makes it easier to maintain the necessary state of focused alertness. If you lie down your mind tends to wander or you fall asleep.
- ❑ If you have a very busy mind, keep a notebook handy and jot down thoughts that won't go away.

Meditation—How To Go About It

1. Find somewhere where you won't be disturbed, whether indoors or outdoors.
2. Make sure you are comfortable and close your eyes.
3. Check over your body for tension and try and relax it. Sit up straight, however, as this is better for your breathing. Take a few deep breaths.

(cont'd)

(cont'd)

4. Concentrate on one thing—see the following box for suggestions. Don't worry about intruding thoughts—just let them come and go and keep returning to whatever it is you are concentrating on. Try not to force your concentration. It will come about of its own accord as your mind calms down.
5. Stop when you feel tired. Give thanks if you feel inspired to do so. Come out of your meditation gently and bring any good feelings with you.

Meditation—Some Suggestions of What To Concentrate On

- ❑ Concentrate on your breathing. Breathe in the new and breathe out the old.
- ❑ Listen to the silence.
- ❑ Imagine yourself in a beautiful place.
- ❑ Remember how glad you are just to be alive.
- ❑ Think of an inspiring word such as *trust* or *love*, or a phrase. Repeat it to yourself or imagine it filling every area of you life.
- ❑ Imagine your mind as a gently rolling sea.
- ❑ Imagine yourself encased in a bubble of light. Feel it warming every part of you.
- ❑ Imagine a divine being protecting you and filling you with joy.

Medium

Someone through whom a spirit being communicates. *Trance* mediums may take on the voice or appearance of the spirit they are working with and remember little or nothing of what they communicated, but not all mediumship is this dramatic. Mediums are best known for the contact they make with people who have died recently in order to bring comfort to the bereaved.

See also **Channeling**, and **Spiritualism**.

Meridian

Energy channel used in **Acupuncture**.

Metamorphic Technique

A therapy developed from **reflexology** in the 1960s. It concentrates on the insides of the feet, which are seen as relating to our nine months in the womb, and is said to be helpful for anyone who feels stuck, whether physically or psychologically.

Money

See **Ethical Consumerism/Investment**, and **LETS**.

Morphogenetic Fields, Morphic Fields, and Morphic Resonance

Genes alone are not enough to explain why we develop as we do. The biologist Rupert Sheldrake compares genes to building materials. Houses can have chemically identical bricks, mortar, and timber but still be different. What makes them different are the architect's plans. Since the 1920s scientists have used the rather vague term *morphogenetic field* to represent the architect's plans in plants and animals—the organizing factor that makes a leg develop into a leg, an eye into an eye, and so on.

Sheldrake suggests that morphogenetic fields might be just one type of field in a much larger group that he calls *morphic fields*. These, he believes, affect not just plants and animals but also crystals, molecules, societies, and cultures, by which he means both animal groups like termite nests and fish shoals, as well as human civilization.

Morphic fields are like habits that a particular species, group, chemical, and so on builds up over time. New habits come into being through creative leaps and are then spread, he suggests, through something he calls *morphic resonance*. This spreads them much more quickly than if each child had to learn them from their parents, for instance, or if an animal in one part of the country had to travel to another part to communicate with other members of the species.

There are many scientific anomalies that could be explained by morphic resonance. For example, glycerin was discovered in the 18th century but for 200 years nobody could get it to become solid (crystallize). Then one batch crystallized of its own accord and soon glycerin crystals were being produced without difficulty all over the world. When milk began to be delivered in bottles in the United Kingdom, blue tits all over the country learned independently to peck through the foil to get at the cream.

Morphic resonance is outside space and time and so could also explain instincts, memory, and **Jung**'s "collective unconscious," as well as skills like **telepathy** and **psychometry**. Sheldrake foresees it being deliberately used to help us learn more quickly or to link computers.

Moxabustion/Moxibustion

A process used by **acupuncturists**. It involves burning a small cone of the herb moxa (Chinese mugwort) on an acupoint (energy point) in order to add energy.

Mu

Another name for the lost continent of **Lemuria**, thought to have been situated in either the Indian or the Pacific Ocean.

Music Therapy

See **Creative Therapies**.

Mystery Tradition

See **Western Mystery Tradition**.

N

Native America

Just as many Europeans are returning to their **Pagan** roots, many people in America—of both settler and native stock—are taking another look at the ancient culture, which was all but destroyed in the 17th to 19th centuries.

When white people first arrived on the continent there were over 2,000 different tribes, representing some 600 ethnic groups, in an area ranging from the jungles of Central America, through the U.S. plains, to the Arctic lands of Canada. Some were hunters, some farmers, and some fishermen, and while traditions varied, they nevertheless had a spirituality in common. This was based around the one creator or Great Spirit, often seen as represented in Mother Earth, Father Sky, Grandmother Moon, and Grandfather Sun. The spirits of ancestors gave protection and guidance, and animals acted as teachers, protective spirits, and allies.

A universal symbol was the circle or *medicine wheel*. This represented life as a whole, or the wholeness of life, as well as the cycles of life such as the seasons and the journey from birth to death. It was engraved on objects like drums, created in temporary form for ceremonies, and built in stones, such as the famous Big Horn Medicine Wheel in Wyoming or the smaller circles, which once covered America.

Native Americans, much like native peoples all over the world, lived in close contact with nature and the spiritual world, and every aspect of their lives was dedicated to maintaining this contact and nourishing the power that created them. **Shamans** or *medicine women/men* (as the settlers called them) led the rituals and interceded with the spirits for the people, but everyone was expected to play their part.

The Sioux visionary Black Elk, remembering the final destruction of his people at the end of the 19th century, said, "the nation's hoop is broken and scattered. There is no center any longer, and the sacred tree is dead." Since then, however, Native America has become an independent nation within the United States, and its spirituality and traditions have been taken up by people of all races. This has not always been welcomed.

The American Indian Movement has accused whites of profiteering from native culture, and some within the movement feel they are being exploited and oppressed all over again. Other Native Americans are even turning to non-natives to preserve their traditions because their own young people are not interested. Sun Bear (1929–1992) believed the "medicine ways" should be taught to all who sincerely want to learn. He started the Sun Bear Tribe in Oregon, open to non-native as well as Native Americans, and holds Medicine Wheel gatherings in both Europe and the United States. The Native American Church combines new forms of native rituals (in particular taking the hallucinogenic cactus, peyote) with Christian ones.

See also **Dreamcatcher**, **Power Animal**, **Smudging**, **Sweat Lodge**, and **Vision Quest**.

Natural Health/Medicine/Therapies

See **Complementary Health**.

Nature Spirits

Throughout the world and across all ages people have reported seeing small and large human-like but nonhuman creatures. (For examples, see *Fairies: Real Encounters with Little People* by Janet Bord.) In northern Europe they are called fairies, pixies, elves, and brownies. The ancient Greeks had satyrs and nymphs. Trolls and Green Men stalk the woods, sylphs grace the air, and mermaids haunt the seas. But what are they?

One theory is that they are nature spirits—creatures who protect and nurture different aspects of the natural world. According to the creators of a garden at **Findhorn** in Scotland who communicated with nature spirits, greater beings called **devas** provide the blueprint and the energy, and nature spirits carry out the work. They have no material form but take on an appearance that suits the folklore of the person perceiving them. This folklore is probably derived from a number of sources including stories about earlier individuals or races, as well as being related to the actual energy form of the being. E. L. Gardner, who wrote about nature spirits in the early 20th century, describes this form as follows:

> *The natural "body" used by elemental [nature spirit] lives seems to be a pulsing globe of light. Streams of force radiating from this centre build up floating figures, "wings" of radiating energy, and filmy shapes of vaguely human likeness.*

According to folklore there are three ways to gain entry to fairyland, or the world of nature spirits:

- ❑ *Time*: Crucial are the four turning points of the day—dusk, midnight, the hour before dawn, and midday—and the four turning points of the year: Halloween (31 October), Yule (21 December), May Eve (30 April) and Midsummer (21 June).
- ❑ *Place*: Some places are more powerful than others and beloved of nature spirits. Try pools, waterfalls, caves, and ancient trees, especially those with stories attached to them, as well as prehistoric standing stones and burial mounds.
- ❑ *State of mind*: Certain plants have a particular affinity with the "little people" and open the sight to them. *(Most can be deadly poisonous, however, in the wrong dose.)* These include liberty cap

("magic mushroom"), fly agaric, henbane, and other plants of the nightshade family.

But beware—nature spirits do not take kindly to unwanted intrusion and have been known to take people away, sometimes forever. (There are similarities between fairy abduction and **abduction by aliens**.)

According to the devas at Findhorn, the proper way to approach spirits is with love and a genuine desire for cooperation. They will then show themselves if we are ready and if the time is right. Curiosity doesn't work and experimentation is harmful. Current agriculture is just the start of our work with nature and as E. L. Gardner says (in the introduction to *Fairies at Work and Play* by Geoffrey Hodson):

> *As we cease to ignore the activities of the devas and nature-spirits, and recognise their partial dependence on human mentality and the amazing response forthcoming when recognition is given, we shall find many of our difficulties and problems solved for us and the world far more wonderful than anything we have yet conceived.*

Naturopathy

Naturopaths are the family doctors of **complementary medicine**. They use a variety of therapies to support the body's own healing powers, especially fasting, **nutritional therapy**, and **hydrotherapy**. They see disease as having three causes—structural, biochemical, or emotional—and emphasize the importance of proper food, clean water and air, exercise, rest, and positive thinking. They use conventional diagnostic techniques such as blood and urine analysis as well as alternative ones like **iridology** (looking at the iris of the eye), **kinesiology** (muscle testing), and hair analysis.

Nazca

On a barren plain below the Andes in Peru lies one of archaeology's great mysteries. Etched into the stony surface are hundreds of straight lines, some many miles long, giant trapezoids, "paperclip" shapes, spirals, and labyrinths, as well as 32 smaller pictures of animals, flowers, and birds. They were discovered when planes began flying over the area in the 1920s and 1930s. There is no sure way to tell how old they are but the people who created the markings are thought to have flourished between 800 BCE and 1400 CE.

The writer Charles Berlitz recounts a local legend that attributes Nazca markings to a goddess who descended to Earth in "a ship of the sky as brilliant as the sun." Erich von Daniken, who believes that extraterrestrials once visited our planet, suggests that some markings at Nazca were made by landing spaceships, and others by bewildered locals over succeeding centuries trying to bring back the "gods" who had come and then gone.

Others have linked the Nazca lines with **ley** lines or wondered if the markings could be a giant astronomical calendar. A recent idea is that the lines and spirals represent **out-of-body** flight and the figures are totem or **power animals**, with the markings as a whole used as ritual pathways.

The best way to see the Nazca markings for yourself is by plane. There are trips from Lima, Ica, and Nazca. From the observation tower some 12 miles north of Nazca, only a few of the shapes can be seen.

Near-Death Experience (NDE)

This term was first coined by an American psychologist, Raymond Moody, who in 1975, published a book called *Life after Life* in which he detailed the remarkably similar experiences reported by many people brought back from death or near death. These experiences went through several stages:

- People first floated out of their bodies, leaving behind any pain or injury and being able to see things that they couldn't have if they were still in their bodies.
- Some then found themselves accompanied by guardian spirits and meeting dead relatives and friends.

- ❑ The next phase was one of transition, often compared to a tunnel, bridge, or mountain pass.
- ❑ The climax was union with unconditional love or the ultimate source of the universe's energy and a sensation of coming home.
- ❑ A life review completed the experience.

John Wren-Lewis of Australia doesn't describe his NDE in the dramatic terms above. He says (in the Natural Death Centre's handbook):

> *I simply entered—or, rather, was—a timeless, spaceless void which in some indescribable way was total aliveness—an almost palpable blackness that was yet somehow radiant.*

This dimension has remained with him and brings the "cheerful equanimity" of knowing that his happiness no longer depends on "satisfying his special preferences" but simply "in being, in the Great Dark."

When Moody first published his book, people saw it as proof of life after death. Because NDEs happen to people who are clinically dead, to scientists they are proof that the mind exists outside the brain. Wren-Lewis's account shows that the near-death dimension is actually a state of being *more* alive and something we can experience here and now.

Neo-Pagans/Neo-Paganism

Modern **Pagans/Paganism**.

Neuro-Linguistic Programming (NLP)

This is a method of personal development popular with businesspeople. It aims to show that most of our problems derive from the models in our heads rather than from the world as it really is. Once we see this and understand how the models work, we can change them. Its main presuppositions are:

- ❑ If what you are doing isn't working, do something else.
- ❑ There is no failure, only feedback.

- It is not what happens to you that matters. It is what you do with what happens to you.
- The meaning of your communication is the response you get.

Nine Star Ki

A type of astrology related to **feng shui**.

Nirvana

A **Buddhist** term meaning the state of complete contentment we reach if we leave behind our consciousness of being separate and individual.

Northern Tradition

This is the general name given to the modern revival of Anglo-Saxon, Norse, and Germanic **Pagan** religions. It is also sometimes called Odinism, after the god Odin, or Asatru, after a group of gods called the Aesir, or Vanatru, after a group of gods called the Vanir. Some followers like to call themselves "heathen" rather than Pagan, heathen meaning *(the beliefs of) the people of the heath*, just as Pagan means *(the beliefs of) the people of the country*, so as to distinguish themselves from other Pagans because they believe their religion has more genuine links with an actual religion of the past.

The main sources of information about Northern myths and deities are the 13th-century *Eddas*, one prose and one poetry. Norse myths are a rumbustious mix of gods, giants, elves, and dwarfs. The universe is seen as a tree, Yggdrasill, and is made up of nine worlds. The human world of Midgard is connected to Asgard, where the gods live, by a rainbow bridge, and under Yggdrasill is Niflheim, a place of freezing mist and darkness which contains the realm of Hel. In Hel is a female monster also called Hel who is half-alive and half-dead, and a dragon called Nidhogg who gnaws at the roots of the tree and chews corpses. Dead warriors are spared Hel and go instead to Valhalla in Asgard. They are taken there by beautiful women called Valkyries. The **runes**, the Norse magical script, were discovered by Odin, chief god, after he spent nine days and nights hanging upside down. A terrible battle, Ragnarok, between the gods and the giants will bring the world to an end.

Some Deities From the Northern Tradition	
Odin	Chief god. God of poetry, battle and death. Discovered runes. Also called Woden and gave his name to Wednesday.
Frigga	Chief goddess. Wife of Odin. Gave her name to Friday.
Thor	God of thunder and law and order. Son of Odin. His hammer, Mjollnir ("crusher"), always returns when thrown. Gave his name to Thursday.
Tui	God of war. Gave his name to Tuesday.
Loki	Troublemaker. God of lies, tricks, evil, and fire.
Freyja	Goddess of fertility. Sister of Freyr.
Freyr	God of fertility. Brother of Freyja.
Norns	Three goddesses of destiny: Skuld (being), Urd (fate), Verdandi (necessity).

Like other Pagans, followers of the Northern tradition time their festivals by the sun and the moon. They have two other special days—Sigurd's Day on April 23, commemorating a dragon-slayer and Heroes' Day on November, 11 when the dead are honored. They meet either outside or indoors in groups called *hearths*. Nine being an important number, they believe in nine noble virtues which are (with variations): courage, truth, honor, fidelity, discipline, hospitality, industriousness, self-reliance, and perseverance. The taking and keeping of oaths is very important, with these often being sworn using the symbol of Thor's hammer (see box). There are three types of **magic**, one using runes, another talismans, and a third more intuitive and **shamanistic** methods.

The Northern tradition has in the past, and still does (in a small minority), have links with Nazism. Some groups only permit men to join and men do dominate.

Nostradamus

A French prophet of the 16th century whose books were bestsellers at the time and have hardly ever been out of print since. Of Jewish ancestry and learned in Hebrew, Greek, and Latin, he worked as an herbalist and surgeon, starting his books in middle age after he began having flashes of precognition. He augmented this natural talent with **astrology** and probably **alchemy** and **cabbalistic** numerology.

The books are written in four-line verses or *quatrains*, which are then grouped into 100-verse sections or *centuries* (nothing to do with years), of which he did nearly ten. In order to exclude the uninitiated he says, but probably for fear of being accused of witchcraft by the Catholic Church, he disguised his predictions by muddling up the date order of the quatrains, using a code for dating and using anagrams and/or letter changes for the names of people and places. The predictions are also written in a mixture of French, local dialect, Greek, and Latin and filled with esoteric symbolism. All this makes them very difficult to understand, even in retrospect, and for any one quatrain there can be numerous interpretations.

Most of his predictions deal with calamities. Among those he may have got right are ones concerning Cromwell, Napoleon, Hitler, and the Great Fire of London. Among his predictions for us are the dethroning of a Pope, widespread earthquakes until 2044, a large comet between 2096 and 2156, a third Antichrist (Hitler having been the second) sometime early in the millennium, and an Asian/Muslim invasion of Europe followed by plague, famine, drought, and floods. However, any of the quatrains could have alternate interpretations (and dating) and we have to bear in mind that he was seeing events with 16th-century eyes, so their real explanations could be quite different.

Numerology

Using numbers for **divination**. The number meanings used most often are those shown in the box. They have developed from the ideas of the Greek mystic and mathematician Pythagoras (6th century BCE), who thought that everything in the universe could be reduced to a number or vibration and that things with the same number or vibration were connected. He also believed that the seven "planets" then known (five planets plus the moon and the Earth) each gave off a different hum according to how far they were from the sun, the eight spheres together making the eight notes of the musical octave. This is known as the "music of the spheres."

Numbers and Their Meanings

Number	Positive Qualities	Negative Qualities	Day Meaning
1	Leadership, independence, masculinity.	Selfishness, loneliness.	A day of opportunity.
2	Cooperation, balance, femininity.	Being two faced, imbalance.	A day for planning rather than action.
3	Creativity, laughter, spiritual power.	Over-indulgence, superficiality.	A lucky day.
4	Endurance, self-discipline, practicality.	Being too materialistic or unadventurous.	A day to catch up on mundane jobs.
5	Sexuality, versatility.	Restlessness.	A day for adventure.
6	Harmony, domesticity.	Irresponsibility, inability to see others' point of view	A day to devote to family or for settling arguments.
7	Mysticism, magic.	Escapism, daydreaming, impracticality.	A day for being alone.
8	Worldly, achievement, power.	Laziness, stress.	A day for big undertakings.
9	Idealism, passion, compassion, mental and spiritual attainment.	Being unable to let go.	A day of fulfillment.

Each letter of the alphabet can be assigned a number equivalent. The simplest way is to go through the alphabet in sequence from one to nine, starting again at one each time you reach nine. However, the more popular system is the one in the following box. This was created from the work of the **cabbalists**, by the 18th-century Italian magician Cagliostro. (This is why there are no letters for the number nine—our alphabet has no equivalents for the Hebrew letters with that number.)

Letters and Their Number Equivalents

1	2	3	4	5	6	7	8
A I Q J Y	B K R	C G L S	D M T	E H N	U V W X	O Z	F P

Using these letter equivalents and the number meanings, you can then gauge influences by finding the following numbers:

- *Name number*: This gives a person's character and current influences. Work out the equivalent number for each letter in their name and add all the numbers together. If the total comes to more than nine, add the figures and keep doing this until you have a number from one to nine. (For example: total = 29, 2+9 = 11, 1+1 = 2.)
- *Birth number*: This gives a person's basic nature and the influences on them at the time of their birth. Add the numbers in their date of birth. For example, if they were born on May 18, 1971, add 1+8+5+1+9+7+1 = 32 = 5.
- *Day number*: This gives the influences on a person on a particular day, past, present, or future. Add their name number, their birth number, and

the number of the day they are interested in (calculated in the same way as the birth number).

Nutritional Therapy

Nutritional therapists believe that poor nourishment contributes to a wide range of physical and some mental problems. They treat these with special short-term diets, supplements, and advice on long-term eating habits.

Don't confuse them with dieticians and nutritionists who offer much more limited advice and do not work **holistically**.

O

Odinism

A **Pagan** religion in the **Northern Tradition**.

Ogham

A symbolic alphabet used by **Druids**. There are 20 letters in the ogham represented by horizontal or slanting lines on one or both sides of a central vertical line (often the corner of a stone monument). Each is named after a different tree and connected to colors, birds, stones, musical notes, and so on. In this way it could be used as a code for secret speech and writing. It was also used for **divination** or *crannchur* with each of the characters carved on sticks of the appropriate wood. These sticks were then thrown and the patterns interpreted.

There are only a few hundred ancient ogham inscriptions still in existence, mostly in Ireland on rocks, stones, and crosses. The earliest may date from about 2000 BCE, that is, pre-**Celtic**. Ogham was superceded by **runes** and by Roman letters.

The Ogham

Authorities differ in their interpretations of the ogham. Those below are adapted from an alphabet compiled by David Smith for the Pagan Federation's Druid information pack and are reproduced with their permission.

Name and Letter	Symbol	English Name	Meaning
Beith (B)	ᚁ	Silver Birch	Beginnings.
Luis (L)	ᚂ	Rowan	Magical protection.
Fearn (F)	ᚃ	Alder	Oracular vision and/or advice.
Saille (S)	ᚄ	Willow	Feminine tides and the moon.
Nuin (N)	ᚅ	Ash	The World Tree; links land, sea, and sky.
Hauthe (H)	ᚆ	Hawthorn	Fertility and the month of May.
Duir (D)	ᚇ	Oak	Strength; a doorway to the Otherworld.
Tinne (T)	ᚈ	Holly	Strength in adverse situations.
Coll (C)	ᚉ	Hazel	Inspiration and poetic vision.
Quert (Q)	ᚊ	Apple	Choices to be made; an Otherworldly fruit.
Muin (M)	ᚋ	Bramble (vine)	Psychic powers.
Gort (G)	ᚌ	Ivy	The spiritual quest.
Ngetal (Ng)	ᚍ	Reed	A time for focused and direct action.
Straif (St)	ᚎ	Blackthorn	Strife and sadness are part of the journey.
Ruis (R)	ᚏ	Elder	Renewal, rebirth, and death.
Ailm (A)	ᚐ	(Scots) Pine	Clear vision, deep into the future.
Ohn (O)	ᚑ	Gorse	Collecting the things needed for the spiritual quest.
Ur (U)	ᚒ	Heather/ Mistletoe	The All-heal; the path to inner peace and healing.
Edhadh (E)	ᚓ	Aspen	The whispering tree of the faery; listen!
Ioho (I)	ᚔ	Yew	The Great Tree of life, death, and rebirth.

Order of the Golden Dawn

See **Hermetic Order of the Golden Dawn**.

Organic Food

Organic (or more accurately organically grown) food is produced without the use of pesticides and artificial fertilizers. This is better for us and better for the environment.

Although there are limits on the chemical residues allowed in foods these are often exceeded. These safe limits neither take into account the effects of eating a cocktail of different chemicals on different foods, nor the effects on children. Animals not reared organically are routinely fed antibiotics, hormones, and other drugs, and these can find their way into the dairy produce and meat that we eat. Plants grown with artificial fertilizer may be deficient in the variety of nutrients (such as minerals) that we need, which are more likely to be found in plants grown with natural fertilizer (such as manure). No organic food is **genetically modified** (GM) and no case of mad cow disease (BSE) has been found in cattle raised organically since before 1985. Organic food tastes better and has a better texture.

Animal welfare is central to organic farming, not least because animals reared with fresh air, space to move, and appropriate food and allowed to grow and breed at their own rate are more likely to be healthy. Organic farmers encourage wildlife as this helps keep pests under control. Recent research by the Soil Association has found that there are five times as many wild plants, nearly twice as many birds, and three times as many butterflies on organic land as on that which is not. It is commonly believed that organic production is less efficient and therefore takes up more space, but this is not necessarily the case. Research at the University of Essex into sustainable farming has found that turning organic has increased yields of coffee in Mexico by 50 percent and doubled yields of maize and wheat in Brazil. Since pesticide use began in the 1940s, the proportion of crops lost to insect damage in the United States has grown by 13 percent. Organic crops may be more resistant to drought, and because organic farmers tend to grow a variety of crops, they are less affected by the vagaries of the weather.

See also **Biodynamic Agriculture**.

Osteopathy

With practitioners trained as doctors in the United States and regulated by law in the United Kingdom, this is a well-established **complementary therapy** that works on the body's bones, muscles, and connective tissue with massage, manipulation, and "thrusts" (sudden movements which improve joint mobility). It can treat a variety of structural and other problems. Practitioners may use x-rays for diagnosis before treatment.

Treatment is not painful, but if necessary, a gentler version called *cranial osteopathy* can be used. This treats the wave-like pulsation of the central nervous system, working mainly on the skull but also on the rest of the body.

Out-of-Body Experience (OOBE)

Sometimes, as a result of intense stress or pain, deep relaxation, sensory deprivation, drugs, during sleep, or for no reason at all, our **energy** body or *astral* body can detach from our physical body. These out-of-body experiences or OOBEs have been externally verified through experiments where numbers are hidden in inaccessible places. People who move out of their body during sleep are able to read the numbers and repeat them when they wake up.

A classic work on OOBEs is *Journeys Out of the Body* by Robert Monroe, who has been experiencing them for most of his life and now runs an institute to study and teach them. On one of his courses, he teaches people to help ghosts, who he believes are people who have died and detached from their body but are unable or unwilling to move on.

Deliberate OOBE is known as **astral projection** or astral travel. An extreme form of OOBE is **near-death experience**.

P

Paganism

Pagan literally means "country-dweller," and the term was used originally by the Romans for the tribes they conquered. As these had non-Roman deities, the term acquired religious connotations and came to be used for non-Christians. Today's Pagans, also sometimes called Neo-Pagans (new Pagans), are inspired by pre-Christian religions such as **Witchcraft/Wicca**, **Druidry**, **Shamanism**, and the **Northern tradition**. However, many people follow their own path, and respect for individual spiritual experience and the many different ways we can approach the divine are an intrinsic part of modern paganism. Other common factors are:

- A love and reverence for nature.
- Honoring the **Goddess**, or female divine principle, as well as the male.
- An individual morality summed up as "If it harms none, do what thou wilt."
- A belief that we can each approach the Divine directly without the need for an intermediary.
- Democratic groups often meeting outdoors and in a Circle, with rituals adapted to meet the needs of the moment.

Until the 1940s and 1950s non-Christian religions were illegal in the West, and Pagans do still suffer persecution from time to time with their practices being labeled "devil worship" or Satanism. This misconception is ironic because the devil is a Christian concept, not a Pagan one. There is a horned Pagan god, but he embodies both good and bad male traits.

Many Pagans worship alone, but if you want to find a group, one of the organizations in the Addresses section may be able to help. The Pagan year is often based on that of the **Celts** with rituals and festivals reflecting the seasons and the phases of the sun and moon. Pagans also have their own ways of marking birth, death, marriage, and entry into a tradition. **Magic** may be used for healing and contacting deeper levels of consciousness. Some groups ("ecopagans") are actively involved in preserving the environment, while others may be concerned with sacred sites. Here there is a conflict between archaeologists who want to dig them up and take bits away, and those who want them left as they are so that we have a direct link with our ancestors.

Paganism—Sowelu's Story

I was brought up in what I would call a secular Christian background. My parents have Christian beliefs but are not churchgoers. I was always encouraged to have an interest in nature and archaeology. In my early teens, I developed an interest in spirituality and found out about a number of religions. None really seemed to fit until I read a book about Wicca by Janet and Stewart Farrar. At once everything made sense and has continued to do so.

When I went to college, I found more books and Pagan magazines, and met a few others who had also recently found Paganism. I joined the Pagan Federation and made a few contacts by letter. It was over a year later that I was put in touch with a coven [group] in Exeter. I mixed with them socially and was given some coursework but I never intended to join. However, the Goddess works in mysterious

(cont'd)

ways. One evening the high priest somewhat dramatically announced his retirement and I was caught up in the resulting chaos. I found myself working closely with other women who were real soul mates, and was initiated as a priestess and later a High Priestess.

So I went from solitary Wicca to working in a group. Both have their benefits and I think there is a time in our lives when we need to work mainly alone. However, a coven is a close emotional and spiritual bond, and this means the magic and the sense of the gods is heightened. My beliefs have had a profound effect on my life. Some Pagans choose simply to believe in the God and Goddess and to celebrate the festivals. But I have been driven to follow the path of the priestess. It is not just something I do on a Sunday morning—Paganism colors my whole life and the way I live day to day. It is a continuing journey, a seeking from within.

So what point am I at now? Well, I am 27, and I continue to work with the coven. My brothers and sisters in the coven are very special to me and we have formed bonds that cannot be easily broken. I have been the Regional Coordinator for the Pagan Federation in Devon for about two years, and feel I have given something back to the organization that helped me at the beginning, although it is hard work on top of a nine to five job.

On my own, I have done some deep spiritual work. A lot of this takes the form of creative projects, from growing magic plants and herbs in the garden, writing articles, meditations, and journals, to charm-making and artwork, and making my own incense, oils, and working tools (like wands). As part of this and with the support of the coven, I have joined the Fellowship of Isis, was ordained as a priestess, have taken a small tangent to the Druid Clan of Dana (part of the FOI) and hope to start my own Grove [group] soon.

Palmistry

See **Handreading**.

Past Lives/Past Life Regression

There are several reasons for reexperiencing past lives. In the same way that we are influenced as adults by our childhood, events from past lives can have repercussions in this one. Phobias, negative attitudes, nightmares, even physical problems can all stem from unresolved incidents in other lives, and understanding this or reliving the incidents can heal us. Experiencing for ourselves the reality of other lives can release us from the fear of death, and give purpose and perspective to our lives here and now. We may also be able to tap into skills and talents from previous lives and draw them into this one. Some people simply want to look into past lives out of curiosity or as a way of learning about other states of consciousness.

See also **Reincarnation**.

Remembering Past Lives

Hypnosis is the usual method of regression, but you may be able to do it for yourself.

1. Decide *why* you want to look at a past life or lives; for example, resolving a fear or "block," going deeper into current relationships by discovering their history in other lives, or tapping into skills or wisdom. Then put that intention to the back of your mind.
2. Put yourself into a meditative state in your usual way or see **meditation**.
3. Imagine time going backwards—that is, by having the hands of a clock or a calendar or the sun going backwards—or imagine yourself in a corridor with many doors and open one of them.
4. Go with whatever images come into your mind. Don't try to direct them consciously. Try to put yourself in the

(cont'd)

scene rather than viewing it from the outside. What are you wearing? What can you smell, hear, feel?

5. Don't worry about whether the scenes are imaginary or real. The question is how deeply the experience touches you. If you feel the visions are just a conscious fantasy, try and relax more, perhaps by concentrating on your breathing. It may be that you are too aware of the purpose of the meditation. If so, try and forget it and just enjoy yourself.
6. Come back the way you went in, bringing with you whatever it was you wanted to resolve or retrieve.

Permaculture

A method of agriculture and living that combines traditional farming and gardening techniques with a modern understanding of ecology. It mimics nature as far as possible by building systems that are self-sustaining. This means:

- ❑ Working *with* local conditions rather than fighting them. Everything can be a positive resource.
- ❑ Encouraging diversity as this leads to greater stability.
- ❑ Aiming towards minimum input for maximum output.
- ❑ Having two or more uses for each element, and achieving each use in two or more ways.
- ❑ Always leaving an area completely wild as this is your creative bank.

An example of a natural ecosystem is a wood, where trees protect the soil from being blown or washed away and nourish it with dead leaves, while the soil feeds and anchors the trees. Modern farming methods on the other hand are very wasteful and destructive. For instance, six tons of topsoil are lost in England for each ton of wheat produced. A system that might be used in permaculture is the reedbed. Reeds are natural water purifiers and so can be used to treat sewage. Fish, shellfish, and birds living in the reedbeds can be used for human food, algae for animal food, and the reeds for thatching. The water left behind is rich in nitrates and can be used to fertilize crops. No waste, no work, and lots of benefits.

Permaculture was devised by the Australian Bill Mollison in the 1970s. However, it can be applied anywhere in the world and is particularly helpful for making the best of degraded areas and bringing them back to health.

Phytotherapy

See **Herbal Medicine**.

Planets

See **Correspondences**.

Polarity Therapy

This gentle therapy, with many women practitioners, was developed by an American doctor, Randolph Stone, in the middle of the last century. He was trained in **chiropractic**, **naturopathy**, and **osteopathy** but was interested in combining these with Eastern systems such as **ayurveda** and **yoga**. There are four aspects to treatment: **bodywork**, diet, exercises, and counseling.

Power Animals

Spirit animals, animal **archetypes**, or animal **devas**. **Native Americans** believe each of us has one special animal spirit who accompanies us all our lives. Others come and go, bringing particular strengths and skills, as we need them. We can meet our power animals in **meditations** and **visualizations** and call on them at any time. We should pay particular attention to the same animal if it turns up in our everyday life. It may have a message for us.

Power animals can be mythical and extinct creatures as well as living ones, native to where we live or not. Even animals normally considered pests could be valuable allies. Totem animals are power animals with which we have had a deep and long-lasting relationship, perhaps over many lifetimes, or animals associated with groups.

Prayer

Shakti Gawain believes there are three stages to a successful **visualization**: desire, belief, and acceptance. The same could be said about prayer. We have to have the simplicity to know what we want and the humility to ask for it. We must have total faith that our prayer will be answered. And we must be prepared to accept the consequences of having what we want.

Marlo Morgan, in *Mutant Message Down Under*, describes how each morning her Aboriginal friends would sing to the universe and imagine anything special they wanted, such as feathers or water:

> *The tribe carried no provisions. They planted no crops; they participated in no harvest. They walked the blazing Australian Outback, knowing each day they would receive bountiful blessings of the universe. The universe never disappointed them.*

Primal Therapy

Intensive **psychotherapy** which deals with the pain of early childhood and can be quite traumatic.

Psi

Paranormal sensory information and a Greek letter (Ψ), pronounced *sigh*. The term was devised by psychic researchers in the early 20th century because of its connection with the Greek word *psyche* (soul), psi being the first letter of the word. It means the same as **extrasensory perception** (ESP).

Psychic Hacking/Spying

The same as **Remote Viewing**.

Psychic Surgery

This is a form of spiritual **healing**. One or more physicians from the spirit world works through a healer in this world to perform operations. The patient may be aware of something touching them or being inside their body but they feel no pain. Blood and diseased tissue is sometimes produced and sometimes not. Sometimes it appears and then disappears. Sometimes surgical instruments are used and sometimes they are not. Operations often take only a few minutes. Although it is obviously all too easy to fake psychic surgery, miraculous cures *have* taken place.

Psychic surgery started in the Philippines in the 1920s and it flourished in South America, particularly Brazil, in the 1960s. According to the British healer Jack Angelo some of the tissue and blood produced by psychic surgery in these countries may be faked, but that doesn't mean healing has not taken place. People often fake this visual evidence because that is what people expect, and also to escape being accused of magic (which can get people into trouble with the authorities).

If it does work, why aren't all patients cured? Stephen Turoff, a psychic surgeon who works in Essex, says (in *Kindred Spirit* magazine):

> *It is down to karma. Two people can visit me with exactly the same condition. One can be healed, the other can't. Before any consultation Dr. Kahn [the spirit doctor he works with] must gain permission from the patient's Higher Self. If the answer is no, then he can't continue. The Higher Self decides when that person has learned sufficiently from their karmic suffering.*

Psychodrama

See **Creative Therapies**.

Psychokinesis (PK)

Also known as telekinesis, this means influencing objects with the mind. It has actually been demonstrated scientifically many times, and animals as well as humans can do it. In one rather grisly experiment (described by the biologist Rupert Sheldrake) young chicks were *imprinted* on a robot (led to believe the robot was their mother) and, although the robot was supposed to make random movements towards and away from their cage, the chicks managed to make it move towards them and stay close.

Another experiment may help to explain why some of us are more prone to having our equipment break down on us, or why it seems to fail just when we need it most. People with nervous disorders such as Parkinson's disease and epilepsy were found to cause increased electrical and mechanical failure in appliances, and when their conditions were treated with drugs, this tendency disappeared.

Psychometry

This is also called "object reading" and means discovering the history or character of objects, or of people who have associated with the objects, by holding them. The term was coined by an American Professor of Medicine in the 19th century who discovered that 80 percent of his students were affected by drugs simply by having them in their hands. Another American academic at around the same time discovered that one in 10 men and four in 10 women could describe something of the geological history of meteorites and fossils by touch alone.

Psychometry—Developing Your Sensitivity to Objects

- ❑ Collect together some objects of the same shape but different colors, such as candles, crayons, or children's building blocks. Try to identify the colors with your eyes shut.
- ❑ With your eyes shut, hold a crystal and feel its qualities—warm/cold, rough/smooth, heavy/light. Put yourself in a meditative frame of mind in your usual way (or see **meditation**) and try to connect with the spirit of the crystal. This could manifest in any way—a scene, a person, or an emotion.

- [ ] When you read a book, try and connect with the author. Pretend that they are a close friend and have written it just for you. Hear their voice. What was happening in their life while they were working on the book? What made them write it? What are they really trying to say?

Psychosynthesis

A *transpersonal* **psychotherapy**—one which deals with the soul as well as the intellect and emotions.

Psychotherapy

This treatment for the mind falls into three main types. The oldest are the *analytic* or *psychoanalytic* therapies, developed from the work of Freud and **Jung**. These use hypnosis, dream analysis, fantasies, and free association to delve into the unconscious. Usually one on one, they can be helpful for people who have had traumatic experiences, particularly in childhood, and therapists are well trained. Critics say that they take too long, concentrate too much on the past, and are too intellectual and pessimistic. More recent kinds of analytic therapy might have the label *psychodynamic*.

Humanistic or *human potential* therapies arose in the 1960s. They have an optimistic view of human nature and treatment is "person centered," which means that people are treated as individuals and encouraged to find their own answers. The emphasis is on emotional expression rather than rational explanation, and on the present rather than the past. Treatment can be individual or in groups, and short or long term. The personal style of the therapist, however, is often more important than the particular type of therapy they practice, and many use one or more types in their work. Useful for a wide range of mental and physical problems, this is also the area where poor training is most likely. The most recent developments in humanistic therapy are *transpersonal* or *psychospiritual* therapies which deal with the spirit as well as the intellect and emotions. These are recommended for those wanting to develop themselves or those seeking meaning in their lives.

Popular today are "behavioral and cognitive" therapies. These teach you to identify unhelpful or destructive ways of thinking or behaving and replace them with better ones. Often used for phobias, obsessions, and addictions, they can also be helpful for depression, panic attacks, and chronic pain. The emphasis is on self-help and you are expected to practice between sessions. Treatment is usually fairly brief, but relapse rates can be higher than for longer-term therapies.

Psychiatry is the medical treatment of mental illness with drugs, surgery, and electric shocks (*electro-convulsive therapy* or *ECT*). Psychology is the study of the mind. "Clinical" psychologists work with patients, often using counseling or behavioral and cognitive therapies.

Psychotherapies Covered in This Book

Analytic Therapies
- Hypnoanalysis

Humanistic Therapies
- Bioenergetics
- Counseling
- Creative Therapies (art, dance, drama, and music)
- Existential Therapy
- Gestalt
- Inner Child Work
- Primal Therapy
- Psychosynthesis
- Rebirthing
- Transactional Analysis

Behavioral and Cognitive Therapies
- Hypnotherapy
- Neuro-Linguistic Programming

Pyramids

Ancient pyramids are found in Central America and **Egypt**. Although the Egyptian pyramids are described by archaeologists as tombs, no bodies have ever been found in any of them, and their real purpose is a mystery.

Many people have been struck by the precise orientation North, South, East and West of the Great Pyramid at Giza near Cairo, its position at the center of the Earth's landmass, and its dimensions both internal and external. These are related to the dimensions of the Earth; the distance of the Earth from the sun; the days of the year; and pi (π), the ratio of the circumference of a circle to its diameter. Peter Lemesurier compares its passages and chambers to the after-death stages described in the Egyptian *Book of the Dead*. He sees in the edifice, as a whole, a description of humankind's spiritual progress, containing detailed prophecies about the collapse of material civilization in 2004–25 (give or take three years) and the birth of a new messiah or spiritual leader on October 21, 2039.

A strange quality of Egyptian pyramids is that the older ones are much bigger and better made than the later ones. The Great Pyramid is still the largest building in the world and even today we would not be able to build it. The conventional dating of the three Giza pyramids at 3000–2000 BCE has been thrown into question by the controversy over the age of the Great Sphinx, which some believe may be as much as 14,000 years old. Are they (and other pyramids) therefore a relic of a previous advanced civilization such as that of the mythical **Atlantis**? They may perhaps have been built by sources of power we don't yet know much about such as sound or **crystals**, or maybe they were energy generators in themselves, part of the crystal technology attributed to the Atlanteans by the 20th-century seer Edgar **Cayce**.

A French visitor to the Great Pyramid of Egypt in the 1930s discovered, in an inner chamber, the bodies of a cat and some small wild animals. Instead of decaying normally in the humid atmosphere, they had actually dried out and become mummified. A Czech engineer managed to create similar effects with a model pyramid, as did the scientist and author Lyall Watson (using eggs, steak, and dead mice). Both also discovered that blunt razor blades left in a model pyramid (on a platform a third of the way up) became sharp again, leading them to conclude that the particular shape of the pyramids has a marked effect on both chemical and physical processes.

Both the Egyptians and Central Americans mummified their dead. It is presumed that this was done in order to preserve their bodies for the afterlife. Erich Von Daniken, however, suggests it is a method of keeping people alive for long space journeys. He says that biologists at the University of Oklahoma confirmed that the skin cells of the mummified Egyptian Princess Mene were still capable of living, several thousand years after her death. He thinks that pyramids might have been giant mummification factories.

In experiments, pyramid shapes placed over people's heads have been found to change their brain waves, and many people including Napoleon and the magician **Crowley** have reported experiencing visions inside the King's Chamber in the Great Pyramid (a third of the way up). Were they therefore built to alter consciousness?

It may be that pyramids were all these things: astronomical, geographical, and mathematical records; sources of power; laboratories; and temples. Everything, in fact, except tombs.

Q

Qabala(h)

See **Cabbala**.

Qi

The same as **Chi**.

Qi Gong

The same as **Chi Kung**.

Quantum Physics

Since the work of Einstein in the early 20th century, the scientific view of the physical world has been shaken to its core and physics itself very nearly toppled. Einstein proved that both space and time, as well as energy and matter, are two sides of a coin. A moving clock runs more slowly as its speed increases and stops running altogether at the speed of light unless you are moving at the same speed as the clock in which case it will appear to behave as normal. As the speed of an object increases, its apparent size decreases and its weight increases until it reaches the speed of light, when it disappears and its weight becomes infinite. Luckily, none of this is really detectable until you approach the speed of light.

In the same way, quantum physics has shown that, although the world at large may appear to function logically and predictably, at the subatomic level (dealing with whatever it is that makes up atoms), things are very different. For example:

- You can prove that subatomic entities are both matter and energy—it just depends which experiments you do. Therefore there is no such thing as a detached observer. What you see is bound up with your own preconceptions.
- You can't predict what a subatomic entity will do—you can only say what it's likely to do. The universe, therefore, can no longer be seen as an inanimate machine following logical rules.
- Entities from a common source remain connected even when apart, so that what happens to one is instantly reflected in the other. In this case relationships between entities are more important than their separate identities and the entire universe may be interconnected.

In order to try and make sense of all this, the physicist David Bohm suggests that reality is not just made up of matter and energy but of matter (*explicate order*), energy (*implicate order*), and meaning (*super implicate order*). Each contains the other two—matter is made up of energy and meaning, energy of matter and meaning, and meaning of matter and energy. Reality, therefore, is not two dimensional like a photograph but multidimensional like a hologram, with each part able to reflect the whole and needing the whole to make sense.

Some people use quantum physics to "prove" the truth of what mystics and magicians have been saying for millennia—but does it really need proving? Moreover, much of quantum physics is just theory. What it has really done is narrow the gap between science and religion. Buddhism is sometimes described as a path to enlightenment for people of intellectual temperament. The same could be said about modern physics. The rest of us will muddle on in our usual way and—who knows?—we may all end up in the same place eventually.

R

Radiesthesia

The same as **Dowsing**.

Radionics

This is a method of **healing** that uses a machine emitting electromagnetic radiation to diagnose and treat. It can be done at a distance and on animals, plants, and the soil, as well as people. Opinion is divided, however, as to whether it works or not. It was developed by a U.S. doctor and professor of medicine at the beginning of the 20th century.

Rebirthing

A **complementary therapy** that uses special breathing techniques to help us replay and, as a result, free ourselves of deep emotional traumas, in particular those we might have experienced while in the womb or being born. The average number of sessions is six to 10, and more advanced rebirthees may further recreate the experience of being in the womb by floating in water. Chronic pain, asthma, depression, schizophrenia, and phobias are said to respond particularly well to rebirthing.

See also **Childbirth**.

Reflexology

This well-established **complementary therapy** consists of gentle massage on the soles of the feet and also sometimes the hands. Exactly how it works is not known, but reflexologists think that the feet are connected to the rest of the body through **energy** channels. The therapy was developed in the 1930s from the work of a surgeon who used pressure on his patients' feet to anaesthetize parts of their bodies. It is relaxing and pleasant in itself and can help a wide range of conditions.

Vacuflex reflexology manipulates the feet through the use of enormous felt boots and suction pads.

Reiki

Reiki (pronounced *ray-key*) is a form of hands-on healing developed in the 19th century from ancient Buddhist texts by Mikao Usui, a Japanese teacher of theology. The name is Japanese for "universal life energy," "ki" being the equivalent of the Chinese **chi**.

Reiki skills are passed on through a structured—and sometimes expensive—program of training, in three stages. The first takes two to four days and involves being *attuned* to reiki energy by a reiki master and learning how to work on yourself, other people, animals, and plants. You are also taught the five reiki principles which are:

- ❑ Just for today, do not worry.
- ❑ Just for today, do not anger.
- ❑ Honor your parents, teachers, and elders.
- ❑ Earn your living honestly.
- ❑ Show gratitude to every living thing.

(There may be slight variations to these, depending on the lineage of your teacher. These come from the United Kingdom Reiki Association.)

The second must be at least three months later to give you a chance to get used to the new energy. Also two to four days in duration, it involves more energy activation and learning how to give distant healing and work with symbols. Becoming a master, the third stage, enables you to teach reiki. Starting at least three years after the first stage, this takes about a year of one-on-one work with a reiki grand master.

Karuna and Tera-Mai reiki are more advanced forms of reiki.

Reincarnation

The belief that we have more than one life is widespread. Of the major world religions, only the orthodox versions of Judaism, Islam, and Christianity exclude it. However, some of Jesus' words can be interpreted as a reference to reincarnation (for example, he says that John the Baptist was Elijah, the Old Testament prophet), and it was a feature of Christianity until the 6th century, when the Council of Constantinople decided to exclude it. It is part of the beliefs of heretical Christian sects, such as the **Rosicrucians**, and of the **cabbala** and **Sufism**, the mystical wings of Judaism and Islam.

There have been attempts to prove reincarnation or to study people professing to remember past lives. In 1966, Dr. Ian Stevenson at the University of Virginia in the United States interviewed 600 children from India, Ceylon, Brazil, Alaska, and Lebanon who claimed they could remember past lives. He started out with no opinions either way, but at the end of his research was convinced that reincarnation was possible.

The **psychotherapist** Roberto Assagioli (the founder of **psychosynthesis**) found that people open to the idea of a spiritual self and reincarnation were three times more likely to recover from psychological illness than those not.

See also **Karma**, and **Past Lives**.

Reincarnation—Frequently Asked Questions

Why don't we remember past lives?

Many do, particularly if their previous lives ended early or suddenly. Instant attraction to people, phobias, and outstanding talents could all be explained by experiences in previous lives. We have to be sufficiently evolved to be able to cope with the memory of past lives. Part of our purpose here is to remember and find our way back to the eternal world.

Can we reincarnate as animals, and might we have been animals in the past?

Probably yes, but not everyone agrees. Some say that once a human, always a human. Others believe that we can take on different forms in different lives, both less evolved and more evolved than humans.

How long do we have between lives?

As long as we want or need. Some say that those who have had fewer lives tend to reincarnate more quickly as they are hungry for experience. Those growing out of the need to incarnate as humans spend longer between lives, maybe using the time to guide people on earth (see **spirit guides**).

With so many people in the world now, how come there are enough souls to go round?

One explanation is that we are having less time between lives. Another is that creation is evolving and more spirits have reached the stage of being human. Another is that we are passing through a special time for humankind and many people have chosen to reincarnate now either in order to take advantage of the times for themselves or in order to help humankind through the transition.

Could some people be incarnating for the first time?

Yes.

(cont'd)

Reincarnation—Frequently Asked Questions ***(cont'd)***

When does the soul enter the body—at conception, birth, or later?

Opinions are divided here. A common view is that the soul starts to enter the body at conception, but that it takes some years for it to be firmly anchored in the Earth plane. This is why children are more likely than adults to remember past lives or to see angels and spirits. Miscarriage or profound mental illness such as schizophrenia may arise because the soul does not incarnate properly.

Do we change sex in different incarnations?

Definitely—and problems can arise when the change is recent. Dr. Stevenson (see text preceding box) found that 10 percent of his subjects had changed sex since a previous incarnation, and that many of those who had done so "had a wavering and ambiguous sense of sexual identity."

Do we meet the same people in different lives?

Certainly, if we want and need to. However, they will not necessarily have the same relationship to us. For instance, a mother could become a daughter. This is so that we can experience all of the permutations of our connection with them.

Do we go on reincarnating forever?

We can stop as soon as we want to. The Hindu and Buddhist view of reincarnation is that it is driven by our *karma* (our unfinished business) and by our individual desires. As soon as we become *enlightened*—learn to identify with our deeper self—we are freed from the cycle of death and rebirth. A modern view is that we incarnate almost for fun, simply in order to have the experience, and in order to evolve. With our deeper self we choose before birth what sort of a life we want to experience. As we evolve, we become able to move freely between worlds without having to go through death and rebirth.

Remote Viewing

Also known as traveling **clairvoyance**, psychic spying, and psychic hacking, this means discovering information, by non-physical (either psychic or intuitive) means, about a person or place distant in space or time. The term was coined at Stamford Research Institute, California, in 1972 when they undertook a research project funded by the CIA (the part of the U.S. government involved in *intelligence* or spying). They discovered that two out of three of people had some degree of talent at remote viewing. The research was then later expanded into the secret Stargate project, which continued until 1995.

Joseph McMoneagle, a remote viewer for the project, believes he was chosen because of his openness to the subject as a result of **near-death experience** in 1970. The detail and accuracy of some of his viewings were as good as a photograph. Dale Graff, who ran Stargate, found that success was the result of physical and psychological health, relaxation, and practice. He says (in *Tracks in the Psychic Wilderness*) remote viewing is "non-rational" but not "irrational" and sees the benefits reaching way beyond simple intelligence gathering:

> *As you uncover your natural* **psi** *talent, you will come to sense aspects of self that reach beyond your surface ego. You will feel a need to share your discoveries and seek ways for using your uncovered abilities to help others. You will sense a link with people and your environment and will be attracted toward activities that promote health, improve interpersonal effectiveness, and support humanitarian causes.*

Right Brain

See **Left Brain/Right Brain**.

Rolfing

A modern **bodywork** system which improves posture by stretching and pressing connective tissue and muscles. It can be quite intense, even painful, but can relieve pain and stress and improve performance in all areas. A standard course is 10 sessions.

Rosicrucianism

An occult movement that flourished in the 17th century and was revived at the end of the 19th century.

In 1614, a pamphlet appeared in Germany telling of a 15th-century monk called Christian Rosenkreutz, who had founded an order to preserve ancient wisdom he had learned while travelling in the East. Groups sprang up all over Europe calling themselves Rosicrucians after the monk, and dedicated to passing on occult wisdom such as **alchemy**, **astrology**, and the **cabbala**, which they tied in with mystical Christianity, geometry, music, and architecture. Because of the threat they presented to conventional Christianity, the groups tended to be highly secret and one of the few openly Rosicrucian texts was written by the English alchemist and doctor, Robert Fludd (1574–1637).

The **Hermetic Order of the Golden Dawn**, founded in 1888, based its rituals on those of Rosicrucianism and freemasonry. The Ancient and Mystical Order of the Rosae Crucis (AMORC) was started in 1915. It is still running courses in "metaphysics, mysticism, psychology, parapsychology, and science not taught by conventional educational systems or traditional religions" from its headquarters in California and Grand Lodges in 100 countries. Other Rosicrucian groups, secret and not so secret, exist across the world.

Roth, Gabrielle

The creator of a "five rhythms" form of **dance therapy**.

Runes

Letters used by Norse and Germanic peoples for magic and divination purposes. They were inscribed on wood, metal, stone, and bone, and so are mostly made up of straight lines, as these are easier to carve. The earliest runic inscriptions date from the 3rd century and were found in Denmark, but there is a written account of *casting* (divination with runes) which dates from 98 CE, and runes may actually date back to the first few centuries BCE. They continued to be used in Scandinavia and Iceland until the Middle Ages. Norse runestones from the 11th century have been found in the United States.

Runes are used today for **divination** and by Pagans of the **Northern tradition**. The *futhark*, a Germanic alphabet with 24 letters, is the oldest and most commonly followed. Each rune or letter has a sound associated with it, a name, and a meaning. It is thought there were also various other associations for each letter such as deities, numbers, trees, and colors.

(See the following table of Runes and their meanings on page 196.)

Runes—the Elder Futhark

The following is a brief summary of the runes and their meanings (adapted from a futhark compiled for the Pagan Federation's Northern Tradition information pack and reproduced with their permission). You will find other meanings attached to them and variations in the names and spellings.

Name and Sound	Rune	Meaning
feoh, fehu (f)	ᚠ	cattle, wealth
ur, uruz (u)	ᚢ	auroch (wild ox, now extinct), strength
thorn, thurisaz (th)	ᚦ	giant, obstacles
as, os, ansuz (a)	ᚨ	god, mouth
rad, raido (r)	ᚱ	wagon, travel
ken, kennaz (k)	ᚲ	torch, knowledge
gyfu, gebo (g)	ᚷ	gift, sex
wyn, wunjo (w)	ᚹ	joy, good news
hagel, hagalaz (h)	ᚺ	hail, bad weather
nid, naudiz (n)	ᚾ	need
isa, isaz (i)	ᛁ	ice
jera, jeraz (j)	ᛃ	harvest, year
eoh, yr, ihwaz (e)	ᛇ	yew, bow, earth
peorth, perthro (p)	ᛈ	birth, unknown
elhaz, algiz (z)	ᛉ	elk, protection
sigil, sowilo (s)	ᛊ	sun
tyr, tiwas (t)	ᛏ	courage, battle
beorth, berkanan (b)	ᛒ	healing, woman
ehwho, ehwaz (eh)	ᛖ	horses, adventure
man, mannaz (m)	ᛗ	man
laguz, laukuz (l)	ᛚ	leek, water
ing, ingwaz (ng)	ᛜ	the god Ing
odai, othala (o)	ᛟ	home, tribe
daeg, dagaz (d)	ᛞ	day, balance

S

Sanskrit

Ancient Indian language found in sacred texts of **Hinduism**.

Seichem, Seichim, Sekhem

Three different types of **healing**, related to **reiki** but said to be more powerful. Sekhem is said to come from ancient **Egypt**.

Sexuality

See **Tantra**, and **Tao**.

Shadow

Our shadow, according to the psychologist **Jung**, is the part of us that we suppressed during our upbringing in order to make ourselves acceptable. Robert A. Johnson in *Owning Your Own Shadow* compares our psyche to a seesaw, with the shadow on one side and our public face or *persona* on the other. Not everything in the shadow is dark—it contains the extremes of our nature, both creative and destructive. It is therefore a very powerful part of us and one we have to reclaim in order to be happy and whole.

According to Jung, we live the first part of our lives according to the way we were brought up—perhaps getting married, having children, following a conventional career—and the second half going inwards, reacquainting ourselves with our shadow. If we don't do this the shadow may erupt and cause havoc, the "middle-age crisis" being the classic example.

The shadow is, of course, a very frightening part of ourselves and one we do our best not to acknowledge. One trick we have is to "project" the shadow outwards, seeing in other people what we refuse to see in ourselves. The people we dislike or disapprove of are the very best guides we have to our own shadow. As Confucius said, "If you see a worthy person, strive to emulate them; if you see an unworthy person, examine your inner self."

There are collective shadows as well as individual ones. The "black sheep" of a family is expressing those parts of the family's character that no one else does. If they start to change, so does the rest of the family. During the Cold War, the U.S. and Russia projected their own fanaticism as countries on to each other. There is also a universal shadow, which we call evil or the devil.

The mature person—someone who, and Jung puts it, has been through the "individuation" process—has no shadow. Everything is in their consciousness.

Shamans/Shamanism

Shamanism is the oldest form of spirituality in existence. Found in almost every corner of the world (under different names), it is usually associated with gatherer-hunter societies. Shamans, women as well as men, are the spiritual leaders of a tribe. They practice healing, prophecy, and magic as well as settling quarrels and leading rituals. Through drumming, rattling, dancing, chanting, meditation, fasting, or consuming "power plants" they are able to travel to the spirit world where they find guidance, meet with their spirit allies, or do battle with harmful spirits. Some people become Shamans through heredity. Others manifest special powers from childhood. Others become Shamans after serious illness, which is often seen as a sign that someone has been chosen for the Shamanic path.

Shamanic practices underlie most **Neo-Pagan** religions and can also be used as a form of **psychotherapy**. Essentially solitary, they involve deep inner experience, altered states of consciousness, and a close relationship with all the forces of nature. A modern Westerner who has come into direct contact with ancient Shamanic traditions is Professor Michael Harner.

He has written several respected books on his experiences with Native Americans and leads workshops in many countries. Two others are Carlos **Castaneda** and Lynn V. Andrews. Castaneda was a Californian academic who wrote about his apprenticeship to a Yaqui sorcerer in the 1960s. Lynn V. Andrews, a Californian art dealer, was trained by Manitoba medicine women and later joined a secret society of women shamans from across the world called the Sisterhood of Shields. Although their books are very readable (or perhaps because they are), there is some doubt as to whether they are true or fictional.

A Glossary of Shamanism

Flying	Travelling to the upper world.
Journeying	Travels to other planes of existence.
Lower,Middle, and Upper Worlds	The three main planes of existence. In the lower world dwell monsters and the spirits of illness. It is often entered through tree roots and caves. Humans dwell in the middle world. The upper or sky world is mostly benevolent and contains the spirits who form the prototypes for the human world. The three worlds are often seen as connected by a tree.
Power Animal	A spirit ally. Shamans often have spirit animals as allies. They can provide special powers, skills, and knowledge. For example, birds, because they fly high, can see things humans can't (See **power animals**).
Power Plants	Hallucinogenic or sacred plants and fungi. Examples are: the peyote cactus used by the natives of Central America; psilocybe mushrooms found in Central America and Europe; the climbing plant, morning glory; and tobacco.
Shaman	The word comes from the Tungus tribe of Siberia, possibly deriving from Sanskrit.
Shamanka	A woman Shaman. (The word is not always used.)
Shapeshifting	Identification with an animal or other living creature that is so extreme the body changes as well.
Soul Loss/Retrieval	Illness and trauma can drive part of the soul away or cause it to lose power. The Shaman journeys on behalf of the sick person to find the missing part of the soul, do battle (if necessary) with whatever is holding it captive, and bring it back.

Shiatsu

This vigorous Japanese **massage** uses the same principles of energy flow as **traditional Chinese medicine** but emphasizes the abdomen or *hara*, which is seen as the center of the body's energy system. It is done on a mat on the floor, with practitioners using their forearms, knees, and feet as well as hands, and the recipient remaining lightly clothed.

Smudging

The use of smoke for the purification of spaces, tools, and people in sacred rituals, particularly **Shamanic** and **Native American** ones. It is traditional to waft the smoke with a large feather or a feather fan rather than your hands. Herbs used in America include plains or desert sage (a completely different plant from the European sage), cedar, and sweetgrass. In the United Kingdom you could use rosemary, which is a traditional spring-cleaning herb, or mugwort, an ancient sacred plant with mind-altering properties.

Socially Responsible Investment (SRI)

The same as **Ethical Investment**.

Sound Therapy

Every cell in the body is thought to have its own particular rate of vibration and to be affected by the different vibrations of different sounds. Sound from vibrating chairs or hand-held machines is sometimes used for healing (particularly pain, muscle weakness, and fractures) and some musicians offer their music as a form of allover sound therapy. Most religions use sounds like drumming or chanting to alter consciousness.

Each of the **chakras** is related to a musical note (from base to crown C, D, E, F, G, A, B) and American sound researcher Sharry Edwards has discovered that each person gives off a particular note. With this note she can find the sound they need in order to be cured of an illness.

Spirit Guides

Spirit beings with which we have a special relationship. There are many different sorts of spirit beings—**angels, power animals, ascended masters, nature spirits, devas, goddesses,** and gods—but we each have a special guide or guides who can help us with our daily life. They are most likely beings who were once human but no longer have any need to incarnate on Earth or to incarnate so often. When we die they are there to help us make the transition.

We communicate with our spirit guides through our soul or *higher self*—this means, through intuition and imagination, through our creativity, and in **meditation** and **visualization**.

See also **Channeling**.

Spiritualism

This stepsister of the orthodox Christian Church arose in mid-19th-century America and was largely concerned with giving physical proof that we live after death. Spiritualists held meetings called seances and invited spirits to communicate through table rapping and the levitation of people and objects. The spirits also communicated through people called mediums at seances, lectures, and church services.

Today spiritualism has dropped the emphasis on physical phenomena. The guiding spirits quoted in *Opening to Channel* by Roman and Packer say physical phenomena were created by spirits in the past to help people believe in the spirit world, but that we don't need such proof any more.

Steiner, Rudolf

Rudolf Steiner (1861–1925), perhaps best known for his contribution to education, has also had an influence on farming, the arts, and medicine. He was originally involved with the **Theosophical** Society, but left in 1913 to form his own *anthroposophical* movement because he felt the theosophists were too concerned with Eastern religions at the expense of

Christianity. Like the theosophists, however, he was concerned with uniting science and spirituality—which he viewed as an essential part of us that we have allowed to fall into disuse. Spirituality, he believed, can be developed in a scientific way by meditation and through imagination, inspiration, and intuition.

He founded a new type of school, called the Waldorf or Steiner Waldorf school, of which there are now 450 throughout the world. These aim to develop the emotions and spirit as well as the mind and body. Steiner-inspired **biodynamic** farming and gardening not only avoids the use of chemicals but also works with cosmic forces. This is said to produce vibrant plants that feed both body and soul.

Anthroposophical doctors base their work on Steiner's ideas about the interaction of body and soul, and use both orthodox and holistic methods, in particular **nutritional therapy**, **massage**, **hydrotherapy**, **creative therapies**, and **counseling**. His eurythmy or eurythmics is a form of dance used as a therapy where each sound has a specific movement associated with it.

Steiner's books tend to be based on his lectures (he delivered over 6000 in 25 years) and are not an easy read. Born in what was then the Austro-Hungarian Empire (now Croatia), he died in Switzerland and this is where the headquarters of the Anthroposophical Society are today. These, along with worldwide branches, continue the work of a remarkable man.

Stonehenge

This most famous of prehistoric monuments stands on the bare windswept plateau of Salisbury Plain in southern England. It was begun 5000 years ago and remodeled several times in the centuries that followed.

The earliest construction was a ditch with a ring of 56 chalk-filled pits (known as the "Aubrey holes") and at the center, a wooden circle, possibly roofed (similar to the one on Overton Hill at **Avebury**). About 2000 BCE, nearly 100 bluestones, weighing about four tons each, were brought to the site from Wales or Ireland to make a double circle. However, this wasn't finished and instead two horseshoe shapes and two circles were put up using both the bluestones and local sarsen stones. This was finished by 1500 BCE and its ruins are what we see today. The so-called altar stone is in fact a fallen bluestone from the inner horseshoe.

Although there's no way of knowing for sure, archaeologists think that Stonehenge was a temple, festival site, and astronomical observatory. At the summer solstice the rising sun is framed by two stones in the outer circle which align with the center of the horseshoes. Gerald Hawkins, an astronomy professor, discovered that the site accurately pinpointed 12 positions of the sun in 1500 BCE and 12 of the moon, and that the Aubrey holes could have been used to predict eclipses.

Others (including Foster Forbes and John Michell) go further, suggesting that the monument may actually have been used to collect, store, and transmit power from heavenly bodies. This is why it was so important to use the right type of stone, even if it had to be brought from far away.

Like many other great ancient monuments, Stonehenge may be on one of the Earth's *acupoints*, places where **Earth energy** can be tapped or altered. This makes it a potent place, ideal for spiritual upliftment and contacting the forces of creation.

How Stonehenge was constructed with primitive technology is an even greater mystery than *why* it was built. Solar power, mind power, and extraterrestrials have all been put forward as possibilities. According to legend, Merlin (King **Arthur**'s counselor) built Stonehenge with magic stones he had brought from Ireland by sea and then on rafts across land.

Normally you have to view Stonehenge from a distance, but special arrangements can be made with English Heritage, the guardians of the site, for individuals and groups to enter the henge itself.

Subtle Body/Energy

Life energy permeates the universe, and because it is invisible to most people and not able to be measured by scientific instruments, it is sometimes called *subtle* energy. Subtle energy is recognized in Eastern philosophy—in China, for example, it is called *chi* and in India *prana*. **Traditional Chinese medicine** and Indian **yoga** both work on this subtle energy, as do some Western **complementary therapies**.

The subtle body is the energy field of a living organism, visible to some as the **aura**. It is also known as the energy, etheric, astral, or dream body.

For us to be healthy, energy should flow through us unobstructed. Unresolved pain from the past, however, can set up blocks in this free-flow of subtle energy and this is the start of all unhappiness and disease. According to James Redfield, in his novel *The Celestine Prophecy*, all human conflict stems from the fact that we try to get energy from each other instead of tapping into the unlimited source that the universe provides. The way to get back in touch with universal energy is to uplift or send out love to nature and everyone we come into contact with. This clears a space in us for more energy to flow in, and starts a benign chain reaction in us and in the world as a whole.

Sufis/Sufism

A spiritual movement that sprang from Islam around the 9th century but is currently enjoying a worldwide revival among both Muslims and non-Muslims.

Sufism is often called a religion of the heart, because it is concerned with direct individual experience of god and surrender to ecstatic worship and love of god. This is done through dance, poetry, music, chanting, prayer, breathing, and meditation. There are no rules or dogma, and any teaching is passed down from person to person. The 13th-century Persian poet Jalal-al-Din Rumi is one of its most beloved influences.

The name *sufi* comes from the Arabic word for wool, a reference to the fact that followers wore wool like the Christian ascetics on whom they modeled themselves. Sufi groups were called dervishes, which also means poor. The famous whirling dervishes were said to be following the example of Rumi, who at the death of his mentor spun on the spot until his grief passed.

Sufism was introduced to the West largely by one man, the Indian Hazrat Inayuat Khan, in the early 20th century. He founded the Sufi Order in the West, wrote many books, and emphasized the universal aspects of Sufism rather than its Islamic connections.

Sweat Lodge

A **Native American** ritual for mental and physical purification. The lodge is a dome 3–4 feet high made from saplings covered with blankets, canvas, or skins. Inside is a hole that is filled with red hot rocks heated in a bonfire outside. Participants may fast beforehand. They wear few or no clothes and crawl in through a small flap. During the ceremony the rocks are splashed with cold water to create steam and sacred herbs are burnt. The ceremony is led by a medicine person (**Shaman**) and has four sessions involving prayer, drumming and chanting between which the flap is opened to let air and coolness in, and for people to leave if they have had enough.

Swedish Massage

Classic Western **massage**, developed in the 19th century by a Swedish gymnast.

Synchronicity

The term coined by the psychologist **Jung** and the **quantum physicist** Wolfgang Pauli for meaningful coincidences. There are several ways of recognizing these and distinguishing them from ordinary coincidences:

- ❑ They fulfill a need. Forgetting something is forgetfulness but forgetting something and returning to the house only to discover you've left the gas on is synchronicity.

- Emotional reaction—you *know* something unusual is going on. The synchronicity is related to something important or makes you realize how important something is to you. You might have a sense of déjà vu. The event might be mirrored in dreams or reinforced with other similar coincidences.
- Humor—synchronicity has been called the "puns of destiny." The astronomer Camille Flammarion was writing a book when some of the pages were whisked away by the wind. They were found by the printer about to work on the book who returned them to the author. And what were the pages about? Wind.
- There is more than one element to the coincidence. For instance, bumping into a friend is a coincidence, but bumping into a friend who happens to mention the book whose title you were trying to remember is synchronicity.

Synchronicity is a sign that there is more to the universe than simple cause and effect and that mind and matter are somehow interconnected. For James Redfield, in his novel *The Celestine Prophecy*, synchronicity shows us that we are connected to divine energy, so awakening to synchronicity is part of our spiritual awakening. The more connected we are, the more we spot the meaningful coincidences at work in our lives and the more we can make them happen. The **remote viewing** expert Dale Graff explains that working with synchronicity alerts us to the unconscious and creative part of our minds. It is also a way to help others. Not only are we more likely to be in the right place at the right time for ourselves, but we are more likely to be in the right place at the right time for them. Above all, as psychotherapist Robert Hopcke writes in *There Are No Accidents*, it "makes us aware, again and again, of the beauty, order, and connectedness of the tales we are living."

Encouraging Synchronicity

- ❑ Accept that it exists. Intense disbelief upsets the workings of the universe. Paranormal researcher Jenny Randles explains that people can be divided into sheep and goats. Sheep accept the paranormal and allow things to happen without challenge. This means that they *do* happen. Goats butt in with endless objections and stop everything in its tracks.
- ❑ Be clear about your needs and do everything you can by *normal* means to fulfill them.
- ❑ Be flexible. Vary your routine and be as open and spontaneous as possible. Don't fight hitches in your plans or berate yourself for forgetfulness—there might be a very good reason for them.
- ❑ Don't force things. Don't jump to the conclusion that the universe is ignoring you just because there is a delay in you getting what you want. Get on with the rest of your life. Be prepared to adapt your needs and wants—old ones may well have been superceded and there is no point hanging on to them just to prove a point.
- ❑ If synchronicity does occur, be grateful and *act on it*. This conveys the message that you are willing to receive more. Keep a diary of meaningful coincidences that happen to you. This reinforces your belief in them.

T

T'ai Chi

Pronounced *tie chee*, full name "t'ai chi chuan," this is graceful, flowing exercise popular in both China and the West. Originally developed in the 13th century as a martial art, it is usually taught simply as a method of achieving balance, concentration, and relaxation.

The exercise sequences, (called *forms*), consist of different postures and movements that flow into each other. These work on every part of the body and ensure that **chi**, or life energy, is circulating freely and that our negative and positive elements, or **yin and yang**, are balanced. The movements have imaginative names like "Bring tiger to the mountain" or "Snake creeps down" and are quite difficult to remember to start with. However, t'ai chi is suitable for people of any age or level of fitness.

Tantra

This is a tradition within both **Hinduism** and **Buddhism** concerned with using sexual, emotional, and imaginative energy for spiritual transformation. Practices include the use of **mandalas**, **mantras**, symbolic gestures (*mudras*) and visualizations of oneself as a deity. Sex, in particular, is seen as a shortcut to enlightenment, with full-body orgasms effectively raising the **kundalini** and bringing instant wholeness.

Tantra may actually predate both religions and derive from ancient **Goddess** worship and **Shamanism** because the name means "fundamental doctrine," acknowledgement and use of female power is an important part of the practices (particularly in Tibetan Buddhism), and the enjoyment of the body is in contrast to the asceticism of **yoga**. It is particularly associated with the worship of Shakti and Shiva, Hindu deities often depicted in sensuous embrace. Practices were secret and passed down from teacher to pupil, with the few texts written in symbolic language to confuse the non-initiated.

Today in India, tantra is almost always associated with spells and black magic. In its modern Western form it is seen as a form of sex therapy and a way to make sex something that involves the whole person—body, mind, and spirit.

Tao/Taoism

This is a fundamental of Chinese thought. Its classic work is the *Tao Te Ching*, a collection of poems and sayings supposed to have been written by someone called Lao Tzu around the 6th century BCE, but was possibly an anthology of work by different people. The title translates as "the classic work about the way and the power." The way, or *tao* is the undefinable reality which underlies all creation. As the book says (translation by D.C. Lau):

The way is to the world as the River and the Sea are to rivulets and streams. (Reproduced with permission of Penguin Books Ltd.)

The tao is ever changing—this is the only constant. Power is gained by acting in accordance with the tao, in other words spontaneously, with flexibility and without force. Nor should one ever go to extremes, since extreme actions produce extreme results and balance between opposites (that is, **yin and yang**) is the ideal:

Rather than fill it to the brim by keeping it upright
Better to have stopped in time; Hammer it to a point
And the sharpness cannot be preserved forever.

Another important concept is "wu-wei," literally non-action but more accurately the effortlessness of right action.

The second taoist classic is the *Chuang Tzu*, named after its supposed author, but this too may be a collection of writings by different people. It dates from around the same time or a little later than the *Tao Te Ching* but is more philosophical and less poetic.

Another strand of taoism was concerned with immortality. Followers would hold their breath since they believed we have a limited number of breaths in a lifetime, and men practiced achieving orgasm without ejaculation since semen was a life-giving force and shouldn't be spent. Interest is reviving in the latter. Daniel Reid, who has written a book called *The Tao of Health, Sex and Longevity*, believes that limited ejaculation can help prevent colds, hair loss, wrinkling, arthritis, and rheumatism. The Healing Tao Centre in London, whose courses are for women as well as men, says:

> *Conservation and transformation of sexual energy can release immense, potentially explosive, internal power...Recirculation of the generative forces from the genital organs to the higher energy centres, invigorates, and rejuvenates all the vital functions, improves health, and slows depletion of your genetic energy-bank.*

Tarot

Tarot cards first surfaced in Europe in the 14th century and the earliest surviving packs date from the 15th century. They may be much older than that, however, since they contain symbolism from many ancient sources including: **astrology**; **numerology**; **witchcraft**; **Egyptian**, **Celtic** and Norse (**Northern**) mythology; the **cabbala**; and Christianity. As far as we know, they were used simply for gaming and **divination**, but many people have suggested that they were actually made as a record of ancient wisdom in picture form, and used for instruction or to preserve such knowledge in the face of persecution. Similarly, today they can be enjoyed on many levels.

In divination the 22 cards called the Major *Arcana* (secrets) are seen as representing our main path through life and our spiritual development. (See the Major Arcana symbolism table that follows on page 212.) The 56 cards of the Minor Arcana are divided into four suits—wands/batons, swords, cups, and pentacles/coins. These are the four aspects, respectively, of human experience: spiritual and creative, mental, emotional, and physical or material. Cards one to 10 in each of these suits are the ups and downs of everyday life. There are four court cards in each of these suits, usually seen as representing people or the particular qualities people have. In older packs these are: knave/page, prince, queen, and king. In newer packs the knave or page is often replaced with a princess to equalize the sexes.

You may be confused when you first try to learn about the cards by the many different and sometimes contradictory interpretations. The answer is, no one really knows what the cards mean, and the best thing to do at first is to learn one system really well, and then to build on it with your own experience of the cards and perhaps other interpretations. Don't worry too much about the symbolism at the beginning—you can learn about this as you go along. There are many different packs in existence today, often introducing new themes such as Arthurian, angelic, inner child, Native American, and Greek mythology. Simply choose a pack that appeals to you and that you won't find too difficult to learn.

You can read for yourself (although this is more difficult) as well as other people, and you can use the cards for meditation and creative inspiration. *Spreads* are the arrangements of cards used in divination. There are many complicated spreads, but these can be more of a hindrance than a help as they make everything too cut and dried and stop you using your own intuition. You can start with just three cards, the first one representing the past, the second the present and the third the future, and gradually build on these.

The Tarot's Major Arcana

This is just one, very simple interpretation of the cards. You may find the order of the cards varies slightly in different packs. The fool comes at both ends of the cycle.

Card		Symbolizes
0	Fool	Risk
I	Magician	Potential
II	High Priestess (Papess)	Intuition
III	Empress	Nurturing
IV	Emperor	Guidance
V	Heirophant (Pope)	Spiritual teaching
VI	Lovers	Options
VII	Chariot	A hard decision
VIII	Justice	A good decision
IX	Hermit	Introversion
X	Wheel of Fortune	Cycles
XI	Strength (Fortitude)	Inner strength
XII	Hanged Man	Sacrifice
XIII	Death	Sudden change
XIV	Temperance	Harmony
XV	Devil	Manipulation
XVI	Tower	Destruction
XVII	Star	Hope
XVIII	Moon	Fluctuation
XIX	Sun	Happiness
XX	Judgement	Opportunity
XXI	World	Accomplishment
0	Fool	Freedom

Teeth

See **Dentistry**.

Telekinesis

The same as **Psychokinesis**.

Telepathy

Telepathy, or thought transference, is one of the most common psychic occurrences and something nearly all of us have experienced at some time in our lives. At its simplest, it is being aware that someone is looking at us, or thinking of someone just before the telephone rings with a call from them. At its most sophisticated, precise information can be transmitted. When the Australian Lindy Chamberlain was in prison, after being accused of killing her baby (a charge that was later dropped), she found that Aborigine women inmates received detailed news, both personal and political, through telepathic contact with relatives and friends on the outside. Pictures, emotions, and physical sensations can also be transmitted.

Perhaps even more common than telepathy between people is that between people and animals. The biologist Rupert Sheldrake has collected together a mass of stories about the sensitivity of animals of all kinds in his book *Dogs That Know When Their Owners Are Coming Home*. Telepathy is vital if we are to communicate with animals. The dog trainer Barbara Woodhouse says, "If you wish to talk to your dog, you must do so with your mind and will power, as well as your voice." Animal communicator Lydia Hiby, who works with sick animals, uses what she calls "mind pictures." She is able to receive detailed information from them about what is wrong and what should be done to put things right, and is able to send back messages of reassurance and explanation.

The younger the child, the better they perform in telepathy tests, which suggests that telepathy is a skill we stop using once we get better at speaking. Gill Edwards, in her book *Stepping Into The Magic*, says that telepathic messages are sent and received by what she calls our "basic self," which consists of our body, our emotions, and our subconscious mind. This is why telepathy is so much more common between people who are physically related or who have close emotional bonds. She suggests a three-stage process to sending messages: First, give your basic self clear (perhaps written) instructions, for example,

"I'd like so-and-so to contact me urgently"; second, build up the energy of your basic self through breathing, relaxation, or sending love to the other person; and third, remove your conscious mind from the process, allowing the basic self to get on with its job.

Teleportation

This means relocating without physical movement—your physical body disappears from one spot and reappears instantaneously in another. Practiced teleporters (and authors of *Teleportation! A Practical Guide for the Metaphysical Traveler*) Gwen Totterdale and Jessica Severn say that to start with you might only achieve partial de- and re-materialization, and your return will be rapid and involuntary, but eventually you can go anywhere you like.

See also **Astral Projection**.

Thai Massage

A vigorous treatment of the **energy** system in which the masseur uses their hands, arms, feet, legs, and body weight to press, stretch, and manipulate different parts of your body. It is done on the floor with the recipient remaining fully clothed, and takes from one and a half to three hours.

Theosophy

Theosophy, or "divine wisdom," is concerned with the mystical truth at the center of all religions and esoteric teachings. It came to prominence at the end of the 19th century when the flamboyant Madame Helena **Blavatsky** founded the Theosophical Society. This had three aims:

- ❑ To form a universal brotherhood without regard to race, religion, sex, class, or color.
- ❑ To encourage a study of comparative religion, science, and philosophy.

- To investigate the unexplained laws of nature and the powers latent in humankind.

The society was enormously influential in bringing Eastern philosophies to the West, in particular **astrology**, which was then virtually unknown, and has even been called the "grandparent of the new age movement." The society rose to its peak under a second woman, Annie Besant, a noted social reformer and writer who became its president in 1907. Another person connected with the society is Krishnamurti, an Indian spiritual teacher, whom Besant saw as the **maitreya** or new messiah. The Austrian mystic Rudolf **Steiner** was a one-time member but left in 1913 to found his own movement, anthroposophy.

The society started in New York but has its headquarters today near Madras in India, and branches in more than 60 countries, including England.

Therapeutic Touch (TT)

A form of **healing** practiced particularly by nurses in hospitals. Involving both hands-on and non-touching work, it tends to be used in extreme situations such as intensive care units and for the dying or mentally ill. One nurse who uses it for premature babies who can't be touched says (in *Here's Health* magazine): "I use TT because it makes babies feel loved and cared for. You can give them all the medical attention in the world, but without love, they fade away and die."

Tibetan Book of the Dead, The

This contains teachings about the after-death state, and was designed to be read to a person when they were dying and for 49 days afterwards. The teachings derive from both **Buddhism** and **Shamanism** and were written down in about the 8th century, when Buddhism first took hold in Tibet. The book was only translated into English in 1927.

The amount of time we spend in the after-death state is 49 days. During this time, we have the opportunity to break out of the circle of death and rebirth and to remain in the "clear light of absolute reality," which is what we first experience when dying. If we have never met this light before, however, it can terrify us or we may just not recognize it, and our mind descends into the next stage or "bardo." This is a stage when we are beset with visions of all kinds. The way to cope with these is to realize they are simply creations of the mind and not real at all. If we are unable to see this, we pass into the next phase and begin to crave a return to the body. Even now, we have the chance to return to our true nature, but if we don't we are reborn in accordance with our **karma**.

There are similarities between these after-death stages and **near-death experiences** (NDEs). The main difference, however, is that people who have been through NDEs report a longing to stay with the light. They return with reluctance to their body because they have unfinished business.

Sogyal Rinpoche, who has written a modern commentary on the book, *The Tibetan Book of Living and Dying*, does not believe NDEs are a true representation of what happens after death. He also points out that the bardos are actually descriptions of different types of consciousness. For example, at a moment of great loss we can have an instant of clarity and relief before our mind and our attachment to "relative reality" kick in again. Death is like falling asleep, the clear light is like deep sleep, the vision stage is like dreaming, and the "bardo of becoming" is like waking life. Not just in the after-death state, but at every moment of existence we have the opportunity to be free.

Touch for Health

A simplified form of **Kinesiology** for use at home.

Traditional Chinese Medicine (TCM)

An umbrella term for a vast and ancient system of healthcare, the three main ingredients of which are **acupuncture**, Chinese **herbal medicine**, and **tui na** massage. It is based on an understanding of human functioning every bit as detailed and profound as Western medicine, if not more so because it takes into account mind, emotions, and spirit, as well as body, and relates these to external factors. Pragmatic rather than fixed and theoretical, it has been extended and refined over the course of perhaps 5,000–6,000 years and today, in the West, is one of the most respected and well-established **complementary therapies**. It continues to be used in China alongside Western medicine.

As with all complementary medicine, and particularly so in TCM, prevention is as important as cure, so it is perfectly in order to visit a practitioner with tiny niggling symptoms—in fact this is the best time to go, before a "pattern of disharmony" has taken hold—and it is common to visit at times of stress or change. Diagnosis is mainly by "looking, hearing, smelling, questioning, and touching." The condition of the skin, hair, and most importantly, the tongue are noted, and the practitioner will take your pulse on both wrists in several positions. It is said that best results come from using two or more TCM components at the same time, for example, acupuncture and herbs.

Some Features of Traditional Chinese Medicine

- Fundamental are the concepts of yin and yang (see **yin and yang**), complementary forces which underlie everything in the universe including us and which need to be kept in balance.
- People have five basic substances that cause illness if they are deficient, disturbed, or obstructed. These are: *shen*, which can be loosely translated as mind or spirit; *chi* (chee), or energy; *jing*, our constitution and our ability to grow, develop and reproduce; *blood*, which nourishes, moistens, and houses shen; and body fluids.
- Chi circulates around the body through 14 main *meridians* and a network of smaller channels. Each of the meridians is concerned with particular

(cont'd)

Some Features of Traditional Chinese Medicine (cont'd)

mental and physical processes. For instance the "kidney" meridian (which passes through the kidneys) regulates yin and yang, controls birth, growth, and reproduction, is involved with short-term memory, and determines willpower.

- ❑ Five Elements—Wood/Tree, Fire, Earth/Soil, Metal and Water—are used to connect parts of the body, states of mind, and symptoms. For example the liver, gallbladder, tendons, eyes, and nails, as well as the emotion anger, are connected with wood. These elements interact with each other. For example, fire melts metal but nourishes earth, water nourishes wood but destroys fire.
- ❑ Unhealthy external influences are divided into wind, cold, damp, fire, summer heat, and dryness (with broader meanings than the Western ones).

Trager

A pain-free and non-invasive type of **bodywork** involving gentle rocking and stroking to release deep-seated physical and emotional tension. It was developed by Milton Trager, a U.S. acrobat and doctor, in the 1930s.

Transactional Analysis

A type of **psychotherapy** based on the idea that we are all a combination of three "ego states"—child, adult, and parent. The aim is to get each of these working as constructively as possible.

Tui Na

Part of **traditional Chinese medicine** and also known as Chinese medical massage, this uses deep vigorous pressure, stretching, and manipulation to work on the body's **energy** system. You either sit or lie on a couch and can remain clothed. It is pronounced *twee-nah*.

𝒰

UFOs

The UFO phenomenon began with two events in 1947. The first took place over Washington State, when a pilot saw nine silvery crescent-shaped aircraft travelling, he calculated, at 1000–2000 miles an hour. The term "flying saucer" was coined by a journalist writing about them. Nine days later a farmer near Roswell in New Mexico found unidentifiable wreckage on his land and informed the police. The wreckage was removed by the Air Force, the area cordoned off and the farmer interrogated. In 1995 it was reported that aliens had been found at another crash in the same area, and film was produced showing an autopsy being carried out on one of them. Most people consider this a hoax.

Since 1947, craft of all shapes and sizes have been seen all over the world, often by many people at the same time and by people who would have nothing to gain by inventing a story. Electrical and atmospheric phenomena could account for some of these stories but Nick Pope, who worked from 1991 to 1994 for the British Ministry of Defence managing the "UFO desk," says that five percent of all sightings are truly inexplicable. Although he started out a skeptic, Pope now believes that extraterrestrial spacecraft are a reality and that the answers are "almost definitely buried somewhere deep within the American government."

UFOs have been linked with the animal mutilation that has been going on since the 1960s. The animals in question, usually cattle, are found dead with their blood drained and organs neatly removed. Scorch marks but no blood, footprints, or tire tracks are found nearby. One farmer in Kansas reported in 1987 that he had actually seen an airship winch up a cow.

"Area 51" or "Dreamland" is a notorious U.S. government installation about 120 miles Northwest of Las Vegas. According to several people who have worked there, it houses extraterrestrial technology that is being "back-engineered" (taken to pieces to see how it works) for military use. Some believe that, in exchange for alien technology, the U.S. government turns a blind eye to the **abductions** and mutilations that are part of the aliens' research.

Strange flying objects have been reported all over the world for thousands of years. In China there are supposed to be 12,000-year-old discs that tell of a crashed alien craft (see *The Chinese Roswell* by Hartwig Hausdorf). The Indian god Indra rode through the air in a disc-shaped golden chariot. In fact some (such as Erich von Daniken) suggest that *all* gods were astronauts. Astrophysicist Dr. Johannes von Buttlar says (in *UFOs: The Secret Evidence*, a video by Michael Hesemann):

> *The statistical probability is immensely high that there is life in other planetary systems. And not only that: Because most stars in the Milky Way are much older than our sun, we can assume that there are many older civilizations. Civilizations which are also technologically far ahead of us.*

A top secret NATO report and a U.S. airforce study both concluded that the Earth is indeed visited by extraterrestrials. According to Nick Pope, there are many UFO papers that the U.S. government refuses to release, and many say that the very fact the U.S. government is so keen to debunk the whole UFO phenomenon shows they have something to hide.

We don't, however, have to assume that all extraterrestrials are out to harm us. The novelist Whitley Strieber wrote of his own abduction in two books called *Communion* and *Transformation*. While he found the experience terrifying, he believes that alien appearances are designed to help human beings undergo spiritual growth. Metaphysician Brad Steiger believes that extraterrestrial or extradimensional beings are overseeing the transformation of the human race. This is one of the reasons for the increase in **channeling** and many of us may in fact be "star people," descendants of these benevolent beings.

UFO Glossary

EBE	Extraterrestrial biological entity; a U.S. government term.
ET	Extraterrestrial.
ETI	Extraterrestrial intelligence.
Foo Fighter	Name given, by pilots in World War II, to the lights that accompanied their aircraft; these are still seen by modern flyers.
IFO	Identified flying object—90 to 95 percent of reported UFOs become IFOs after investigation.
SETI	The search for extraterrestrial intelligence.
UAP	Unidentified atmospheric phenomenon; a description used by UFOlogist (see the following entry) for sightings that can probably be explained by natural processes yet unknown to science.
UFO	Unidentified flying object; a term invented by the U.S. government in 1952.
UFOlogist	Someone who studies UFOs and reported sightings; nearly always amateur, as the subject is not considered suitable for paid research.
UFOnaut	Someone who travels in a UFO.

Uluru

This is the **Aborigine** name for Ayers Rock, the magnificent sandstone monolith that rises from the desert in the center of Australia. It is the Aborigines' most sacred site and a place of pilgrimage for people of all races and nationalities.

In Aborigine myth there was a major battle here which marked the end of the Dreamtime, or creation time, and the beginning of our own age. Uluru is crossed by many songlines and is one of the homes of the great ancestral being called the Rainbow Snake.

Only 25 miles away is another extraordinary, but much less well-known, rocky outcrop known as Katatjuta, or the Olgas. This is sacred to Aboriginal women.

A symbol of the Aborigines' struggle for land rights, the rock has been returned to them and the area made a national park. However, it is leased back to the state and serviced by the Yulara Tourist Resort, the third largest community in the Northern Territory with an airport, shopping precinct, and campsite for 4000 people.

Whatever their background and in spite of the numbers of other visitors, few people remain unmoved by Uluru. The British comic writer and skeptic Howard Jacobson, who traveled round Australia with his wife, says in *In the Land of Oz*:

> *I hadn't got very far with it myself as a religious totem; by and large I didn't hold with sacred sites and was left quite cold by the various taboos and other unspeakables vested in Uluru.... Coming at it from a different angle, I think Ros felt similarly. We had both been happy at Ayers Rock. It was a question we put to ourselves with some seriousness as we left: Would we ever be as happy again?*
> (Reproduced by permission of Penguin Books Ltd.)

V

Vaccination

Vaccinations are supposed to protect us from infectious diseases. However, many people are questioning whether they are really necessary, and there is growing concern about their safety.

Infectious disease began to die out way before vaccines were introduced, as a result of better housing and sanitation, clean drinking water, and improved nutrition, and it is not clear in any case how much protection vaccinations actually offer. In the case of tuberculosis (TB), for example, the rate of decrease in deaths has not changed since vaccination became common, and in trials in India (reported in 1980) more people developed TB in a vaccinated group than in a nonvaccinated group. Travel vaccines have the poorest record of success of all vaccines, and 95 percent of the diseases you are likely to catch abroad are not preventable by them anyway.

Some children have suffered brain damage as a direct result of vaccination, and sometimes the risks of the vaccine are greater than those of the disease being vaccinated against. Other illnesses that may be related to vaccinations include cot death, dyslexia, autism, irritable bowel syndrome, epilepsy, asthma, multiple sclerosis, and AIDS. Many **complementary health** practitioners believe that it is wrong to suppress childhood illnesses as these develop the immune system and stop children from the risk of more serious illness later in life.

The yearly vaccinations we are encouraged to give our pets have been linked to skin problems, allergies, seizures, warty growths, tumors, and bone and joint disorders.

There is not a single vaccine that does not involve animal testing. Even types that have been in use for many years are subject to safety, potency, and purity tests before being sold. Many contain animal products as well as noxious substances such as mercury, formaldehyde, and aluminum. They may also contain antibiotics.

When deciding whether or not to be vaccinated, you have to look at vaccinations individually, as the risks and effectiveness vary. Something else to take into consideration is the seriousness of the illness and whether it can be treated. You may already be immune; a blood test will confirm this. When travelling abroad you need to find out how likely you are to come into contact with a disease. A yellow fever vaccination certificate is now the only certificate required in international travel, and then only for a limited number of travelers.

An alternative to vaccination is **homeopathy**, which can be used for prevention as well as cure in both animals and humans. The best protection for children is breastfeeding as the mother's antibodies are then passed on.

Vacuflex

A type of **reflexology** (foot massage) using boots and suction pads.

Vanatru

A **Pagan** religion in the **Northern tradition**.

Vastu vidya

The Indian art of placement, similar to **feng shui**.

Veganism/Vegans

Vegans eat no animal products at all. While not eating meat, this also means excluding fish, dairy produce, or eggs and, for some, honey or additives derived from animals (for example, cochineal, gelatin). Most also choose to avoid animal products in other areas of their lives. While simply replacing meat with cheese (as many vegetarians do) brings few advantages, there are ethical, compassionate, environmental, and health reasons for veganism.

Some people believe that all animal exploitation is wrong, however well the animals are treated. Keeping animals in captivity, instead of letting them live free and wild, is keeping them as slaves.

In both the meat and dairy industries animals may be transported for long distances, have an unnatural and restricted lifestyle, and suffer inexpert castration, dehorning, and slaughter. Since World War II when farming became intensive, the dairy cow in particular has been subjected to a harsh regime. Mother and calf are likely to be separated a few hours after birth and the average milk yield of the dairy cow is two or even three times what it was 60 years ago. This can lead to chronic lameness and liver damage. Another common problem is udder infection (mastitis) from damage by milking machines. The cow's natural life span is 20 years, but most are worn out and slaughtered at age 2 to 7. Even under an **organic** regime, her circumstances are much the same.

Rearing animals for food is a very wasteful form of land use. Ten acres of soybeans can provide protein for 60 people, while 10 acres of grazing for cattle provides for only two. Rearing animals also uses massive quantities of water—100 times as much as growing vegetables. Farm animals produce nearly a third of the greenhouse gas methane and 90 percent of water pollution by sewage is due to farm animals.

Research has shown that a varied and balanced vegan diet provides all the nutrients necessary at all stages of life, from weaning through childhood, adolescence, and adulthood including pregnancy and breastfeeding, and old age. (See for example *Vegan Nutrition: A survey of research* by Gill Langley.) However, some doctors remain unconvinced, particularly where children are concerned. (For more on this issue and for information on what to feed the young see *Pregnancy, Children and the Vegan Diet* by Dr. M. Klaper, and *Vegetarian Baby* and *Vegetarian Children* by Sharon K. Yntema.) The vegan diet is low in fat, especially saturated fat, high in fiber, and rich in vitamins and minerals, so reducing the risk of high blood pressure, heart disease, cancer, gallstones, diabetes, and being overweight. It may also help allergies, asthma, and rheumatoid arthritis. The risk of osteoporosis may be less as exclusion of meat helps the body conserve calcium.

As well as in food and leather, animal products may be found in cosmetics, household cleaners, fertilizers, brushes, nutritional supplements, drink additives, condoms, medical drugs, surgical stitching, and stringed musical instruments to name but a few. Some suppliers of animal-free products are listed in the mail order section (see Resources) and further details on all aspects of vegan living are available from the Vegan Society (see Addresses).

Veganism—What to Eat

Carbohydrates

It's important to eat wholegrain foods, as these contain protein as well as starch.

- ❑ Whole wheat bread.
- ❑ Whole-grain crispbreads and biscuits.
- ❑ Whole wheat pasta.
- ❑ Brown rice.
- ❑ Other grains—for example, oats, corn, millet, quinoa.

Protein and essential fatty acids

Most vegetable protein is "incomplete" so you need to eat it with whole-grain foods that make up the deficit, preferably at the same meal. Oils must be cold pressed and nonhydrogenated to keep their EFAs. If frying with oils, don't let them smoke and use them once only.

- ❑ Pulses—for example, baked beans, lentils, kidney beans, peas, hummus (tahini and chick peas).
- ❑ Nuts, nut creams and butters, nut oils (cold pressed).
- ❑ Seeds—for example, tahini (sesame seed paste), sunflower seeds, seed oils (cold pressed).
- ❑ Soy products—soy milk, soy cream, soy yogurt, tofu, miso (paste for flavoring), soy sauce (additive-free Japanese versions: shoyu and tamari).
- ❑ Vegetable margarine (nonhydrogenated).
- ❑ Vegetable stock cubes and powder.

Vegetables and fruit

Vegetables contain some protein and are a rich source of minerals as well as vitamins. Have as fresh as possible and steam lightly, stir fry, or use in soups and salads to preserve nutrients.

- ❑ Variety of fresh or frozen vegetables.
- ❑ Sprouted beans and seeds.
- ❑ Fresh herbs.
- ❑ Sea vegetables.
- ❑ Fresh fruit.
- ❑ Dried fruit.

Sweeteners

White sugar actually depletes our body of nutrients. The items that follow contain nutrients as well as sweetness.

- ❑ Concentrated apple juice.
- ❑ Maple syrup.
- ❑ Molasses.
- ❑ Malt.
- ❑ Dark brown sugar.

Vegetarianism

Vegetarians eat food from live animals (dairy produce, eggs) but not from dead ones (meat and fish). This has few benefits in terms of animal welfare, our health, or the environment. A more logical option for those who really want to make a difference is **veganism**.

Vibrational Medicine

See **Complementary Medicine, Subtle Energy**.

Vision Education/Therapy

This is based on the premise that poor sight and many eye problems are caused by bad physical and mental habits, *not* irreversible physical characteristics, and that these habits can be changed.

The first vision educator, William Bates, was an American eye specialist working at the start of the 20th century. Having cured himself of the long sight that is supposed to be an inevitable part of growing older, he went on to develop a series of exercises that still form the basis of much vision therapy (see on page 229).

Teachers today have gone on to link eye problems with psychology and have shown that there are physiological changes in the eye in response to unpleasant situations. In other words, we don't see because we don't want to see. As well as physical exercises, they use **psychotherapeutic** techniques to take us back to a time when we *could* see properly and to reprogram our responses. Two leaders in this field are Meir Schneider and Jacob Liberman. Meir Schneider cured himself of near-blindness and recounts his remarkable story in *Self Healing: My Life and Vision*. Jacob Liberman had a miraculous healing of his eyesight after a mystical experience. He has written an inspiring book called *Take Off Your Glasses and See* and says, for example, that short sight is caused by fear in childhood, and long sight by anger.

Vision educators have worked successfully with short sight, long sight, astigmatism, squints, lazy eyes, cataracts, and glaucoma as well as rarer conditions (amblyopia, macular degeneration, iritis, and optic neuritis). The therapy can also be used for people with normal sight to prevent deterioration and by people who do a lot of eye work, such as computer users. It works particularly well with children, as bad habits can be stopped before they take too much hold. It is also worth considering for other conditions where eye strain may be a contributing factor, such as with headaches and migraines, or for illnesses that can affect the eyes, such as MS and ME.

Looking After Your Eyes

- ❑ Glasses and contact lenses perpetuate problems, so wear them as little as possible, but don't strain to see things without them as this can also make matters worse. Lenses are slightly better than glasses, but more likely to be worn for long periods.
- ❑ Blink as much as possible and massage round your eyes.
- ❑ When reading and at the end of a page, look up and focus on something distant.
- ❑ Rest your eyes every 10 minutes or so when using a computer.
- ❑ Be aware of tension in your neck and shoulders as this is liable to be connected to eye tension.

Some Bates Eye Exercises

Palming

Probably the most important exercise of all, this involves rubbing your hands together to warm them and then closing your eyes, placing your palms over them to block out all light, and relaxing.

Stunning

This is done to teach the eye to accept strong light without tensing. Don't do it in very strong (midday) sun. While outside, close your eyes and raise your face to the sun. Move your head and shoulders from side to side, keeping your eyes closed, so that you face towards and away from the sun.

Swaying and swinging

In swaying, you look at one point and sway your body. In swinging, you move your eyes, or your eyes together with your body. Both these exercises hone focusing skills and get the eyes working together.

Vision Quest

A **Native American** practice, usually for adolescent males but also for anyone seeking inner guidance. It involves fasting and purification (for example, in a **sweat lodge**) beforehand and then spending several days alone in a sacred place in nature, without food and water and resisting sleep. Through these rigors young people gain insight about their purpose in life, perhaps meeting their **power animal** or discovering special objects or songs that will be important to them throughout their lives and remind them of their vision.

Visualization

Everything we do starts with a thought or image, from picking up a cup to writing a book. So if we want to change our lives, we have first to imagine or *visualize* the change. With our imagination we connect to our deeper self and to the cosmos, and set the wheels in motion for change to come about. There are three types of visualization:

1. Visualizing something you want, whether a new car, being able to get on with a friend, or having more confidence. This type of visualization is rather like an **affirmation**. You imagine what you want in as much detail as possible and you then imagine it actually in your life now. You can use the affirmation exercise to deal with all the reasons your mind comes up with as to why you can't or shouldn't have what you want.
2. Guided visualizations, sometimes called *meditations*, on tape or in books. These have specific focuses such as meeting a spirit guide or lowering your blood pressure. With the written kind you have to read them through first and then remember them. If you can't manage this you can put them on tape yourself, remembering to leave lots of gaps for your thoughts.
3. Creative or active visualizations. These are rather like waking dreams and are good for problem-solving or confronting fears. You can even use them to replay dreams and alter the endings. First you need to decide what your focus is and put yourself in as relaxed a frame of mind as possible, and then you allow your unconscious to surface and present you with an image, scene, or drama. Try to participate in the visualization yourself as much as possible, and if you get stuck call on your **spirit guide** or **power animal** to help.

See also **prayer**.

Vivisection

Vivisection is experimentation on animals. This is done for all sorts of reasons: to test the safety of drugs, food additives, cosmetics, toiletries, household products, chemicals, and industrial waste; during the routine manufacture of drugs; to try out and teach surgical procedures; to study disease and injury; in **biotechnology**; and in weapons research.

Few would deny that it is cruel. In 1995, nearly three million experiments were carried out on mice, rats, rabbits, cats, dogs, horses, monkeys, birds, fish, goats, sheep, cattle, pigs, ferrets, and others. These involved animals being burned, scalded, electrocuted, addicted to drugs, infected with serious disease, shot, gassed, poisoned, subjected to freezing temperatures, reared in darkness, having irritating substances put on their skin and in their eyes, having their eyes removed, their brains damaged, and their bones broken. Three-quarters of these experiments were done without anaesthetic.

However, what most people don't know is that vivisection is scientifically unsound and that there are many better procedures available. It is impossible to judge the effect of drugs on humans by testing them on animals because humans and animals are different, because animals can't tell us about any psychological symptoms (such as depression, hallucinations), and because anything can be proved "safe"—it just depends which animal you test it on. Surgical procedures are better learned on models or corpses, and under the tuition of an experienced surgeon. Human disease and injury are better studied on humans. Other alternatives to vivisection include: test-tube research; cell, tissue, and organ culture; computer modeling; X-rays and scans; and autopsies.

Few medical advances have come about through vivisection and it can even have a reverse effect. X-rays, anesthetics, and penicillin were discovered by accident (that is, intelligent observation). The heart drug digitalin and aspirin both derive from long-standing herbal remedies (that is, tested on humans for centuries). Infectious disease declined before the advent of **vaccination** because of better sanitation and nutrition, and vaccination may even be causing disease. For many years the links between coal dust and asbestos and lung disease, and between smoking and cancer, were denied because of animal research. Half a million anticancer compounds were tested on animals between 1970 and 1985 that produced a short list of 12, all of which were, in fact, already known to be beneficial. So long as chemicals are tested separately one by one for their effects, we will continue to pollute the environment as a whole with substances whose cumulative and long-term dangers are only discovered when it is too late.

Money is thought to be the reason vivisection continues—too many people have made it their career, from animal breeders and equipment suppliers to research scientists and pharmaceutical workers. Animal tests allow drug companies to put their products on to the market as quickly as possible.

(For advice on avoiding cruelty to animals, see **animals** and **veganism**.)

W

Western Mystery Tradition

A blanket term for all forms of Western spirituality that depart from orthodox Christianity. The word *mystery* is used both because these traditions are frequently mystical in character and also because they were condemned by the Church and forced underground. The terms *occult* (hidden) and *esoteric* (inner, for a select few) are also sometimes used for similar reasons. The tradition is said to have come down to us from **Atlantis** via **Egypt**.

See **Divination**, **Gnosticism**, **Hermeticism**, **Paganism**, **Rosicrucianism.**

Wicca

An Old English word for **witchcraft**, often used for the modern revival of the religion in order to avoid the negative connotations of the other name.

Witchcraft/Witches

Also called the Craft, the Way of the Wise, the Old Religion, and **Wicca**, this is believed to be the prehistoric fertility religion of Europe. It was revived in Britain in the 1950s when antiwitchcraft laws were repealed and is now a thriving arm of modern **Paganism**.

The suggestion that witchcraft represents a remnant of an ancient and widespread tradition was first put forward by the anthropologist Margaret Murray in her two books *The Witch-Cult in Western Europe* (1921) and *The God of the Witches* (1931). The tradition is said to have been driven deep underground by persecution, in particular the trials and executions of the 16th and 17th centuries, but kept alive within families and by being passed down from individual to individual.

Although not generally accepted by scholars, Margaret Murray's ideas paved the way for Gerald Gardner who joined a semitraditional coven (group) in 1939–40. He went on to develop the tradition and wrote about it in his influential *Witchcraft Today* (1954) and *The Meaning of Witchcraft* (1959). Another witch, who was initiated by his grandmother, is Alex Sanders. He founded many covens and his type of witchcraft is detailed in the books of Janet and Stuart Farrar. The mother of modern witchcraft was Doreen Valiente, who was initiated by Gardner and wrote many incantations that are still in use today.

Modern witches, both men and women, base their practices around worship of the **Goddess** and her horned consort. Covens are small, and entry is by initiation after a probationary period. There are also solo or "hedge" witches. **Magick** and **divination** are important and rituals are conducted at the full moon (*esbats*) and at the eight seasonal festivals (*sabbats*), which have come down to us from the **Celts**. Nakedness may be a feature, depending on the coven, as this helps people to be themselves and close to nature, and sexual rites may be practiced for their energy—a sort of Western **tantra** as Doreen Valiente calls it (in *Far Out: The dawning of new age Britain, Akhtar and Humphries*). The Book of Shadows is the record a witch keeps of their rituals, spells, experiences, and so on.

For women, witchcraft can be enormously liberating. Doreen Valiente explains (in *Far Out*):

In most ceremonial magic the women just did as they were told, but in witchcraft it was the women who had the power. The full moon was very important for magic and it was called the feminine light with which women instinctively had a relationship because the moon cycle is the same as the feminine cycle.

Witchcraft is now one of the West's fastest growing religions.

Y

Yidake/i

Another name for the Australian Aboriginal musical instrument, the **didgeridoo**.

Yin and Yang

According to Chinese philosophy, these two complementary forces are present in each of us, in everything around us and in everything we do. Balance between the two is the ideal, but as the world is in a constant state of flux this is seldom achieved. However, as each force reaches its extreme, nature or the **tao** takes over, and it becomes its opposite, thereby restoring balance.

In the Chinese ***I Ching***, or Book of Changes, the different strengths of yin and yang are rendered mathematically in 64 hexagrams, which are then used to gauge the current disposition of the world so that action can be taken in harmony with it.

Yin and yang are further divided into five elements (wood or tree, fire, earth or soil, metal, and water), which are important in both **traditional Chinese medicine** and the Chinese art of landscaping, **feng shui**.

In the West we tend to think in extremes and in terms of good and bad—"action is better than doing nothing," "men/women are better than women/men," "positive is better than negative," and so on. Yin and yang remind us to seek the middle way.

See also **Left Brain/Right Brain**, and **Macrobiotics**.

Yin and Yang

Yin	Yang
Darkness	Light
Negative	Positive
Earth	Heaven
Feminine	Masculine
Receptive	Creative
Stillness	Action
Moon	Sun
Winter	Summer
Wet	Dry
Cold	Hot
Space	Time
Plants	Animals
Intuition	Logic
Spirituality	Religion
Cooperation	Competition
Means	Ends
Depression	Anger
Chronic disease	Acute disease
Sugar	Salt

Yoga

This is the practical part of **Hinduism**—physical, mental, and spiritual exercises that date back to at least 3000 BCE. The word means *union* and refers to the ultimate aim of yoga—harmony of body, mind, and spirit and union with the divine. There are several different types, including: **karma** yoga, the way of action; bhakti yoga, the way of love and devotion, especially to a deity; and **tantra**, which uses sexual and imaginative energy. There are eight stages, covering ethical conduct, physical exercises, breathing exercises, concentration and meditation.

The type best known in the West is *hatha yoga*. "Ha" means sun and "tha" means moon, referring to the fact that hatha yoga aims to balance the flow of **subtle energy** as it enters and leaves our body. This is done through physical exercises or "postures" and breathing exercises known as *pranayama* ("prana" meaning subtle energy). Hatha yoga ensures that the body is healthy and relaxed and prepares a person for the higher practices of concentration and meditation.

Hatha yoga works on every area of the body and on the internal organs as well as the outer ones, creating suppleness, strength, and stamina. It is noncompetitive and can be done by people of all ages and levels of fitness. Practice can be geared to specific conditions such as pregnancy and old age or problems like back pain and asthma. It is best learned from a teacher to start with and not a book or tape, as you risk injuring yourself if you don't do the postures properly or strain too much at them. Ideally, you should then practice a little at home every day. No special equipment or clothes are needed.

See also **Chakras**.

Z

Zen

A type of Buddhism, related to **taoism**, that flourished in Japan in the 12th century and continues to influence Japanese culture. The word means *meditation* and the art of zen is to turn your whole life into a meditation or, as Fritjof Capra puts it in *The Tao of Physics*, to live with "spontaneity, simplicity and total presence of mind."

There were two schools of zen. One emphasized *zazen* or sitting meditation, a type of meditation in which the mind is left to settle like mud in a pool of water. Another used shock tactics to overload and cut through the mind. Sometimes the disciples were hit, at other times they were presented with riddles or anecdotes called *koans*. For example, in one anecdote a monk asked his master about a buddha who had sat in meditation for 10 cycles of existence and still not reached enlightenment. "Why was this?" he asked. "He was not a buddha," came the answer. Everyday life was another training ground. A monk asked a master when he was weighing some flax, "What is buddha?" The master answered, "This flax weighs three pounds."

The zen outlook permeates many aspects of Japanese life: the martial arts, poetry, painting, calligraphy, flower arranging, the tea ceremony, and gardening. As in taoism, the point of all these pastimes is effortless action. With perfection of technique and complete absorption, the separation between you and what you are doing disappears. Things just happen.

Through all these means we can experience *satori*, those flashes of intuition that make us see everything in a completely new light and are actually glimpses of our true nature.

Zero Balancing

This gentle **bodywork** uses finger pressure and held stretches to release tension. The stretches are called fulcrums because they provide “a point of stillness around which energy and structure can reorganize”, that is, become perfectly or “zero” balanced. You remain fully clothed and an average session takes about half an hour; three are recommended to start with.

Zero balancing was developed in the 1970s by Fritz Smith, an American **osteopath**, doctor, and **acupuncturist** who was interested in combining Eastern and Western massage systems.

Resources

Recommended Reading

Books

Some classics and some of my favorites.

Albery, Nicholas, Gil Elliot, and Joseph Elliot (eds), *The New Natural Death Handbook*. Rider, 1977. A moving and practical guide to preparing for dying, caring for the dying, living wills, green burial, and DIY funerals.

Andrews, Lynn V., *Medicine Woman*. Harper & Row, San Francisco, 1981. A vivid first-hand account of Shamanism from the female perspective.

Black Elk (ed. John G. Neihardt), *Black Elk Speaks*. Abacus 1974, (first pub. USA, 1932). The moving story of the death of a Native American nation from one of its medicine men.

Bradley, Marion, *The Mists of Avalon*. Sphere, 1984 (first pub. USA, 1982). British Paganism as it might have been at the time of Arthur.

Capra, Fritjof, *The Tao of Physics*. HarperCollins, 1992 (first pub. 1975). This classic is a useful introduction to both modern physics and Eastern philosophy.

Castaneda, Carlos, *The Teachings of Don Juan*. Penguin, 1970 (first pub. USA, 1968). A U.S. academic drawn into the disturbing world of Mexican shamanism. This is the first in a series of books—for details on the others, see Bibliography.

Chernak McElroy, Susan, *Animals as Teachers and Healers*. Rider, 1997 (first pub. USA, 1996). True stories of all kinds.

Eisler, Riane, *The Chalice and the Blade*. Thorsons, 1998 (first pub. USA, 1987). Goddess-centered versus non-goddess-centered cultures—scholarly but impassioned.

Findhorn Community, *The Findhorn Garden*. Findhorn Press, 1988 (first pub. 1976). The extraordinary tale of how three people worked with angels and nature spirits to create a garden on a sandy, windswept promontory off the north-east coast of Scotland.

Gawain, Shakti, *Creative Visualization*. Novato, Calif.: New World Library, 1995. How to create the sort of life we want—a simple, inspiring workbook.

Hay, Louise L., *You Can Heal Your Life*. New York: Eden Grove Editions, 1988 (first pub. USA, 1984). Symptoms as signs from the soul, and how to deal with them.

Lynn, Denise, *Signposts*. Rider, 1996. How to tune into portents and messages in our dreams and the world around us.

Morgan, Marlo, *Mutant Message Down Under*. Thorsons, 1995 (first pub. USA, 1994). An American woman doctor's adventure with a band of Aborigines in the Australian outback.

Pope, Nick, *Open Skies, Closed Minds*. Simon & Schuster, 1996. UFOs, alien abduction, and crop circles from someone in the know.

Redfield, James, *The Celestine Prophecy*. Bantam, 1994 (first pub. USA, 1994). A deceptively simple novel about finding our spiritual path.

Roman, Sanaya and Duane Packer, *Opening to Channel*. Tiburon, Calif.: H.J. Kramer, 1987. Channeling and spirit guides made easy, with uplifting messages from the authors' own guides.

Sheldrake, Rupert, *The Rebirth of Nature*. Century, 1990. Mysticism and science brought together by a scientist who writes with elegant English.

Magazines

Awareness Magazine
(Devoted to improving your life and the life of the planet)
7441 Garden Grove Blvd., Suite C
Garden Grove, CA 92841
Tel: 800 758 3223 or 714 894 5133
Fax: 714 890 1664
E-mail: *awarenessmag@earthlink.net*
www.awarenessmag.com

Ayurveda for All
D-56, Sector-55, Noida, U.P.
Tel: 95-120-4314221, 4314220, 25837024
E-mail: *ayur@homoeopathyforall.com*

Ayurveda for Holistic Age
Dayanand Ayurvedic College
GT Road
Jalandhar 144 008
Tel: 0181 2471146, 2253571

Body & Soul
(Inspires you to live a healthy, balanced, and fulfilling life)
42 Pleasant Street
Watertown, MA 02472
Tel: 800 782 7006 or 617 926 0200
Fax: 617 926 5021
E-mail: *editor@bodyandsoulmag.com*
www.bodyandsoulmag.com

Circle Magazine
(Filled with a variety of articles, rituals, meditations, illustrations, invocations, contents, news, photos, herbal formulas, reviews, magical development exercises, chants, and other material)
PO Box 219
Mt. Horeb, WI 53572
Tel: 608 924 2216
E-mail: *circle@mhtc.net*
www.circlesanctuary.org

Continuum Magazine
(A magazine of Higher Consciousness)
Tel: 507 368 4485
E-mail: *anna@continum-magazine.com*
www.continuum-magazine.com

Down to Earth
(Society of Environmental Communication)
41, Tuglakabad Institutional Area,
New Delhi 110062
Tel: 011 29955124
email: editor@downtoearth.org.in
www.downtoearth.in

Eternal Solutions
(Manual of Life)
Editorial and Marketing Office:
B-6/91, Safdarjung Enclave,
New Delhi 110029
Tel: 011 41651841/42
Fax: 011 41651843
email: editor@theeternalsolutions.com
wecare@theeternalsoulutions.com
www.theeternasolutions.com

Ethical Consumer
(Looks at social and environmental records of companies behind brand names)
Unit 21
41 Old Birley Street
Manchester M15 5RF
Tel: 0161 226 2929
Fax: 0161 226 6277
www.ethicalconsumer.org

Fortean Times
(Strange phenomena worldwide)
From newsagents or:
John Brown Publishing
The New Boathouse
136–142 Bramley Road
London W10 6SR
Tel: 020 7565 3000
Fax: 020 7565 3050
E-mail: *info@johnbrown.co.uk*
www.forteantimes.com, www.johnbrown.co.uk

Here's Health
(Complementary health including detalils of practitioner organizations)
From newsagents or:
Freepost
Subscriptions Dept
Emap Consumer Magazines
Leicestershire LE87 4AB
Tel: 01858 438869

In Light Times
(Metaphysics, Alternative Health, Astrology, New Age Spirituality, Hypnosis, Reincarnation, Regression, Astral Journeys, Dreams, Psychic & Paranormal Phenomena, Love & Relationships, Earth Changes, Inspirational Life Stories, Holistic Philosophies, and so much more)
PO Box 35798
Las Vegas, NV 89133
Tel: 702 795 4801
E-mail: *ilt@inlighttimes.com*
www.inlighttimes.com

Kindred Spirit
(All new age subjects; also book and CD mail order)
From new age and wholefood shops or:
Foxhole
Dartington
Totnes
Devon TQ9 6EB
Tel: 01803 866686
Fax: 01803 866591
E-mail: *subs@kindredspirit.co.uk*
mailorder@kindredspirit.co.uk
www.kindredspirit.co.uk

The Ley Hunter
(Leys and other earth mysteries; mail order books)
PO Box 258
Cheltenham
Glos. GL53 0HR

The Light Connection
914 S. Santa Fe Ave. #L
Vista, CA 92084
Tel: 760 631 1177
Lightconnection@cox.net

Life Positive
153, Okhla Industrial Area,
Phase I
New Delhi 110020
Email: *india@lifepositive.net*
lifepositive@vsnl.com
www.lifepositive.com

Magical Blend—MB Media
(Magical Blend exists to embrace the hopes, transform the fears, and assist people in achieving their highest spiritual awareness)
PO Box 600
Chico, CA 95927-0600
Tel: 530 893 9037
Fax: 530 893 9076
E-mail: *info@magicalblend.com*
www.magicalblend.com

Modern Sage
(spiritual, holistic, and alternative health)
PO Box 158
Merrick, NY 11566
Tel: 516 867 6666
E-mail: *modrnsage@aol.com*
www.modernsage.com

Natural Health
(Information that embraces a natural and holistic approach to health)
70 Lincoln Street
Boston, MA 02111
www.naturalhealth.com

New Moon Rising
(To be a vital stimulus in the continuing international Pagan Renaissance)
1630 Williams Hwy, PMB 148
Grants Pass, OR 97527-5660
E-mail: *info@nmrising.com*
www.nmrising.com

Nexus
(Hidden history and science; mail order books)
From newsagents or:
55 Queens Rd
East Grinstead
West Sussex RH19 1BG
Tel: 01342 322854
Fax: 01342 324574
E-mail: *nexus@ukoffice.u.net.com*
www.nexusmagazine.com

New Witch Magazine
(A magazine dedicated to, featuring, and partially written by young or beginning Witches, Wiccans, Neo-Pagans, and other Earth-based, ethnic, pre-Christian, Shamanic, and magical practitioners.)
PO Box 641
Point Arena, CA 95468
Tel: 707 882 2052
Fax: 707 882 2793
E-mail: *info@newwitch.com*
www.newwitch.com

Nexus Magazine
2940 E. Colfax #131
Denver, CO 80206
Tel: 888 909 7474 or 303 321 5006
Fax: 603 754 4744
E-mail: *nexususa@earthlink.net*
www.nexusmagazine.com

PanGaia Magazine
(A quarterly magazine that explores Pagan and Gaian Earth-based spirituality at home and around the world.)
PO Box 641
Point Arena, CA 95468
Tel: 888 724 3966
E-mail: *info@pangaia.com*
www.pangaia.com

Parabola
(a quarterly journal devoted to the exploration of the quest for meaning as it is expressed in the world's myths, symbols, and religious traditions, with particular emphasis on the relationship between this store of wisdom and our modern life)
656 Broadway
New York, NY 10012
Tel: 800 783 403
E-mail: *orders@parabola.org*
www.parabola.org

Positive News
(Quarterly newspaper of good news rather than bad)
From new age and wholefood shops or:
No. 5 Bicton Enterprise Centre
Clun
Shropshire SY7 8NF
Tel: 01588 640 022
Fax: 01588 640 033
E-mail: *posenquiries@positivenews.org.uk*
www.positivenews.org.uk

Psychic News
(Weekly spiritualist newspaper)
Available from newsagents or:
Psychic Press Ltd
The Coach House
Standsted Hall
Stansted
Essex CM24 8UD
Tel: 01279 817050
Fax: 01279 817051

Sagewoman Magazine
(In our pages, you'll be supported, uplifted, and challenged to envision the Goddess in all women, especially in yourself.)
PO Box 641
Point Arena, CA 95468
Tel: 707 882 2052
Fax: 707 882 2793
E-mail: *info@sagewoman.com*
www.sagewoman.com

Sedona Journal of Emergence!
c/o Light Technology Publications
PO Box 3540
Flagstaff, AZ 86003
www.sedonajournal.com/sje/

Vedic Astrology
72, Gagan Vihar
Delhi 110051
India
Ph: 011 22543563
E-mail: *vedastrology@yahoo.com*
www.vedicastro.com

What Doctors Don't Tell You
(Information on conventional and complementary medicine)
77, Grosvenor Avenue
London N5 2BR
Tel/Fax: 0800 146054 (subscription freefone)
www.wddty.co.uk

What is Enlightenment?
(To present our ongoing investigation into this question, and to share our discoveries with those who are also interested in this vast and most subtle subject)
PO Box 2360
Lenox, MA 01240
Tel: 800 376 3210 or 413 637 6000
E-mail: *wie@wie.org*
www.wie.org

Yoga Life
c/o ICYER, 16-A
Mettu Street Chinnamudaliarchavady
Kottakuppam (via Pondicherry)
605 104
Tamil Nadu
India
Tel: 2622902, 2241561
E-mail: *yognat2001@yahoo.com*
www.icyer.com

Additional Resources

Most of the following organizations are small and charitable/not for profit, so send return postage if writing. I haven't personally tested all of them so please use your own judgement when dealing with them.

Altered states of consciousness

Lucidity Institute
(Lucid dreaming—research, courses, books, products)
2555 Park Blvd, Suite 2
Palo Alto, CA 94306
Tel: 415 321 9969
Fax: 415 321 9967
www.lucidity.com

Monroe Institute
(Training in and research into altered states of consciousness and OOBE)
62 Roberts Mountain Road
Faber, VA 22938–2317
USA
Tel: 804 361 1252
Fax: 804 361 1237
E-mail: *monroeinst@aol.com*
www.monroeinstitute.org/

Animal Welfare

American Anti-Vivisection Society
(Society dedicated to ending experimentation on animals)
801 Old York Road #204
Jenkintown, PA 19046-1685
Tel: 215 887 0816
E-mail: *aavs@aavs.org*
www.aavs.org

American Vegan Society
(Information on all aspects of living without cruelty to animals)
56 Dinshah Lane
PO Box 369
Malaga, NJ 08328
Tel: 856 694 2887
Fax: 856 694 2288
www.americanvegan.org

The American Society for the Prevention of Cruelty to Animals (ASPCA)
424 E. 92nd Street
New York, NY 10128
Tel: 212 876 7700
E-mail: *information@aspca.org*
www.aspca.org

Animal Aid
(Animal-rights charity)
The Old Chapel
Bradford Street
Tonbrideg
Kent TN9 1AW
Tel: 01732 364546
Fax: 01732 366533
E-mail: *info@animalaid.co.uk*
www.animalaid.org.uk

Animal Defenders
(Particularly concerned with animals in circuses and trade in endangered species)
261 Goldhawk Road
London W12 9PE
Tel: 020 8846 9777
Fax: 020 8846 9712
E-mail: *navs@cygnet.co.uk*
www.cygnet.co.uk/navs

Animal Legal Defense Fund
127 Fourth Street
Petaluna, CA 94952-3005
Tel: 707 769 7771
Fax: 707 769 0785
E-mail: *Info@aldf.org*
www.adlf.org

British Anti-Vivisection Association
PO Box 82
Kingswood
Bristol BS15 1YF
Tel/Fax: 0117 909 5048
E-mail: *bava@esmail.net*
www.eurosolve.com/charity/bava

Campaign Against Fraudulent Medical Research
(Anti-vivisection organization)
PO Box 234
Lawson, New South Wales 2783
Australia
Tel: 02 4758 6822
www.pnc.com.au/ ~cafmr

Comapssion in World Farming
Charles House
5A Charles Street
Petersfield
Hampshire GU32 3EH
Tel: 01730 264208/268863
Fax: 01730 260791
E-mail: *compassion@ciwf.co.uk*
www.ciwf.co.uk

Humane Society of the United States
2100 L Street, NW
Washington DC 20037
Tel: 202 452 1100
www.hsus.org

National Anti-Vivisection Society
261 Goldhawk Road
London W12 9PE
Tel: 020 8846 9777
Fax: 020 8846 9712
E-mail: *info@navs.org.uk*
www.navs.org.uk

The Nature of Wellness (SUPRESS)
(Anti-vivisection organization)
PO Box 10400
Glendale, CA 91209-3400
Tel: 818 790 6384
Fax: 818 790 9660
E-mail: *info@animalresearch.org*
www.animalresearch.org

People for the Ethical Treatment of Animals (PETA)
501 Front St.
Norflok, VA 23510
Tel: 757 622 PETA (7832)
Fax: 757 622 0457
E-mail: *info@peta-online.org*
www.peta-online.org

Royal Society for the Prevention of Cruelty to Animals (RSPCA)
(Monitors treatment of animals)
Causeway
Horsham
West Sussex RH12 1HG
Tel: 0870 3335 999
0870 5555 999 (24hour hotline for reporting cruelty)
www.rspca.org.uk

Vegan Society
(Information on all aspects of living without cruelty to animals)
Donald Waston House
7 Battle Road
St Leonards-on-Sea
East Sussex TN37 7AA
Tel: 01424 427393
Fax: 01424 717064
E-mail: *info@vegansociety.com*
www.vegansociety.com

World Society for the Protection of Animals
(Promotes animal welfare and conservation worldwide)
34 Deloss Street
Framingham, MA 01702
Tel: 508 879 8350
Fax: 508 620 0786
E-mail: *wspa@wspausa.com*
www.wspa-international.org

Birth and Death

Active Birth Centre
(Natural childbirth—advice, classes, teachers, products; birthing pool hire)
25 Bickerton Raod
London N19 5JT
Tel: 020 7482 5554
Fax: 020 7267 9683
E-mail: *mail@activebirthcentre.com*
www.activebirthcentre.com

Childbirth.org
(Help for mothers to know what to expect and to make decisions about her birthing process)
www.childbirth.org

Final Passages
PO Box 1721
Sebastopol, CA 95473
Tel: 707 824 0268
E-mail: *Info@finalpassages.org*
www.naturaldeathcare.org

Natural Death Centre
(Help with caring for the dying, bereavement, living wills, green burial, DIY funerals; Handbook £13.50 inc.p.&p. and update sheets)
20 Heber Road
London NW2 6AA
Tel: 020 8208 2853
Fax: 020 8452 6434
E-mail: *rhino@dial.pipex.com*
www.naturaldeath.org.uk

Natural Family Site
(Information on alternative medicine paths available for childbirth)
www.bygpub.com/natural

Communities and Complementary Currencies

Cohousing Network
1504 Franklin Street, Suite 102
Oakland, CA 94612
Tel: 510 844 0790
E-mail: *webmaster@cohousing.org*
www.cohousing.org

Cohousing Communities Foundation
(Advice on setting up schemes; individual and group contacts)
6 Scraptoft Lane
Leicester

UK Cohousing Network
(Details of eight UK Projects)
E-mail: *stuart@cohousing.co.uk*
www.cohousing.co.uk

Ego-Village Network for the UK
(Advice and directory)
PO Box 1410
Bristol BS99 3JP
E-mail: *evnuk@gaia.org*
www.ecovillages.org

Federation of Egalitarian Communities
138 Twin Oaks Road
Lousia, VA 23093
Tel: 540 894 5126
E-mail: *secretary@thefec.org*
www.thefec.org

Fellowship for International Community
(Publishes the directory of communities in North America and other countries)
RR 1 Box 156-W
Rutledge, MO 63563-9720
Tel: 660 883 5545
E-mail: *fic@ic.org*
Fic.ic.org
www.ic.org

Findhorn Foundation
(Famous community offering range of residential courses; ecovillage; open to visitors and new members)
The Park
Findhorn
Forres
Morayshire IV36 3TZ
Tel: 01309 690311
Fax: 01309 691301
E-mail: *reception@findhorn.org*
www.findhorn.org

Global Eco village Network
(Promotion and shared information for ecovillages)
www.gaia.org/services/Profie/The_Americas/

LETS-linkup
(International Traders)
E-mail: *jtaris@nex.net.au*
www.lets-linkup.com/71-USA/htm

LETSLINK UK
(Guidelines and contacts for LETS; links worldwide)
56 Campbell Road
Southsea
Hants PO5 1RW
Tel: 01705 730 639
E-mail: *lets@letslinkuk.org*
www.trendmonitor.com/LETSLINKUK

Complementary Health

Al-Anon Family Group Headquarters, Inc.
1600 Corporate Landing Parkway
Virginia Beach, VA 23454-5617
Tel: 757 563 1600
Fax: 757 563 1655
E-mail: *wso@al-anon.org*
www.al-anon.alateen.org

Al-Anon
(Worldwide organization offering help to the families of alcoholics)
61 Great Dover Street
London SE1 4YF
Tel: 020 7403 0888 (24 hour helpline)
Fax: 020 7378 9910
www.hexnet.co.uk/alanon

Alternative Medicine
1650 Tiburon Boulevard
Tiburon, CA 94920
Tel: 800 515 4325
www.alternativemedicine.com

American Herbalists Guild
(Organization aimed at revitalizing herbal traditions)
1931 Gaddis Road
Canton, GA 30115
Tel: 770 751 6021
Fax: 770 751 7472
E-mail: *ahgoffice@earthlink.net*
www.americanherbalistsguide.com

American Holistic Health Association
(Dedicated to connecting individuals with vital wellness solutions)
PO Box 17400
Anaheim, CA 92817-7400
Tel: 714 779 6152
E-mail: *mail@ahha.org*
www.ahha.org

Animal Reiki Ltd
(Courses, training, healing)
PO Box 1867
Yeovil
Somerset BA22 7YU
Tel: 0709 1214524
E-mail: *animalreikitherapy@x-stream.co.uk*

American Society for the Alexander Technique
PO Box 60008/
Florence, MA 01062
Tel: 800 473 0620 or 413 584 2259
Fax: 413 584 3097
E-mail: *alexandertech@earthlink.net*
www.alexandertech.org

Anthroposophical Society
c/o Park Attwood Clinic
Trimpley, Bewdley
Worcester DY12 1RE
United Kingdom

Association of Light Touch Therapists
(Information and list of practitioners for over thirty healing and bodywork therapies)
6 Combermere Road
St Leonards on Sea
East Sussex TN38 0RR
Tel/Fax: 01424 430001
E-mail: *lighttouch@callnetuk.com*
www.internethealthlibrary.com

Association of Vision Educators
735 Earthship Landing
Bayfield, CO 81122
E-mail: *kate@simwell.com*
www.visioneducators.org

Ayurvedic Company of Great Britain
(Clinic, products, list of practitioners, information on training)
81 Wimpole Street
London W1M 7DB
Tel: 020 7224 6070
Fax: 020 7224 6080
E-mail: *acgb@compuserve.com*
www.ayurvediccompanyofgreatbritain.co.uk

Ayurvedic Institute
(Training, products, books)
11311 Menaul NE
Albuquerque, NM 87112
Tel: 505 291 9698
Fax: 505 294 7572
www.ayurveda.com

Bates Association for Vision Education
(Newsetter, courses, and list of teachers)
PO Box 25
Shoreham-by-Sea
West Sussex BN43 6ZF
United Kingdom
Tel: 01273 422090
Fax: 01273 279983
E-mail: *info@seeing.org*
www.seeing.org

Biomagnetic Therapy Association
(Magnetic Therapy: ethics, medicine, library infromation, books, and advances)
PO Box 394
Lyons, CO 80540
Tel: 303 823 0307
E-mail: *info@biomagnetic.org*

British Association of Homoeopathic Vets
(List of practitioners)
Chinham House
Stamford-in-the-Vale
Farringdon
Oxon SN7 8NQ

British Biomagnetic Association
(Magnet therapy on acupoints)
31 St Marychurch Road
Torquay
Devon TQ1 3JF
Tel: 01803 293346

British Complementary Medicine Association
(Information, training details and lists of practitioners for sixteen lesser-known therapies)
Kensington House
33 Imperial Square
Cheltenham GL50 1QZ
Tel: 01242 519911
Fax: 01242 227765
E-mail: *info@bcma.co.uk*
www@bcma.co.uk

British Homoeopathic Dental Association
(List of practitioners)
2B Frankin Road
Watford
Herts WD1 1QD
Tel: 01923 233336
www.bhda.org

British Society for Mercury Free Dentistry
(Advice on testing and removing fillings)
221 Old Brompton Road
London SW5 0EA

British Wheel of Yoga
(Information on yoga and classes; teacher training)
1 Hamilton Place
Boston Road
Sleaford
Lincs NG34 7ES
Tel: 01529 306851
Fax: 01529 303233
www.members.aol.com/wheelyoga

Canine Health Concern
(Information free of commercial interest about pet food, vaccinations and drugs for dogs and other animals, US link)
PO Box 1
Longnor
Derbyshire SK17 0JD
Tel: 07071 226482
Fax: 01382 320719
www.asr-svcs.diron.co.uk/www chc

Citizens for Health
(National, non-profit grassroots organization protecting health choices and promoting wellness)
E-mail: *citizenshf@healthfreedom.com*
www.healthfreedom.com/

Complementary and Alternative Veterinary Medicine
www.altvetmed.com

Confederation of Healing Organisations
(Sixteen healing associations and worldwide affiliations; details of practitioners and training)
Suite J, Second Floor
The Red and White House
113 High Street
Berkhamsted
Herts HP4 2DJ
Tel: 01441 870660
Fax/answerphone: 01442 870667
E-mail: *Cho.healing@virgin.net*
www.users.globalnet.co.uk/~ sos/cho

Council for Complementary and Alternative Medicine
(Information on major therapies)
63 Jeddo Road
London W12 9HQ
Tel: 020 8735 0632

Empulse
(Electromagnetic therapy; worldwide network of therapists)
Cobbs Yard
St Nicholas Street
Diss, Norfolk IP22 3LB
Tel: 01379 64423
0116 277 2051
www.empulse.com

Healing Arts Network
(Information on Alternative Medicine, Holistic Health, and Shamanic Practice)
www.healingartsnetwork.com

Health World Online
(24-hour health resource center—a virtual health village where you can access information, products, and services to help create your wellness-based lifestyle)
171 Pier Avenue, Suite 160
Santa Monica, CA 90405
E-mail: *info@healthy.net*
www.healthy.net/welcome/index.asp

Holistic Dental Association
(List of practitioners)
Box 5007
Durango, CO 81301
Tel: 970 259 1091
E-mail: *hda@frontier.net*
www.holisticdental.org

Institute for Complementary and Alternative Medicine
(Information on therapies and training; lists of practitioners)
PO Box 194
London SE16 1QZ
Tel: 020 7237 5165
Fax: 020 7237 5175
E-mail: *icm@icmedicine.co.uk*
www.icmedicine.co.uk

Institute for Optimum Nutrition
(Nutritional therapy: list of therapists, training, information)
Blades Court
Deodar Road
London SW15 2NU
Tel: 020 8877 9993
Fax: 020 8877 9980
www.ion.ac.uk

International Association of Reiki Professionals
PO Box 104
Harrisville, NH 03450
Tel: 603 827 3290
Fax: 603 827 3737
E-mail: *Info@iarp.org*
www.iarp.org

International Center for Reiki Training
21421 Hilltop Street, Unit #28
Southfield, MI 48034
Tel: 800 332 8112
Fax: 248 948 9534
E-mail: *center@reiki.org*
www.reiki.org

International Register of Consultant Herbalists and Homoeopaths
(General Council and Register of Consultant Herbalists)
(Training and list practitioners)
32 King Edward Road
Swansea SA1 4LL
Tel/Fax: 01792 655886

Iridologists International
24360 Old Wagon Road
Escondido, CA 92027
Tel: 619 749 2727
Fax: 619 749 1248

Kushi Institute
(Macrobiotics—information, courses, training, and mail order)
PO Box 7
Becket, MA 01223-0007
Tel: 888 547 2663
Fax: 413 623 8827
E-mail: *programs@kushiinstitute.org*
www.kushiinstitute.org

Macrobiotic Association of Great Britain
(Information, events, register of consultants)
99 Yeldham Road
London W6 8JQ
Tel: 020 8741 0279
www.macrobiotic.co.uk

Macrobiotics America
PO Box 1874
Oroville, CA 95965
Tel: 877 622 2637
Fax: 310 388 6019
E-mail: *info@macroamerica.com*
www.macroamerica.com

Meir Schneider School for Self-Healing
(Particularly concerned with eye/vision problems)
1718 Taraval Street
San Francisco, CA 94116
Tel: 415 665 9574
Fax: 415 665 1318
E-mail: *info@self-healing.org*
www.self-healing.org

National Center for Complementary and Alternative Medicine
National Institutes of Health
Bethesda, MD 20892
E-mail: *info@nccam.nih.gov*
Nccam.nih.gov

National Institute of Medical Herbalists
(Training and list of practitioners)
56 Longbrook Street
Exeter
Devon EX4 6AH
Tel: 01392 426022
Fax: 01392 498963
www.btinternet.com/~ nimh

National Vaccination Center
421-E Church Street
Vienna, VA 22180
Tel: 800 909 7468
www.909shot.com

NaturalDoctors.org
(International end-to-end Internet alternative medical healthcare company)
915 Branch Drive
Alpharetta, GA 30004
Tel: 770 777 1299
Fax: 770 740 0099
E-mail: *Info@naturaldoctors.org*
www.naturaldoctors.org

Register of Chinese Herbal Medicine
(Information, training and list of practitioners)
PO Box 400
Wembley
Middlesex HA9 9NZ
Tel: 020 8904 1357
www.rchm.co.uk

Reiki Association
(Information on therapy and training; list of masters)
Cornbrook Bridge House
Cornbrook
Clee Hill
Ludlow
Shropshire SY8 3QQ
Tel/Fax: 01584 891 197
E-mail: *reikiassoc_ admin@compuserve.com*

Reiki Blessings Academy
PO Box 2000
Byron, GA 31008
Tel: 478 825 0877
Fax: 801 705 1802
E-mail: *reikiblessings@msn.com*
www.reikiblessings.homestead.com

Society of Teachers of The Alexander Technique
(List of teachers (therapists), books, videos)
20 London House
266 Fulham Road
London SW10 9EL
E-mail: *enquiries@stat.org.uk*
www.stat.org.uk

Van UK
National Vaccination Information Centre
(Information on all types—childhood, animal and travel)
178 Mansfield Road
Nottingham NG1 3HW
Tel: 0870 444 0894
Fax: 0870 741 8415
E-mail: *enquiries@van.org.uk*
www.van.org.uk

Yoga Finder
(Largest yoga directory on the web)
www.yogafinder.com

Yoga Research Education Center
(Serves reserachers, educators, and practitioners)
2400A Country Center Drive
Santa Rosa, CA 95403
Tel: 707 566 9000
E-mail: *mail@yrec.org*
www.yrec.org

Yoga Site
(Postures, retreat centers, styles, teachers, products, and organizations)
www.yogasite.com

Divination and Channelling

Academy for Psychic Studies
(Officers ongoing programs about the Psychic Arts)
c/o Spiritual Rights Foundation
PO Box 14341
Brekeley, CA 94712
Tel: 800 642 WELL (9355)
E-mail: *Arcana@celestia.com*
www.celestia.com

American Association of Professional Psychics
(Develop standards and certify psychics)
c/o Enchanted Forest
PO Box 7118
Ellicott City, MD 21042
Tel: 410 750 0077
Fax: 410 750 0010
E-mail: *comments@certifiedpsychics.com*
www.certifiedpsychics.com

American Federation of Astrologers, Inc.
(Information and meeting place for astrologers)
6535 S. Rural Road
Tempe, AZ 85283
Tel: 888 301 7630 or 480 838 1751
Fax: 480 838 8293
E-mail: *afa@msn.com*
www.astrologers.com

Association of Professional Astrologers
(Information and list of practitioners)
5 Greenway
Woodford Green
Essex IG8 7RD
Tel: 020 8498 9850
E-mail: *peta@5greenway.freeserve.co.uk*

Association for Research and Enlightenment
(Continues work of Cayce: transcripts, books, newletters, lectures, and study groups)
215 67th Street
Virginia Beach, VA 23451
Tel: 800 333 4499 or 757 428 3588
E-mail: *are@edgarcayce.org*
www.are-cayce.com

British Astrological and Psychic Society
(Information, courses and list of practitioners for wide range of skills)
Robert Denholm House
Bletchingley Road
Nutfield
Surrey RH1 4HW
Tel: 07071 780796
E-mail: *BAPS@tlpplc.com*

College of Psychic Studies
(Wide range of courses and talks; library)
16 Queensberry Place
London SW7 2EB
United Kingdom
Tel: 020 7589 3293
Fax: 020 7589 2824
E-mail: *cpstudies@aol.com*
www.psychic-studies.org.uk

Kepler College of Astrological Arts and Sciences
(Issues BA or MA in Astrological Studies)
4630 200th SW, Suite A-1
Lynnwood, WA 98036
Tel: 425 673 4292
Fax: 425 673 4983
www.keplercollege.org

LuminEssence Productions
(Newsletter, workshops, and tapes by authors of Opening to Channel)
PO Box 19117
Oakland, CA 94619
Tel: 510 482 4560

National Council of Geocosmic Research
(Education and Research)
c/o Terry Lamb
712 Concepcion Avenue
Spring Valley, CA 91977
Tel: 619 303 9236
E-mail: *execsec@geocosmic.org*
www.geocosmic.org

Spritualist Association of Great Britain
(Services, lectures, mediums for private appointments, healing, counselling and psychic development classes)
33 Belgrave Square
London SW1X 8QB
Tel: 020 7235 3351
Fax: 020 7245 9706

Universal Spiritualist Association
(Organization of believers and practitioners of the religion of Spiritualism)
4905 West University Avenue
Muncie, In 47304-3460
Tel: 765 286 0601
www.spiritualism.org

Earth Mysteries, Paranormal

American Society for Psychical Research
(supports scientific investigation of unexplained phenomena)
5 West 73rd Street
New York, NY 10023
Tel: 212 799 5050
Fax: 212 496 2497
www.aspr.com

American Society of Dowsers
PO Box 24
Danville, VT 05828
Tel: 800 711 9530
E-mail: *asd@downsers.org*
www.dowsers.org

Association for the Scientific Study of Anomalous Phenomena (ASSAP)
(Advice on researching all paranormal phenomena; local groups, talks, magazine and postal library)
20 Paul Street
Frome
Somerset BA11 1DX
Tel: 01373 451777
Fax: 01373 452888
www.assap.org

Balance of Logic and Science in the UFO Debate
E-mail: *Admin@ufoskeptic.org*
www.ufoskeptic.org

British Society of Dowsers
(Register of practising dowsers; local groups offering lectures and courses)
The British Society of Dowsers
Sycamore Barn
Hastingleigh
Ashford
Kent TN25 5HW
Tel/Fax: 01233 750253
E-mail: *bsd@dowsers.demon.co.uk*
www.dowsers.demon.co.uk

British UFO Research Organisation (BUFORA)
(Research, journal, lectures, library, help for abductees)
70 High Street
Wingham
Canterbury
Kent CT3 1BJ
Tel: 0891 121886
www.bufora.org.uk

Centre for Crop Circle Studies
12 Tintagel Close
Exeter EX4 9EH
Tel: 01392 677462
E-mail: *su2261@eclipse.co.uk*

Crop Circle Research
(Resource Center for the latest findings)
E-mail: *pvigay@cropcircleresearch.com*
www.cropcircleresearch.com

CSICOP—Committee for Scientfic Investigation of Claims of the Paranormal
(Encourages the critical investigation of paranormal and fringe science claims from a scientific viewpoint)
Box 703
Amherst, NY 14226
Tel: 716 636 1425
E-mail: *info@csicop.org*
www.csicop.org

NASA
Headquarters
Washington, DC 20546
E-mail: *Comments@nasa.gov*

National Institute for Discovery Science
4975 S. Polaris Ave
Las Vegas, NV 89118-1629
Tel: 702 798 1700
Fax: 702 798 1970
E-mail: *nids@anv.net*
www.nidsci.org

National UFO Reporting Center
PO Box 45623
University Station
Seattle, WA 98145
Tel: 206 722 3000
E-mail: *webmaster@ufocenter.com*
www.ufocenter.com

Research into Lost Knowledge Organisation (RILKO)
(Journal, lectures, library, mail-order books)
8 The Drive
New Southgate
London N11 2DY
www.members.aol.com/rilko

Skywatch International
(Non-profit UFO researching)
PO Box 4243
Lancaster, CA 93539-4243
www.dreaman.org/usufoircl.html

UFO Seek
(Paranormal and UFO Search Engine)
E-mail: *ufoseek@ufoseek.com*
www.ufoseek.com

United States UFO Information and Research Center
Post Office Box 153
Unicoi, TN 37692
Tel: 423 735 0848
E-mail: *usufocenter@usufocenter.com*

World UFO News
www.aufosg.org/page6.html

Eastern Spirituality

Buddha Net
(Buddhist information & education network)
Buddha Dharma Education Association Inc.
E-mail: *support@buddhanet.net*
www.buddhanet.net

Dechen
(Tibetan Buddhism; centres throughout UK)
Tel: 020 7281 5340
www.dechen.org

Friends of the Western Buddhist Order
(Information, classes and retreats throughout UK and rest of world; mail order books)
Padmaloka Retreat Centre
Lesingham House
Surlingham
Norwich NR14 7AL
Tel: 01508 538112/0121 449 8272 (liaison office)
E-mail: *info@lbc.org.uk (London centre)*
www.fwbo.org

Healing Tao Centre
(Tai, chi, chi kung, shiatsu and tao/tantra, taught in London and occasionally elsewhere)
188 Old Street
London EC1V 9BP
Tel: 0700 078 1195
E-mail: *enquiries@healing-tao.co.uk*
www.healing-tao.co.uk

Healing Tao USA
PO Box 24
Lodi, NJ 07644-0024
Tel: 888 999 0555 or 973 777 4442
Fax: 973 777 3753
E-mail: *support@healingtao.com*
www.healingtaousa.com

Hindu Net
www.hindunet.org

Kreative World
Attn: SkyDancing Tantra
732 Montecillo Road
San Rafael, CA 94903
Tel: 415 789 8339
E-mail: *register@skydancingtantra.com*
www.skydancing.com

Ramakrishna Vedanta Society
(Lectures, classes and books on Hinduism; worldwide links)
Unity House
Blind Lane
Bourne End
Bucks SL8 5LG
Tel: 0162 8526464
Fax: 0162 8532437
E-mail: *vedantauk@talk21.com*
www.vedanta.org

SkyDancing
(Tantra for healing/holistic sexuality—teachers, seminars and videos)
47 Maple Road
Horfield
Bristol BS7 8RE
Tel/fax: 0117 983 0958
E-mail: *skydancing@cableinet.co.uk*

Sufi Movement International of the USA
Tel: 510 594 1729
Fax: 510 655 9032
E-mail: *smiusa@earthlink.net*
www.sufimovement.net

Sufi Order (UK)
(Classes, courses and retreats; mail order books)
Beauchamp Lodge
2 Warwick Crescent
London W2 6NE
Tel: 020 7266 3099

Sufi Order International
North American Secretariat
PO Box 30065
Seattle, WA 98103
Tel: 206 525 6992
Fax: 206 525 7013
E-mail: *sufiorderintl@cs.com*
www.sufiorder.org

Tantra.com
Tel: 707 823 3063
E-mail: *staff@tantra.com*
www.tantra.com

A Tribute to Hinduism
E-mail: *Info@atributetohinduism.com*
www.atributetohinduism.com

Universal Tao Center
E-mail: *universaltao@universaltao.com*
www.universalttao.com

Environment

Biodynamic Farming and Gardening Association, Inc.
(Information, regional groups, products, planting calender)
Building 1002B, Thoreau Center, The Presidio
PO Box 29135
San Francisco, CA 94129-0135 USA
Tel: 888 516 7797
Fax: 415 561 7796

Campaign for Environmentally Responsible Tourism
(Details of tour operators; research programmes)
1 Hydeway
Thundersley
Essex SS7 3BE
Tel: 01268 795772
Fax: 01268 759834
E-mail: *info@c-e-r-t.org*
www.c-e-r-t.org

Campaign for Food Safety
(Global clearing house for information on GE)
Highway 61
Little Marias, MN 55164
Tel: 218 226 4164
Fax: 218 226 4157
E-mail: *alliance@mr.net*
www.purefood.org/index.htm

Centre for Alternative Technology
(Sustainable Living—infromation, exhibitions, courses, consultancy, and mail order)
Machynlleth
Powys SY20 9AZ
United Kingdom
Tel: 01654 705981
Fax: 01654 703 605

EcoMall
(Earth's Largest Environmental Shopping Center)
www.ecomall.com

EcoWorld Nature & Technology
4526 Kenneth Avenue
Fair Oaks, CA 95628
Tel: 916 961 6770
E-mail: *contact@ecoworld.com*
www.ecoworld.org

Friends of the Earth
(Information on major issues including ethical investment, GE; local groups)
26–28 Underwood Street
London N1 7JQ
Tel: 020 7490 1555
Fax: 020 7490 0881
E-mail: *info@foe.co.uk*
www.foe.co.uk

Friends of the Earth International
(Network of environmental organizations in sixty-one countries)
www.foei.org

Green Globe 21
(Info on sustainable travel for businesspeople and holidaymakers)
www.greenglobe21.com

Greenpeace USA
702 H Street NW, Suite 300
Washington, DC 20001
Tel: 202 462 1177
Fax: 202 462 4507
E-mail: *greenpeace.usa@wdc.greenpeace.org*
www.greenpeace.org

Hemptech
(Information on growing and marketing hemp; mail order books; international directory of companies selling hemp products, seed, and equipment)
PO Box 1716
Sebastopol, CA 97473
Tel: 707 823 2800
Fax: 707 823 2424

The International Ecotourism Society
PO Box 668
Burlington, VT 05402
Tel: 802 651 9818
Fax: 802 651 9819
E-mail: *Ecomail@ecotourism.org*
www.ecotourism.org

International Permaculture Institute
PO Box 1
Tyalgum
NSW 2484
Australia
Tel: 066 793 442
E-mail: *perminst@peg.apc.org*

Occidental Arts & Ecology Center
15290 Coleman Valley Road
Occidental, CA 95465
Tel: 707 874 1557
Fax: 707 874 1558
E-mail: *inquiry@oaec.org*
www.oaec.org

Organic Consumers Association
6101 Cliff Estates Road
Little Marais, MN 55614
Tel: 218 226 4164
Fax: 218 226 4157
www.organicconsumers.org

Permaculture Association
BCM Permaculture Association
London WC1N 3XX
Tel: 07041 390170
E-mail: *office@permaculture.org.uk*
www.permaculture.org.uk

Permaculture Institute of Northern CA
PO Box 341
Point Reeves Station, CA 94956
Tel: 415 663 9090
E-mail: *info@permacultureinstitute.com*
www.permacultureinstitute.com

Picoturbine
(Renewable energy education)
146 Henderson Road
Stockholm, NJ 07460
Fax: 973 208 2478
E-mail: *comments@picoturbine.com*
www.picoturbine.com

Soil Association
(Information on organic food and farming)
Bristol House
40–56 Victoria Street
Bristol BS1 6BY
Tel: 0117 929 0661
Fax: 0117 925 2504
E-mail: *info@soilassociation.org*
www.soilassociation.org

Women's Environmental Network
87 Worship Street
London EC2A 2BE
Tel: 020 7247 3327
Fax: 020 7247 4740
E-mail: *testtube@gn.apc.org*
www.gn.apc.org/wen

Ethical Consumerism and Investment

The Ethical Investor
(Ethical Investment News & Information)
Netherlands
www.theethicalinvestor.com

Paganism, Shamanism, and Native Spirituality

Ár nDraíocht Féin (ADF)
PO Box 17874
Tucson, AZ 85731-7874
E-mail: *ADF-Office@ADF.ORG*
www.adf.org

Bear Tribe
(Native American books, teaching, and gatherings)
PMB 223
3750-A Airport Blvd
Mobile, AL 36608-1618
Tel: 334 663 0499
www.ewebtribe.com

British Druid Order
(Events, workshops, talks, magazine, mail order books)
PO Box 29
St Leonards-on-Sea
East Sussex TN37 7YP
E-mail: *office@druidorder.demon.co.uk*
www.druidorder.demon.co.uk

Carlos Castaneda's Magical Passes
c/o Cleargreen, Incorporated
10812A Washington Blvd.
Culver City, CA 90232
Tel: 310 839 7150
Fax: 310 839 7155
www.castaneda.org

Church of All Worlds
(The first Pagan Church founded in the United States)
E-mail: *office@caw.org*
ww.caw.org

Covenant of the Goddess
(International organization of cooperating, autonomous Wiccan congregations and solo practitioners)
537 Jones Street #2887
San Francisco, CA 94102
E-mail: *info@cog.org*
www.cog.org

Eagle's Wing Centre for Contemporary Shamanism
(Shamanistic healing and courses)
58 Westbere Road
London NW2 3RU
Tel/Fax: 020 7435 8174
E-mail: *eagleswing@shamanism.co.uk*
www.shamanism.co.uk

Fellowship of Isis
(Worldwide goddess-worshipping network)
Clonegal Castle
Enniscorthy, Eire
Republic of Ireland
www.fellowshipofisis.com

Foundation for Shamanic Studies
(Founded by Michael Harner; courses worldwide, information, and products)
PO Box 1939
Mill Valley, CA 94942
Tel: 415 380 8282
E-mail: *info@shamanicstudies.com*
www. shamanism.org

The Four Winds Society (Alberto Villoldo)
PO Box 680675
Park City, UT 84068-0675
Phone 888 437 4077 or 435 647 5988
Fax: 435 647 5905
E-mail: *fourwinds@thefourwinds.com*
www.thefourwinds.com

Gwyddonic Order
E-mail: *Gwyddoniad@gwyddoniad.org*
www.gwyddoniad.org

The Henge of Keltria
(Neo-Pagan Druidism)
PO Box 48369
Minneapolis, MN 55448
E-mail: *Henge-office@keltria.org*
www.keltria.org

Institute for Contemporary Shamanic Studies
238 Davenport Road
Box 393
Toronto, Ontario M5R 1J6
Canada
Tel: 416 603 4912
Fax: 416 603 4913
E-mail: *jump@icss.org*
www.icss.org

Issac Bonewits's Homepage
(one of the leaders of the Neo-Pagan movement)
E-mail: *ibonewits@neopagan.net*
www.neopagan.net

Odinshof
(Northern tradition: hearths, newsletter and charity for buying woodland; one-third women
BCM Tercel
London WC1N 3XX
www.gippeswic.demon.co.uk/odinshof.html

Order of Bards, Ovates, and Druids
(Full training by post)
PO Box 1333
Lewes
East Sussex BN7 3ZG
United Kingdom
www.druidry.org

Pagan Educational Network
(Dedicated to educating the public about Paganism and building community)
PO Box 586
Portage, IN 46368
E-mail: *info@PaganEdNet.org*
www.PaganEdNet.org

Pagan Federation
(Information on all types including wicca/witchcraft, druidry, Northern tradition, shamanism, goddess worship and men's traditions; contacts, conferences, magazine)
BM Box 7097
London WC1N 3XX
E-mail: *Secretary@paganfed.demon.co.uk*
E-mail (USA): *Mthorn@aol.com*
www.paganfed.demon.co.uk

Pagan Federation
(Range of information including Wicca/Witchcraft, Druidry, Northern tradition, Shamanism, Goddess worship, and men's tradition, contacts, conferences, and magazines)
E-mail: *paganfedus@aol.com*
members.aol.com/paganfedus

A Pagan Nation
www.pagannation.com

Pagan Pride Project
(Fosters pride in Pagan identity through education, activism, charity, and community)
E-mail: *webmaster@paganpride.org*
www.paganpride.org

Sacred Trust
(Courses in various parts of UK; mail order)
PO Box 16
Uckfield
East Sussex TN22 5WD
Tel: 01825 840574
Fax: 01825 841153
E-maill: *mail@sacredtrust.org*
www.sacredtrust.org

Shamanic Circles
(Dedicated to fostering global Shamanic community)
E-maill: *swanwoman@kconline.com*
www.shamaniccircles.org

The Wiccan Pagan Times
(Officers feature articles, recipes, events, and coven life information)
E-mail: *boudica@twpt.com*
www.twpt.com

Witch's League for Public Awareness
PO Box 909
Rehoboth, MA 02769
E-mail: *Hernesson@aol.com*
www.celticcrow.com

The Witches Voice, Inc.
(Neo-Pagan news & Networking)
PO Box 4924
Clearwater, FL 33758-4924
www.witchvox.com

Psychotherapy

The American Council of Hypnotist Examiners
Tel: 800 894 9766

American Counseling Association
(Layperson's guide to counselor ethics, help in finding a counselor, coping with crisis)
5999 Stevenson Ave.
Alexandria, VA 22304
Tel: 800 347 6647
Fax: 800 473 2329
E-mail: *webmaster@counseling.org*
www.counseling.org/consumers/consumers.htm

American Group Psychotherapy Association
(Information about group therapy and the benefits of it for different troubles)
25 East 2st Street, 6th Floor
New York, NY 10010
Tel: 877 668 2472 or 212 477 2677
Fax: 212 979 6627
E-mail: *info@agpa.org*
www.groupsinc.org/group/consumersguide2000.html

Association for Neuro-Linguistic Programming (ANLP)
PO Box 10
Porthmadog LL48 6ZB
Tel: 0870 870 4970
Fax: 0870 444 0790
E-mail: *admin@anlp.org*
www.anlp.org

British Academy of Graphology
(Training and reserach)
11 Roundacre
London SW19 6DB
Tel: 020 8778 3289
Fax: 020 8778 4729
www.graphology.co.uk

British Association for Counselling
(List of practitioners, training)
1 Regent Place
Rugby
Warwickshire CV21 2PJ
Tel: 0178 550899
Fax: 01788 562189
E-mail: *bac@bac.co.uk*
www.bac.co.uk

British Hypnotherapy Association
(Information and list of practitioners)
14 Crown Street
Chorley
Lancashire PR7 1DX
www.zednet.co.uk/bhahypnotherapy

UK Council for Psychotherapy
(List of practitioners, training)
167–169 Great Portland Street
London W1N 5FB
Tel: 020 7436 3002
Fax: 020 7436 3013
E-mail: *ukcp@psychotherapy.org.uk*
www.psychotherapy.org.uk

College of Past Life Regression Studies
(Courses and therapists)
42 Borden Avenue
Enfield
Middlesex EN1 2BY
Tel: 018 372 3124
E-mail: *helen.wozniak@btclick.com*
www.glassmandala.co.uk

Handwriting Research Corporation
(History, uses of, services)
4445 North 24th Street
Phoenix, Arizona 85016-5518
Tel: 602 957 8870
Fax: 602 957 8656
E-mail: *info@handwriting.com*
www.handwriting.com

Hypnotherapy Training Institute
4730 Alta Vista Avenue
Santa Rosa, CA 95404
Tel: 800 256 6448 or 707 579 9023
Fax: 707 578 1033
E-mail: *info@hypnoschool.com*
www.sonic.net/hypno/

Institute of Integral Handwriting Studies
228 Commercial Street, #268
Nevada City, CA 95959-2507
Tel: 530 470 0991
E-mail: *teachers@vimalarodgers.co*
www.iihs.com

International Association for Regression Research
(Dedicated to increasing the acceptance and use of professional and responsible past-life therapy through education, association, and research)
PO Box 20151,
Riverside, CA 92516
Tel: 909 784 1570
Fax: 909 784 8440
E-mail: *info@iarrt.org*
www.aprt.org

International Association of Hypno-Analysts
PO Box 417
Hills Road
Cambridge CB2 1WE
United Kingdom
Tel: +44 1763 261181
Fax: +44 1763 260214
E-mail: *training@theiah.com*
www.hypno-analysis.com

International Association of Past Life Therapies
PMB #356
19744 Beach Blvd.
Huntington Beach, CA 92648
Tel: 714 536 1935
Fax: 714 960 1343
www.pastlives.net

International Graphoanalysis Society
111 N. Canal St., Suite 955
Chicago, IL 60606
Tel: 312 930 9446
Fax: 312 930 5903
E-mail: *headquarters@igas.com*
www.igas.com

Western Spirituality

Aetherius Society
(Group dedicated to working with higher beings from outer space)
6206 Afton Place
Los Angeles, CA 90028
Tel: 800 800 1354
E-mail: *info@aetherius.org*

Anthroposophical Society in America
(Association of people who would foster the life of the soul, both in the individual and in human society, on the basis of a true knowledge of the spiritual world)
1923 Geddes Ave
Ann Arbor, MI 48104-1797
Tel: 734 662 9355
Fax: 734 662 1727
E-mail: *information@anthroposophy.org*
www.anthroposophy.org

Authentic Hermetic Order of the Golden Dawn
(Initiatic and magical order which were founded by high-ranking Freemasons)
E-mail:
hermeticorder@golden-dawn.com.test.levoline.com
www.golden-dawn.com

Builders of the Adytum
(Teaching in cabbala and tarot)
5010-05 N Figueroa St
Los Angles
CA 90042, USA
www.bota.org

Hermetic Order of the Golden Dawn
(Continued preservations of that body of knowledge known as Hermeticism)
PO Box 1757
Elfers, FL 34680
E-mail: *hogdmail@netscape.net*
www.hermeticgoldendawn.org/index.shtml

Lectorium Rosicrucianum
(Worldwide temples and teachings)
PO Box 95241
Seattle, WA 98145-2421
Tel: 206 932 7093
E-mail: *info@lectoriumrosicrucianum.org*
www.lectoriumrosicrucianum.org

Order of the Thelemic Golden Dawn
(Magical/religious/scientific order dedicated to the teachings of Aleister Crowley)
E-mail: *info@thelemicgoldendawn.org*
www.thelemicgoldendawn.org

Rosicrucian Order, AMORC
(Courses in one hundred countries)
1342 Naglee Avenue
San Jose, CA 95191
Tel: 408 947 3600
Fax: 408 947 3677

Dept INTUI
PO Box 35
Crowborough
East Sussex TN6 1ZX
Tel: 01892 653197
Fax: 01892 667432

Dept ZIN
PO Box 1087
Burwood North
NSW 2134, Australia
E-mail: *amorc@ozemail.com.au*

Theosophical Society in America
(Talks, courses, library, branches world wide)
PO Box 270
Wheaton, IL 60189-0270
Tel: 630 668 1571
Fax: 630 668 4976
E-mail: *olcott@theosmail.net*
www.theosophical.org

Society of the Inner Light
(Correspondence teaching, especially cabbala and Arthurian)
38 Steele's Road
London NW3 4RG
E-mail: *sil@innerlight.org.uk*
www.innerlight.org.uk

Supplies

Azuregreen
(Supplies for Your Occult, Metaphysical, and Witchcraft Needs)
PO Box 48-WEB
Middlefield, MA 01243-0048
Tel: 413 623 2155
Fax: 413 623 2156
www.azuregreen.net

Capricorn's Lair
(Wicca Pagan Gothic Metaphysical Superstore)
2446 & 2450 Washington Blvd.
Ogden, Utah 84401
E-mail: *coinutah@aol.com*
www.capricornslair.com

Hamilton Supplies
PO Box 1258 I
Moorpark, CA 93021
Tel: 805 529 5900
Fax: 805 529 2934

Original Publications
(African Spirituality, Occult books and supplies)
22 East Mall
Plainview, NY 11803
Tel: 888 622 8581
Fax: 516 454 6829
E-mail: *OriginalPub@aol.com*

Triple Moon Witchware
(Complete source for everything magical)
15 Powder House Circle
Needham, MA 02492
Tel: 781 453 0363
Fax: 781 449 4963
E-mail: *info@witchware.com*
www.triplemoon.com

Bibliography

Akhtar, Miriam and Steve Humphries. *Far Out: The Dawning of New Age Britain*. Sansom & Co./Channel Four Television, 1999.

Albery, Nicholas, Gil Elliot, and Joseph Elliot (eds). *The New Natural Death Handbook*. London: Rider, 1997.

Allen, J.M. *Atlantis, The Andes Solution*. Gloucestershire, England: Windrush, 1998.

Alper, Frank. *An Evening with Christos*. Phoenix, Ariz.: Arizona Metaphysical Society, 1979.

Anderson, Luke. *Genetic Engineering, Food, and Our Environment*. Totnes, England: Green Books, 1999.

Andrews, Lynn V. *Medicine Woman*. London: Penguin Arkana, 1989 (first pub. USA, 1981).

——. *Flight of the Seventh Moon*. San Francisco: Harper & Row, 1984.

——. *Jaguar Woman*. San Francisco: Harper & Row, 1985.

——. *Star Woman*. New York: Warner Books, 1986.

——. *Crystal Woman*. New York: Warner Books, 1987.

Angelo, Jack. *Spiritual Healing, Energy Medicine for Today*. Rockport, Mass.: Element, 1991.

Bailey, Alice. *The Reappearance of Christ*. New York: Lucis Publishing, 1969.

——. *Seventh Ray: Revealer of the New Age*. New York: Lucis Publishing, 1996.

Bates, William H. *Better Eyesight Without Glasses*. London: Thorsons, 2000 (first pub. 1919).

Berlitz, Charles. *The Mystery of Atlantis*. London: Souvenir Press, 1976 (first pub. USA, 1969).

Berry, Ruth. *Working with Dreams*. How To Books, 1999.

Besant, Annie. *The Ancient Wisdom*. Wheaton, Ill.: Theosophical Publishing House, 1928 (first pub. 1897).

——. *Esoteric Christianity*. Wheaton, Ill.: Theosophical Publishing House, 1901.

Black Elk, ed. John G. Neihardt. *Black Elk Speaks*. London: Abacus, 1974 (first pub. USA, 1932).

Blavatsky, H.P. *Collected Writings*. Wheaton, Ill.: Theosophical Publishing House, 1950–85 (*Isis Unveiled*, first pub. USA, 1877; *The Secret Doctrine*, first pub. 1888; *The Key to Theosophy*, first pub. 1889).

Bohm, David. *Wholeness and the Implicate Order*. London: Routledge & Kegan Paul, 1983.

Bord, Janet. *Fairies: Real Encounters with Little People*. London: Michael O'Mara, 1997.

Bord, Janet and Colin Bord. *Mysterious Britain*. London: Paladin, 1974 (first pub. 1972).

Bradley, Marion. *The Mists of Avalon*. London: Michael Joseph, 1983 (first pub. USA, 1982).

Brennan, Herbie. *The Atlantis Enigma*. London: Piatkus, 1999.

Brennan, J.H. *The Astral Projection Workbook*. Northamptonshire, England: Aquarian, 1989.

Bunker, S. et al (ed.). *Diggers & Dreamers, 2000–01 Ed*. London: Diggers & Dreamers Publications, 1999.

Capra, Fritjof. *The Tao of Physics*. London: HarperCollins, 1992 (first pub. 1975).

Castaneda, Carlos. *The Teachings of Don Juan*. London: Penguin Arkana, 1990 (first pub. USA, 1968).

——. *A Separate Reality*. London: Penguin Arkana, 1990 (first pub. USA, 1971).

——. *Journey to Ixtlan*. London: Penguin Arkana, 1990 (first pub. USA, 1972).

——. *Tales of Power*. London: Penguin Arkana, 1990 (first pub. USA, 1974).

——. *The Second Ring of Power*. London: Penguin Arkana, 1990 (first pub. USA, 1977).

——. *The Eagle's Gift*. London: Penguin Arkana, 1992 (first pub. USA, 1981).

——. *The Fire from Within*. New York: Touchstone Books, 1998 (first pub. USA, 1984).

——. *The Power of Silence*. New York: Simon & Schuster, 1987.

——. *The Art of Dreaming*. Northamptonshire, England: Aquarian, 1994 (first pub. USA, 1993).

——. *Magical Passes*. London: Thorsons, 1998.

——. *The Wheel of Time*. London: Allen Lane The Penguin Press, 1998 (first pub. USA, 1998).

——. *The Active Side of Infinity*. London: Thorsons, 1999.

Cayce, Edgar. *Atlantis: Fact or Fiction?* Virginia Beach, Va.: ARE Press, 1962.

——. *Edgar Cayce on Atlantis*. New York: Paperback Library, 1968.

Chamberlain, Lindy. *Through My Eyes*. Portsmouth, N.H.: Heinemann, 1991 (first pub. Australia, 1990).

Chatwin, Bruce. *The Songlines*. London: Pan, 1988 (first pub. 1987).

Cheiro. *Cheiro's Language of the Hand: The Classic of Palmistry*. New York: Simon & Schuster, 1987 (first pub. USA, 1897).

Chernak McElroy, Susan. *Animals as Teachers and Healers*. London: Rider, 1997 (first pub. USA, 1996).

Childress, David Hatcher. *Lost Cities of Ancient Lemuria & the Pacific*. Stelle, Ill.: Adventures Unlimited Publishing, 1999.

Chopra, Deepak. *Ageless Body, Timeless Mind*. London: Rider, 1998 (first pub. 1993).

Chuang Tzu, edited by Martin Palmer and Man-Ho Kwok. *Chuang Tzu*. London: Penguin Arkana, 1996.

Churchward, James. *The Lost Continent of Mu*. London: Spearman, 1959 (first pub. USA, 1926).

Collins, Doris. *The Power Within*. London: Grafton, 1986.

Cowan, James G. *The Elements of the Aborigine Tradition*. Rockport, Mass.: Element, 1992.

Cremo, Michael A. and Richard L. Thompson. *Forbidden Archeology: The Hidden History of the Human Race*. San Diego, Calif.: Bhaktivedanta Institute, 1993.

Croce, Pietro. *Vivisection or Science: A Choice to Make*. Zurich, Switzerland: CIVIS, 1991.

Crowley, Aleister. *Moonchild*. York Beach, Maine: Samuel Weiser, 1970 (first pub. 1917).

——. *Diary of a Drug Fiend*. London: Sphere, 1972 (first pub. 1922).

——. *Magick in Theory and Practice*. Thame, England: IHO Books, 1999 (first pub. 1929).

——. *The Book of Thoth*. New York: Weiser, 1981 (first pub. 1944).

De Leon, Moses, translated by H. Sperling and M. Simon. *The Zohar*. Soncine Press, 1970.

Devereux, Paul. *Shamanism and the Mystery Lines*. London: Quantum, 1992.

Devereux, Paul and Nigel Pennick. *Lines on the Landscape: Leys and Other Linear Enigmas*. London: Robert Hale, 1989.

Donnelly, Ignatius. *Atlantis: The Antediluvian World*. New York: Dover, 1977 (first pub. USA, 1882).

Douthwaite, Richard. *The Ecology of Money*. Totnes, England: Green Books, 1999.

Edwards, Gill. *Stepping Into The Magic*. London: Piatkus, 1993.

Eisler, Riane. *The Chalice and the Blade*. London: Thorsons 1998 (first pub. USA, 1987).

Fadali, Moneim A. *Animal Experimentation: A Harvest of Shame*. Los Angeles, Calif.: Hidden Springs Press, 1996.

Farrar, Janet and Stewart. *The Witches' Way*. London: Hale, 1990.

Farrar, Stewart. *What Witches Do*. London: Hale, 1971.

Flem-Ath, Rose and Rand. *When the Sky Fell—In Search of Atlantis*. Orion, 1996.

Fludd, Robert. *Apologia*. Basson, 1616.

Forbes, Foster. *The Unchronicled Past*. London: Simpkin Marshall, 1938.

Fordham, Frieda. *An Introduction to Jung's Psychology*. New York: Viking Penguin, 1953.

Fortune, Dion. *The Mystical Qabalah*. York Beach, Maine: Samuel Weiser, 1997 (first pub. 1936).

——. *The Cosmic Doctrine*. London: SIL Trading, 1995 (first pub. 1924).

——. *Avalon of the Heart*. Northamptonshire, England: Aquarian, 1971 (first pub. 1934).

——. *The Goat Foot God*. Golden Gates, 1992 (first pub. 1936).

Freke, Tim and Peter Gandy. *The Jesus Mysteries*. London: Thorsons, 1999.

Gardner, Edward L. *Fairies: A Book of Real Fairies*. Wheaton, Ill.: Theosophical Publishing House, 1945.

Gardner, Gerald B. *Witchcraft Today*. Thame, England: IHO Books, 1999 (first pub. 1954).

——. *The Meaning of Witchcraft*. York Beach, Maine: Samuel Weiser, 1975 (first pub. 1959).

Gardner, Laurence. *Bloodline of the Holy Grail*. Rockport, Mass.: Element, 1996.

Gauquelin, Françoise. *Psychology of the Planets*. New York: Astro Computing Services, 1982.

Gauquelin, Michel. *Cosmic Influences on Human Behavior*. Santa Fe, N. Mex.: Aurora, 1986.

Gawain, Shakti. *Creative Visualization*. Novato, Calif.: New World Library, 1995 (first pub. USA, 1979).

Graff, Dale E. *Tracks in the Psychic Wilderness*. Rockport, Mass.: Element, 1998.

Graves, Tom. *Needles of Stone*. London: Turnstone, 1978.

Gyatso, Geshe Kelsang. *Introduction to Buddhism*. London: Tharpa, 1993 (first pub. 1992).

Harner, Michael. *Hallucinogens and Shamanism*. New York: Oxford University Press, 1973.

——. *The Way of the Shaman*. San Francisco: Harper & Row, 1980.

Hausdorf, Hartwig, translated by Evamarie Mathaey and Walraut Smith. *The Chinese Roswell*. Boca Raton, Fla.: New Paradigm Books, 1998.

Hawkins, Gerald S. *Stonehenge Decoded*. London: Souvenir Press, 1966.

Hay, Louise L. *You Can Heal Your Life*. New York.: Eden Grove Editions, 1988 (first pub. USA, 1984).

Hiby, Lydia with Bonnie S. Weintraub. *Conversations with Animals*. Troutdale, Oreg.: New Sage Press, 1998.

Hodson, Geoffrey. *Fairies at Work and at Play*. Leominster, Mass.: Quest, 1982 (first pub. USA, 1925).

Hopcke, Robert H. *There are No Accidents: Synchronicity and the Stories of Our Lives*. New York: Macmillan, 1997 (first pub. USA, 1997).

Hughes, Robert. *The Fatal Shore*. London: Pan, 1988 (first pub. 1987).

Jacobson, Howard. *In the Land of Oz*. London: Penguin, 1988 (first pub. 1987).

Johnson, Robert A. *Owning Your Own Shadow*. New York: HarperCollins, 1991.

Khan, Hazrat Inayat. *The Music of Life*. Santa Fe, N. Mex.: Omega Press, 1983.

Kitzinger, Sheila. *Homebirth, and Other Alternatives to Hospital*. New York: Dorling Kindersley, 1991.

Klaper, M. *Pregnancy, Children and the Vegan Diet*. Umatilla, Fla.: Gentle World Inc., 1987.

Krishnamurti, Jiddu, edited by Mary Lutyens. *The Penguin Krishnamurti Reader*. New York: Penguin, 1970.

Kübler-Ross, Elisabeth. *On Death and Dying*. London: Routledge, 1989 (first pub. USA, 1969).

Kushi, Aveline. *Aveline Kushi's Complete Guide to Macrobiotic Cooking*. New York: Warner, 1985.

Kushi, Michio. *The Book of Macrobiotics*. Tokyo: Japan Publications, 1977.

LaBerge, Stephen. *Lucid Dreaming*. New York: Ballantine Books, 1985.

Langley, Gill. *Vegan Nutrition: a survey of research*. London: Vegan Society, 1988.

Lao Tzu, translated and edited by Gia-fu Feng and Jane English. *Tao Te Ching*. London: Wildwood House, 1973.

——, translated by D.C. Lau. *Tao Te Ching*. London: Penguin, 1963.

Leboyer, Frederick. *Birth without Violence*. Glasgow, Scotland: Fontana, 1977 (first pub. France, 1974).

Lemesurier, Peter. *The Great Pyramid Decoded*. Rockport, Mass.: Element, 1993 (first pub. 1977).

Liberman, Jacob. *Take Off Your Glasses and See*. New York: Crown, 1995.

Lovelock, J.E. *Gaia: A new look at life on earth*. Oxford, England: Oxford University Press, 1979.

Mack, John E. *Abduction: Human Encounters With Aliens*. New York: Simon & Schuster, 1994.

Malory, Sir Thomas, edited by Janet Cowen. *Le Morte D'Arthur*. New York: Penguin, 1986 (first pub. 1485).

Malory, Sir Thomas (abridged Michael Senior). *Sir Thomas Malory's Tales of King Arthur*. London: Collins, 1980.

McMoneagle, Joseph W. *Mind Trek*. Charlottesville, Va.: Hampton Roads, 1997 (first pub. 1993).

Meera, Mother. *Answers*. London: Rider, 1991 (first pub. USA, 1991).

Melody. *Love is in the Earth*. Wheat Ridge, Colo.: Earth-Love Publishing House, 1995 (first pub. USA, 1991).

Michell, John. *The View over Atlantis*. London: Abacus, 1975 (first pub. 1969).

——. *The New View over Atlantis*. London: Thames and Hudson, 1983.

Mollison, Bill and Reny Mia Slay. *Introduction to Permaculture*. Tyalgum, Australia: Tagari Publishers, 1991.

Monmouth, Geoffrey of, translated by Lewis Thorpe. *The History of the Kings of Britain*. London: Peguin, 1966 (first pub. *c.* 1136).

Monroe, Robert. *Journeys Out of the Body*. New York: Doubleday, 1971.

Moody, Raymond. *Life after Life*. New York: Bantam, 1975.

Morgan, Marlo. *Mutant Message Down Under*. London: Thorsons, 1995 (first pub. USA, 1994).

——. *Message From Forever*. London: Thorsons, 1998 (first pub. USA, 1998).

Morton, Christ and Ceri Louise Thomas. *The Mystery of the Crystal Skulls*. London: Thorsons, 1997.

Mudrooroo. *Aboriginal Mythology*. Northamptonshire, England: Aquarian, 1994.

Murray, Margaret. *The Witch-Cult in Western Europe*. Oxford, England: Oxford University Press, 1971 (first pub. 1921).

——. *The God of the Witches*. Oxford, England: Oxford University Press, 1970 (first pub. 1931).

Myss, Caroline. *Why People Don't Heal and How They Can*. New York: Bantam, 1998 (first pub. USA).

Ohsawa, George. *Guidebook for Living*. Los Angeles: Ohsawa Foundation, 1967.

Pennick, Nigel and Paul Devereux. *Lines on the Landscape: Leys and Other Linear Enigmas*. London: Hale, 1989.

Poems of the Elder Edda, translated by Patricia Terry. Philadelphia, Pa.: University of Pennsylvania Press, 1990.

The Poetic Edda, translated by Carolyne Larrington. Oxford, England: Oxford University Press, 1999.

Pope, Nick. *Open Skies, Closed Minds*. New York: Simon & Schuster, 1996.

Randles, Jenny. *The Paranormal Source Book*. London: Piatkus, 1996.

Redfield, James. *The Celestine Prophecy*. New York: Bantam, 1994 (first pub. USA, 1994).

Reid, Daniel. *The Tao of Health, Sex and Longevity*. New York: Simon & Schuster, 1989.

Restall Orr, Emma. *Principles of Druidry*. London: Thorsons, 1998.

Rinpoche, Sogyal. *The Tibetan Book of Living and Dying*. London: Rider, 1992.

Roberts, Jane. *Seth Speaks: The eternal validity of the soul*. San Rafael, Calif.: Amber-Allen Publishing/Novato, Calif.: New World Library, 1994 (first pub. USA, 1972).

Roberts, Peter, and Helen Greengrass. *The Astrology of Time-Twins*. Pentland Press, 1993.

Robinson, Rowan, ed. *The Great Book of Hemp*. Rochester, Vt.: Park Street Press, 1996.

Roman, Sanaya and Duane Packer. *Opening to Channel*. Tiburon, Calif.: H.J. Kramer, 1987.

Rumi, Jalal-al-Din, translated by James Cowan. *Where Two Oceans Meet*. Rockport, Mass.: Element, 1992.

Schneider, Meir. *Self Healing: My Life and Vision*. London: Penguin Arkana, 1989.

Sheldrake, Rupert. *The Rebirth of Nature*. London: Random Century, 1990.

——. *Dogs That Know When Their Owners Are Coming Home*. London: Hutchinson, 1999.

Shine, Betty. *My Life as a Medium*. London: HarperCollins, 1999.

Starhawk. *The Spiral Dance: A Rebirth of the Ancient Religion of the Great Goddess*. New York: HarperCollins, 1989 (first pub. USA, 1979).

Steiger, Brad. *Revelation: The Divine Fire*. Englewood Cliffs, N.J.: Prentice Hall, 1973.

Steiger, Brad and Francie. *The Star People*. New York: Berkley Books, 1981.

Steiner, Rudolf. *The Course of My Life*. Hudson, N.Y.: Anthroposophic Press, 1970.

Stelle, Robert. *An Earth Dweller's Return*. Milwaukee, Wisc.: Lemurian Press, 1940.

Stevenson, Ian. *Twenty Cases Suggestive of Reincarnation*. New York: American Society for Psychical Research, 1966.

Stòkes, Doris. *Host of Voices*. London: Macdonald, 1984.

Strieber, Whitley. *Communion*. New York: Beech Tree Books/ William Morrow, 1987.

——. *Transformation*. New York: Avon Books, 1989.

Sturluson, Snorri, translated by Anthony Faulkes. *Edda*. London: Everyman, 1995.

Sun Bear and Wabun. *The Medicine Wheel*. Englewood Cliffs, N.J.: Prentice Hall, 1980.

Tennyson, Alfred. *Idylls of the King*. London: Penguin, 1983 (first pub. 1891).

Thun, Maria and M.K. *Working with the stars: biodynamic sowing and planting calendars*. East Grinstead: Lanthorn Press, (pub. annually).

The Tibetan Book of the Dead. W.Y. Evans-Wentz, comp./ed. Oxford, England: Oxford University Press, 1960 (first pub. 1927).

The Tibetan Book of the Dead, translated by Francesca Fremantle and Chogyam Trungpa. Boston, Mass.: Shambhala, 2000.

Totterdale, Gwen and Jessica Severn. *Teleportation! A Practical Guide for the Metaphysical Traveler*. San Antonio, Tex.: Words of Wizdom, 1996.

Underwood, Guy. *The Pattern of the Past*. London: Abacus, 1972.

Valiente, Doreen. *Natural Magic*. London: Hale, 1983.

——. *The Rebirth of Witchcraft*. London: Hale, 1989.

Von Daniken, Erich. *Chariots of the Gods?* Souvenir, 1989 (first pub. Germany, 1968).

——. *Arrival of the Gods: Revealing the Alien Landing Sites of Nazca*. Rockport, Mass.: Element, 1998 (first pub. Germany, 1977).

Walsch, Neale Donald. *Conversations with God*. London: Hodder and Stoughton, 1997 (first pub. USA, 1995).

Watkins, Alfred. *The Old Straight Track*. London: Abacus, 1990 (first pub. 1925).

Watson, Lyall. *Supernature*. London: Coronet, 1974 (first pub. 1973).

——. *Earthworks*. London: Hodder and Stoughton, 1986.

West, John Anthony. *The Case for Astrology*. New York: Viking, 1991.

Yntema, Sharon K. *Vegetarian Baby*. London: Thorsons, 1981 (first pub. USA, 1980).

——. *Vegetarian Children*. London: Thorsons, 1989.

BOOKS OF RELATED INTEREST FROM NAB

ANCIENT ROOTS MANY BRANCHES
Energetics of Healing Across Cultures & Through Time
—Darlena L'Orange & Gary Dolowich

The quest to understand the individual and human conditions has led to a reevaluation of health care practices from indigenous cultures around the world. This book searches for such models of therapy and healing which have stood the test of time, and how these can be integrated effectively in our lives.

ISBN: 81-7822-126-8

THE ART AND SCIENCE OF PSYCHIC HEALING
—Larry M. McDaniel & Phyllis G. McDaniel

This book illustrates in detail just how psychic power may be utilized for greater personal relationship and sexual harmony. The book exhorts: Open your mind to new methods, open your sensitivities to new experiences and be prepared to see an entirely new world and undergo magnificent revelations of the world we live in.

ISBN: 81-7822-030-x

A COMPLETE GUIDE TO HEALING
Elements of Energy Therapies
—Ted Andrews

With the help of this book you can take your first step towards developing your innate ability to heal. The straightforward techniques detailed here will serve to pinpoint what you can control in yourself, what you need to change to become healthier on all levels: emotional, mental, spiritual and physical.

ISBN: 81-7822-119-5